Algebra II Practice Workbook

2024

The Most Comprehensive Review of Algebra II

By

Reza Nazari

Copyright © 2023

Effortless Math Education Inc.

All rights reserved. No part of this publication may be reproduced, stored in a retrieval system, or transmitted in any form or by any means, electronic, mechanical, photocopying, recording, scanning, or otherwise, except as permitted under Section 107 or 108 of the 1976 United States Copyright Ac, without permission of the author.

All inquiries should be addressed to:

info@EffortlessMath.com

www.EffortlessMath.com

ISBN: 978-1-63719-423-2

Published by: Effortless Math Education Inc.

For Online Math Practice Visit www.EffortlessMath.com

Welcome to
Algebra II Prep

We wholeheartedly appreciate your choice to select Effortless Math as your trusted companion for Algebra II preparation. Taking the Algebra II course is indeed an exceptional step you have taken, a step that deserves high recognition and respect.

This commendable journey you've embarked on underscores the importance of utilizing all available resources to achieve optimal success in your final examination. Our comprehensive practice workbook stands as an invaluable instrument, meticulously designed to propel you to your highest possible score. Trust in its ability to guide you through your studies, refining your understanding and ultimately ensuring your success.

The Algebra II Practice Workbook is expertly curated to encapsulate the entire spectrum of topics traditionally found within an Algebra II course. This carefully designed guide offers a myriad of practice problems and quizzes, all aimed at testing and reinforcing your comprehension of the material.

Complementing the workbook are robust online resources that offer a step-by-step guide, a plethora of video tutorials, intuitive lessons, clear examples, and rigorous exercises for each topic. This abundance of resources enables you to validate your solutions, while also enhancing your capacity to independently tackle similar problems.

Crafted with utmost clarity and simplicity, this practice workbook ensures effortless understanding, even for those who have previously faced challenges with mathematics. The inclusion of diverse visual aids such as diagrams, graphs, and charts further facilitates comprehension, providing a more tangible grasp of the abstract concepts.

The Algebra II Practice Workbook's flexible structure allows it to effortlessly supplement a traditional classroom environment or serve as an autonomous resource for self-study. This meticulously designed workbook equips you with the foundational knowledge necessary to conquer the material and excel in your Algebra II course.

Effortless Math's Algebra II Online Center

Effortless Math Online Algebra II Center offers a complete study program, including the following:

- ✓ Step-by-step instructions on how to prepare for the Algebra II test

- ✓ Numerous Algebra II worksheets to help you measure your math skills

- ✓ Complete list of Algebra II formulas

- ✓ Video lessons for all Algebra II topics

- ✓ Full-length Algebra II practice tests

- ✓ And much more…

No Registration Required.

Visit **EffortlessMath.com/Algebra2** to find your online Algebra II resources.

How to Use This Book Effectively

Look no further when you need a comprehensive practice book to improve your math skills to succeed on the Algebra II course. Each chapter of this workbook to the Algebra II will provide you with the knowledge, tools, and understanding needed for every topic covered on the course.

It is absolutely crucial to thoroughly comprehend each topic before transitioning to the next, as this sequential mastery underpins your academic success. Each topic is accompanied by a **QR code** which, when scanned, transports you to a dedicated online page.

This page, abundant with instructional resources, offers a trove of enriching videos, practical examples, and a detailed, step-by-step guide to every concept. These invaluable resources aid in deepening your understanding, offering clarity and comprehensive insight into the course material. This interactive learning style ensures not just a basic understanding, but also imparts a solid grasp on the content that you will encounter throughout the course.

To get the best possible results from this book:

- **Practice consistently.** Study Algebra II concepts at least 30 to 40 minutes a day. Remember, slow and steady wins the race, which can be applied to preparing for the Algebra II test. Instead of cramming to tackle everything at once, be patient and learn the math topics in short bursts.
- Whenever you get a math problem wrong, **mark it off, and review it later** to make sure you understand the concept.
- Start each session by **looking over the previous material.**
- Once you've reviewed the book's chapters, **take a practice test at the back of the book** to gauge your level of readiness. Then, review your results. Read detailed answers and solutions for each question you missed.
- **Take another practice test** to get an idea of how ready you are to take the actual exam. Taking the practice tests will give you the confidence you need on test day. Simulate the Algebra II testing environment by sitting in a quiet room free from distraction. Make sure to clock yourself with a timer.

Looking for more?

Visit EffortlessMath.com/Algebra2 to find hundreds of Algebra II worksheets, video tutorials, practice tests, Algebra II formulas, and much more.

Or scan this QR code.

No Registration Required.

Contents

Chapter 1: Fundamentals and Building Blocks 1
- Order of Operations 2
- Scientific Notation 3
- Exponents Operations 4
- Simplifying Algebraic Expressions 5
- Evaluating Expressions 6
- Sets 7
- Answers – Chapter 1 8

Chapter 2: Equations and Inequalities 11
- Multi–Step Equations 12
- Slope and Intercepts 13
- Using Intercepts 14
- Transforming Linear Function 15
- Solving Inequalities 16
- Graphing Linear Inequalities 17
- Solving Compound Inequalities 18
- Solving Absolute Value Equations 19
- Solving Absolute Value Inequalities 20
- Graphing Absolute Value Inequalities 21
- Solving Systems of Equations 22
- Solving Special Systems 23
- Systems of Equations Word Problems 24
- Answers – Chapter 2 25

Chapter 3: Quadratic Function 33
- Solving a Quadratic Equations 34
- Graphing Quadratic Functions 35
- Axis of Symmetry of Quadratic Functions 36
- Solve a Quadratic Equation by Graphing 37
- Solving Quadratic Equations by Using Square Roots 38
- Build Quadratics from Roots 39
- Solving Quadratic Inequalities 40

Contents

    Graphing Quadratic Inequalities 41

    Factoring the Difference between Two Perfect Squares... 42

    Answers – Chapter 3 43

Chapter 4: Complex Numbers 51

    Adding and Subtracting Complex Numbers 52

    Multiplying and Dividing Complex Numbers 53

    Rationalizing Imaginary Denominators 54

    Answers – Chapter 4 55

Chapter 5: Matrices 57

    Using Matrices to Represent Data... 58

    Adding and Subtracting Matrices 59

    Matrix Multiplications 60

    The Inverse of a Matrix 61

    Solving Systems with Matrix Equations 62

    Finding Determinants of a Matrix 63

    Answers – Chapter 5 64

Chapter 6: Polynomial Operations.. 67

    Writing Polynomials in Standard Form.. 68

    Simplifying Polynomials.. 69

    Adding and Subtracting Polynomials.. 70

    Multiplying and Dividing Monomials... 71

    Multiplying a Polynomial and a Monomial 72

    Multiplying Binomials... 73

    Factoring Trinomials 74

    Choosing a Factoring Method for Polynomials 75

    Factors and Greatest Common Factors 76

    Operations with Polynomials 77

    Even and Odd Functions 78

    End Behavior of Polynomial Functions 79

    Remainder and Factor Theorems 80

    Polynomial Division (Long Division).. 81

    Polynomial Division (Synthetic Division) 82

    Finding Zeros of Polynomials.. 83

Polynomial Identities 84

Answers – Chapter 6 85

Chapter 7: Functions Operations 93

Function Notation 94

Adding and Subtracting Functions 95

Multiplying and Dividing Functions 96

Composition of Functions... 97

Writing Functions 98

Parent Functions 99

Function Inverses 100

Inverse Variation 101

Graphing Functions 102

Domain and Range of Function 103

Piecewise Function 104

Positive, Negative, Increasing, and Decreasing Functions on Intervals........................... 105

Answers – Chapter 7 106

Chapter 8: Exponential Functions 113

Exponential Function... 114

Linear, Quadratic and Exponential Models 115

Linear vs Exponential Growth 116

Answers – Chapter 8 117

Chapter 9: Logarithms 119

Evaluating Logarithms 120

Properties of Logarithms 121

Natural Logarithms 122

Solving Logarithmic Equations 123

Answers – Chapter 9 124

Chapter 10: Radical Expressions 127

Simplifying Radical Expressions 128

Multiplying Radical Expressions 129

Simplifying Radical Expressions Involving Fractions 130

Adding and Subtracting Radical Expressions 131

Domain and Range of Radical Functions 132

Contents

Solving Radical Equations 133

Answers – Chapter 10 134

Chapter 11: Rational and Irrational Expressions 139

Rational and Irrational Numbers 140

Simplifying Rational Expressions 141

Graphing Rational Expressions 142

Multiplying Rational Expressions 143

Dividing Rational Expressions 144

Adding and Subtracting Rational Expressions 145

Rational Equations 146

Simplify Complex Fractions 147

Maximum and Minimum Points 148

Solving Rational Inequalities 149

Irrational Functions 150

Direct, Inverse, Joint, and Combined Variation 151

Answers – Chapter 11 152

Chapter 12: Conics 159

Equation of a Parabola 160

Finding the Focus, Vertex, and Directrix of a Parabola 161

Standard From of a Circle 162

Finding the Center and the Radius of Circles 163

Equation of Ellipse 164

Hyperbola in Standard Form 165

Classifying a Conic Section (in Standard Form) 166

Answers – Chapter 12 167

Chapter 13: Sequences and Series 173

Arithmetic Sequences 174

Geometric Sequences 175

Arithmetic Series 176

Finite Geometric Series 177

Infinite Geometric Series 178

Pascal's Triangle 179

Binomial Theorem 180

Sigma Notation (Summation Notation) 181
Alternating Series 182
Answers – Chapter 13 183

Chapter 14: Trigonometric Functions 187

Trig Ratios of General Angles 188
Trigonometric Ratios 189
Right-Triangle Trigonometry 190
Angles of Rotation 191
The Unit Circle, Sine, and Cosine 192
The Reciprocal Trigonometric Functions 193
Function Values of Special Angles 194
Function Values from the Calculator 195
Reference Angles and the Calculator 196
Coterminal Angles and Reference Angles 197
Angles and Angle Measure 198
Evaluating Trigonometric Function 199
Missing Sides and Angles of a Right Triangle 200
Arc Length and Sector Area 201
The Inverse of Trigonometric Functions 202
Solving Trigonometric Equations 203
Answers – Chapter 14 204

Chapter 15: More Topics Trigonometric Functions 211

Pythagorean Identities 212
Domain and Range of Trigonometric Functions 213
Cofunctions 214
Law of Sines 215
Law of Cosines 216
Sum and Difference Identities 217
Double-Angle and Half-Angle Identities 218
Using the Law of Cosines to Find Angle Measure 219
Answers – Chapter 15 220

Chapter 16: Graphs of Trigonometric Functions 225

Graph of the Sine Function 226

Contents

- Graph of the Cosine Function 227
- Amplitude, Period, and Phase Shift 228
- Writing the Equation of a Sine Graph 229
- Writing the Equation of a Cosine Graph 230
- Graph of the Tangent Function 231
- Graph of the Cosecant Function 232
- Graph of the Secant Function 233
- Graph of the Cotangent Function 234
- Graph of Inverse of the Sine Function 235
- Graph of Inverse of the Cosine Function 236
- Graph of Inverse of the Tangent Function 237
- Sketching Trigonometric Graphs 238
- Answers – Chapter 16 239

Chapter 17: Statistics 251
- Frequency and Histograms 252
- Box-and-Whisker Plots 253
- Measures of Dispersion 254
- Organizing Data 255
- Data Distribution 256
- Central Limit Theorem and Standard Error 257
- Answers – Chapter 17 258

Chapter 18: Probability 263
- Independent and Dependent Events 264
- Compound Events 265
- Conditional and Binomial Probabilities 266
- Theoretical Probability 267
- Experimental Probability 268
- Answers – Chapter 18 269

Time to Test 270

Algebra II Practice Test 1 271

Algebra II Practice Test 2 285

Algebra II Practice Tests Answers and Explanations 300

Chapter 1: Fundamentals and Building Blocks

Math Topics that you'll learn in this Chapter:

- ✓ Order of Operations
- ✓ Scientific Notation
- ✓ Exponents Operations
- ✓ Simplifying Algebraic Expressions
- ✓ Evaluating Expressions
- ✓ Sets

Chapter 1: Fundamentals and Building Blocks

Order of Operations

✎ *Calculate.*

1) $16 + (30 \div 5) =$

2) $(3 \times 9) \div (-3) =$

3) $57 - (3 \times 8) =$

4) $(-12) \times (7 - 3) =$

5) $(18 - 7) \times (6) =$

6) $(6 \times 10) \div (12 + 3) =$

7) $(13 \times 2) - (24 \div 6) =$

8) $(-5) + (4 \times 3) + 8 =$

9) $(4 \times 2^3) + (16 - 9) =$

10) $(3^2 \times 7) \div (-2 + 1) =$

11) $[-2(48 \div 2^3)] - 6 =$

12) $(-4) + (7 \times 8) + 18 =$

13) $(3 \times 7) + (16 - 7) =$

14) $[3^3 \times (48 \div 2^3)] \div (-2) =$

15) $(14 \times 3) - (3^4 \div 9) =$

16) $(96 \div 12) \times (-3) =$

17) $(48 \div 2^2) \times (-2) =$

18) $(56 \div 7) \times (-5) =$

19) $(-2^2) + (7 \times 9) - 21 =$

20) $(2^4 - 9) \times (-6) =$

21) $[4^3 \times (50 \div 5^2)] \div (-16) =$

22) $(3^2 \times 4^2) \div (-4 + 2) =$

23) $6^2 - (-6 \times 4) + 3 =$

24) $4^2 - (5^2 \times 3) =$

25) $(-4) + (12^2 \div 3^2) - 7^2 =$

26) $(3^2 \times 5) + (-5^2 - 9) =$

27) $2[(3^2 \times 5) \times (-6)] =$

28) $(11^2 - 2^2) - (-7^2) =$

29) $(2^2 \times 5) - (64 \div 8) =$

30) $2[(3^2 \times 4) + (35 \div 5)] =$

31) $(4^2 \times 3) \div (-6) =$

32) $3^2[(4^3 \div 16) - (3^3 \div 27)] =$

Chapter 1: Fundamentals and Building Blocks

Scientific Notation

✎ Write each number in scientific notation.

1) $0.114 =$

2) $0.06 =$

3) $8.6 =$

4) $30 =$

5) $60 =$

6) $0.004 =$

7) $78 =$

8) $1,600 =$

9) $1,450 =$

10) $31,000 =$

11) $2,000,000 =$

12) $0.0000003 =$

13) $554,000 =$

14) $0.000725 =$

15) $0.00034 =$

16) $86,000,000 =$

17) $62,000 =$

18) $97,000,000 =$

19) $0.0000045 =$

20) $0.0019 =$

✎ Write each number in standard notation.

21) $2 \times 10^{-1} =$

22) $8 \times 10^{-2} =$

23) $1.8 \times 10^3 =$

24) $9 \times 10^{-4} =$

25) $1.7 \times 10^{-2} =$

26) $9 \times 10^3 =$

27) $6 \times 10^4 =$

28) $2.18 \times 10^5 =$

29) $5 \times 10^{-3} =$

30) $9.4 \times 10^{-5} =$

Chapter 1: Fundamentals and Building Blocks

Exponents Operations

✍ **Simplify and write the answer in exponential form.**

1) $3 \times 3^2 =$

2) $4^3 \times 4 =$

3) $2^2 \times 2^2 =$

4) $6^2 \times 6^2 =$

5) $7^3 \times 7^2 \times 7 =$

6) $2 \times 2^2 \times 2^2 =$

7) $5^3 \times 5^2 \times 5 \times 5 =$

8) $2x \times x =$

9) $x^3 \times x^2 =$

10) $x^4 \times x^4 =$

11) $x^2 \times x^2 \times x^2 =$

12) $6x \times 6x =$

13) $2x^2 \times 2x^2 =$

14) $3x^2 \times x =$

15) $4x^4 \times 4x^4 \times 4x^4 =$

16) $2x^2 \times x^2 =$

17) $x^4 \times 3x =$

18) $x \times 2x^2 =$

19) $5x^4 \times 5x^4 =$

20) $2yx^2 \times 2x =$

21) $3x^4 \times y^2 x^4 =$

22) $y^2 x^3 \times y^5 x^2 =$

23) $4yx^3 \times 2x^2 y^3 =$

24) $6x^2 \times 6x^3 y^4 =$

25) $3x^4 y^5 \times 7x^2 y^3 =$

26) $7x^2 y^5 \times 9xy^3 =$

27) $7xy^4 \times 4x^3 y^3 =$

28) $3x^5 y^3 \times 8x^2 y^3 =$

29) $6x \times y^5 x^2 \times y^3 =$

30) $yx^3 \times 3y^3 x^2 \times 2xy =$

31) $5yx^3 \times 4y^2 x \times xy^3 =$

32) $6x^2 \times 3x^3 y^4 \times 10yx^3 =$

Chapter 1: Fundamentals and Building Blocks

Simplifying Algebraic Expressions

✍ *Simplify each expression.*

1) $3(2x + 1) =$

2) $2(4x - 6) =$

3) $4(3x + 3) =$

4) $2(4x + 5) =$

5) $-3(8x - 7) =$

6) $2x(3x + 4) =$

7) $3x^2 + 3x^2 - 2x^3 =$

8) $2x - x^2 + 6x^3 + 4 =$

9) $5x + 2x^2 - 9x^3 =$

10) $7x^2 + 5x^4 - 2x^3 =$

11) $-3x^2 + 5x^3 + 6x^4 =$

12) $(x - 3)(x - 4) =$

13) $(x - 5)(x + 4) =$

14) $(x - 6)(x - 3) =$

15) $(2x + 5)(x + 8) =$

16) $(3x - 8)(x + 4) =$

17) $-8x^2 + 2x^3 - 10x^4 + 5x =$

18) $11 - 6x^2 + 5x^2 - 12x^3 + 22 =$

19) $3x^2 - 4x + 4x^3 + 10x - 21x =$

20) $10 - 6x^2 + 5x^2 - 3x^3 + 2 =$

21) $3x^5 - 2x^3 + 8x^2 - x^5 =$

22) $(5x^3 - 1) + (4x^3 - 6x^3) =$

Chapter 1: Fundamentals and Building Blocks

Evaluating Expressions

✍ *Evaluate each expression using the values given.*

1) $3x + 5y$
   $x = 3, y = 2$

2) $6x + 5y$
   $x = 1, y = 5$

3) $18a + 2b$
   $a = 2, b = 8$

4) $4x \div 3y$
   $x = 3, y = 2$

5) $-2a + 4b$
   $a = 6, b = 3$

6) $4x + 7 - 2y$
   $x = 7, y = 6$

7) $5z + 12 - 4k$
   $z = 5, k = 2$

8) $2(-x - 2y)$
   $x = 6, y = 9$

9) $2x + 15 + 4y$
   $x = -2, y = 4$

10) $4a - (15 - b)$
    $a = 4, b = 6$

11) $5z + 19 + 8k$
    $z = -5, k = 4$

12) $xy + 12 + 5x$
    $x = 7, y = 2$

13) $2x + 4y - 3 + 2$
    $x = 5, y = 3$

14) $6 + 3(-2x - 3y)$
    $x = 9, y = 7$

15) $2x + 14 + 4y$
    $x = 6, y = 8$

16) $4a - (5a - b) + 5$
    $a = 4, b = 6$

17) $\left(-\frac{12}{x}\right) + 1 + 5y$
    $x = 6, y = 8$

18) $(-4)(-2a - 2b)$
    $a = 5, b = 3$

19) $10 + 3x + 7 - 2y$
    $x = 7, y = 6$

20) $9x + 2 - 4y + 5$
    $x = 7, y = 5$

21) $(3a + 6b) - 5b - 9$
    $a = -2, b = 3$

22) $-3x - 14 + 7y + 3$
    $x = -2, y = -7$

Chapter 1: Fundamentals and Building Blocks

Sets

✎ *Write the following sets in the roster form.*

1) The set of all even numbers less than 14.

2) The set of the first 5 odd numbers.

3) The set of all factors of 24.

4) The set of all factors of 36.

5) The set of integers that is between -2 and 3.

6) The set of all prime numbers greater than 1 but less than 30.

7) The set of unique letters in the word "CHOICE".

8) The set of multiples of 4 that are less than 28.

9) The set of prime numbers less than 18.

10) Write the following set in Roster form.

    $A = \{x | x \text{ is an odd number and is greater than } 11 \text{ and less than } 19\}$

11) Write the following set in Roster form.

    $A = \{x | x \text{ is a factor of } 45\}$

12) The set of all $2-$digit numbers whose sum of digits is 8.

Chapter 1: Fundamentals and Building Blocks

Answers – Chapter 1

Order of Operations

1) 22
2) −9
3) 33
4) −48
5) 66
6) 4
7) 22
8) 15
9) 39
10) −63
11) −18
12) 70
13) 30
14) −81
15) 33
16) −24
17) −24
18) −40
19) 38
20) −42
21) −8
22) −72
23) 63
24) −59
25) −37
26) 11
27) −540
28) 166
29) 12
30) 86
31) −8
32) 27

Scientific Notation

1) 1.14×10^{-1}
2) 6×10^{-2}
3) 8.6×10^{0}
4) 3×10^{1}
5) 6×10^{1}
6) 4×10^{-3}
7) 7.8×10^{1}
8) 1.6×10^{3}
9) 1.45×10^{3}
10) 3.1×10^{4}
11) 2×10^{6}
12) 3×10^{-7}
13) 5.54×10^{5}
14) 7.25×10^{-4}
15) 3.4×10^{-4}
16) 8.6×10^{7}
17) 6.2×10^{4}
18) 9.7×10^{7}
19) 4.5×10^{-6}
20) 1.9×10^{-3}
21) 0.2
22) 0.08
23) 1,800
24) 0.0009
25) 0.017
26) 9,000
27) 60,000
28) 218,000
29) 0.005
30) 0.000094

Effortless Math Education

Chapter 1: Fundamentals and Building Blocks

Exponents Operations

1) 3^3
2) 4^4
3) 2^4
4) 6^4
5) 7^6
6) 2^5
7) 5^7
8) $2x^2$
9) x^5
10) x^8
11) x^6
12) $36x^2$
13) $4x^4$
14) $3x^3$
15) $64x^{12}$
16) $2x^4$
17) $3x^5$
18) $2x^3$
19) $25x^8$
20) $4x^3y$
21) $3x^8y^2$
22) x^5y^7
23) $8x^5y^4$
24) $36x^5y^4$
25) $21x^6y^8$
26) $63x^3y^8$
27) $28x^4y^7$
28) $24x^7y^6$
29) $6x^3y^8$
30) $6x^6y^5$
31) $20x^5y^6$
32) $180x^8y^5$

Simplifying Algebraic Expressions

1) $6x + 3$
2) $8x - 12$
3) $12x + 12$
4) $8x + 10$
5) $-24x + 21$
6) $6x^2 + 8x$
7) $-2x^3 + 6x^2$
8) $6x^3 - x^2 + 2x + 4$
9) $-9x^3 + 2x^2 + 5x$
10) $5x^4 - 2x^3 + 7x^2$
11) $6x^4 + 5x^3 - 3x^2$
12) $x^2 - 7x + 12$
13) $x^2 - x - 20$
14) $x^2 - 9x + 18$
15) $2x^2 + 21x + 40$
16) $3x^2 + 4x - 32$
17) $-10x^4 + 2x^3 - 8x^2 + 5x$
18) $-12x^3 - x^2 + 33$
19) $4x^3 + 3x^2 - 15x$
20) $-3x^3 - x^2 + 12$
21) $2x^5 - 2x^3 + 8x^2$
22) $3x^3 - 1$

Chapter 1: Fundamentals and Building Blocks

Evaluating Expressions

1) 19
2) 31
3) 52
4) 2
5) 0
6) 23
7) 29
8) −48
9) 27
10) 7
11) 26
12) 61
13) 21
14) −111
15) 58
16) 7
17) 39
18) 64
19) 26
20) 50
21) −12
22) −54

Sets

1) {2, 4, 6, 8, 10, 12}
2) {1, 3, 5, 7, 9}
3) {1, 2, 3, 4, 6, 8, 12, 24}
4) {1, 2, 3, 4, 6, 9, 12, 18, 36}
5) {−1, 0, 1, 2}
6) {2, 3, 5, 7, 11, 13, 17, 19, 23, 29}
7) {C, H, O, I, E}
8) {4, 8, 12, 16, 20, 24}
9) {2, 3, 5, 7, 11, 13, 17}
10) $A = \{13, 15, 17\}$
11) $A = \{1, 3, 5, 9, 15, 45\}$
12) {17, 71, 26, 62, 35, 53, 44, 80}

Chapter 2: Equations and Inequalities

Math Topics that you'll learn in this Chapter:

- ✓ Multi–Step Equations
- ✓ Slope and Intercepts
- ✓ Using Intercepts
- ✓ Transforming Linear Function
- ✓ Solving Inequalities
- ✓ Graphing Linear Inequalities
- ✓ Solving Compound Inequalities
- ✓ Solving Absolute Value Equations
- ✓ Solving Absolute Value Inequalities
- ✓ Graphing Absolute Value Inequalities
- ✓ Solving Systems of Equations
- ✓ Solving Special Systems
- ✓ Systems of Equations Word Problems

Chapter 2: Equations and Inequalities

Multi–Step Equations

✏️ **Solve each equation.**

1) $4x - 7 = 13 \Rightarrow x =$ ____

2) $26 = -(x - 4) \Rightarrow x =$ ____

3) $-(5 - x) = 19 \Rightarrow x =$ ____

4) $35 = -x + 14 \Rightarrow x =$ ____

5) $2(3 - 2x) = 10 \Rightarrow x =$ ____

6) $3x - 3 = 15 \Rightarrow x =$ ____

7) $32 = -x + 15 \Rightarrow x =$ ____

8) $-(10 - x) = -13 \Rightarrow x =$ ____

9) $-4(7 + x) = 4 \Rightarrow x =$ ____

10) $22 = 2x - 8 \Rightarrow x =$ ____

11) $-6(3 + x) = 6 \Rightarrow x =$ ____

12) $-3 = 3x - 15 \Rightarrow x =$ ____

13) $-7(12 + x) = 7 \Rightarrow x =$ ____

14) $8(6 - 4x) = 16 \Rightarrow x =$ ____

15) $18 - 4x = -9 - x \Rightarrow x =$ ____

16) $6(4 - x) = 30 \Rightarrow x =$ ____

17) $15 - 3x = -5 - x \Rightarrow x =$ ____

18) $9(-7 - 3x) = 18 \Rightarrow x =$ ____

19) $16 - 2x = -4 - 7x \Rightarrow x =$ ____

20) $14 - 2x = 14 + x \Rightarrow x =$ ____

21) $21 - 3x = -7 - 10x \Rightarrow x =$ ____

22) $8 - 2x = 11 + x \Rightarrow x =$ ____

23) $10 + 12x = -8 + 6x \Rightarrow x =$ ____

24) $25 + 20x = -5 + 5x \Rightarrow x =$ ____

25) $16 - x = -8 - 7x \Rightarrow x =$ ____

26) $17 - 3x = 13 + x \Rightarrow x =$ ____

27) $22 + 5x = -8 - x \Rightarrow x =$ ____

28) $-9(7 + x) = 9 \Rightarrow x =$ ____

29) $12 + 2x = -4 - 2x \Rightarrow x =$ ____

30) $12 - x = 2 - 3x \Rightarrow x =$ ____

31) $19 - x = -1 - 11x \Rightarrow x =$ ____

32) $14 - 3x = -5 - 4x \Rightarrow x =$ ____

Chapter 2: Equations and Inequalities

Slope and Intercepts

✏️ **Find the slope of each line.**

1) $y = 2x - 8$, Slope = ____

2) $y = -6x + 3$, Slope = ____

3) $y = -x - 5$, Slope = ____

4) $y = -2x - 9$, Slope = ____

5) $y = 5 + 2x$, Slope = ____

6) $y = 1 - 8x$, Slope = ____

7) $y = -4x + 3$, Slope = ____

8) $y = -9x + 8$, Slope = ____

9) $y = -2x + 4$, Slope = ____

10) $y = 9x - 8$, Slope = ____

11) $y = \frac{1}{2}x + 4$, Slope = ____

12) $y = -\frac{2}{5}x + 7$, Slope = ____

13) $-x + 3y = 5$, Slope = ____

14) $4x + 4y = 6$, Slope = ____

15) $6y - 2x = 10$, Slope = ____

16) $3y - x = 2$, Slope = ____

✏️ **Find the slope of the line through each pair of points.**

17) $(4, 4), (8, 12)$, Slope = ____

18) $(-2, 4), (0, 6)$, Slope = ____

19) $(6, -2), (2, 6)$, Slope = ____

20) $(-4, -2), (0, 6)$, Slope = ____

21) $(6, 2), (3, 5)$, Slope = ____

22) $(-5, 1), (-1, 9)$, Slope = ____

23) $(8, 4), (9, 6)$, Slope = ____

24) $(10, -1), (7, 8)$, Slope = ____

25) $(16, -3), (13, -6)$, Slope = ____

26) $(12, 5), (8, 1)$, Slope = ____

27) $(6, 6), (8, 10)$, Slope = ____

28) $(10, -1), (8, 1)$, Slope = ____

Chapter 2: Equations and Inequalities

Using Intercepts

✍ *Find the x and y intercepts for the following equations.*

1) $y = -\frac{1}{3}x - 1$

   x−intercept:_____

   y−intercept:_____

2) $y = 5x + 10$

   x−intercept:_____

   y−intercept:_____

3) $2x + 8y = -8$

   x−intercepts:_____

   y−intercepts:_____

4) $3x - 2y = 24$

   x−intercepts:_____

   y−intercepts:_____

5) $-3x + 5y = -15$

   x−intercepts:_____

   y−intercepts:_____

6) $8x - 2y = 10$

   x−intercepts:_____

   y−intercepts:_____

7) $5x - 3y = 18$

   x−intercepts:_____

   y-intercepts:_____

8) $9x - 2y = 24$

   x−intercepts:_____

   y−intercepts:_____

9) $-4x + 2y = 24$

   x−intercepts:_____

   y−intercepts:_____

10) $8x + 4y = -40$

    x−intercepts:_____

    y−intercepts:_____

Chapter 2: Equations and Inequalities

Transforming Linear Function

✎ *Graph.*

1) Graph $f(x) = x$ and find $g(x) = x + 3$.

2) Graph $f(x) = x$ and find $g(x) = x - 1$.

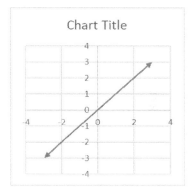

3) Graph $f(x) = x$ and find $g(x) = x - 2$.

Chapter 2: Equations and Inequalities

Solving Inequalities

✎ *Solve each inequality for x.*

1) $x - 9 < 20 \Rightarrow$ _____

2) $14 \leq -6 + x \Rightarrow$ _____

3) $x - 31 > 9 \Rightarrow$ _____

4) $x + 28 \geq 36 \Rightarrow$ _____

5) $x - 24 > 17 \Rightarrow$ _____

6) $x + 5 \geq 3 \Rightarrow x$ _____

7) $x + 14 < 12 \Rightarrow$ _____

8) $26 + x \leq 8 \Rightarrow$ _____

9) $x + 9 \geq -18 \Rightarrow$ _____

10) $x + 24 < 11 \Rightarrow$ _____

11) $17 \leq -5 + x \Rightarrow$ _____

12) $x + 25 > 29 \Rightarrow x$ _____

13) $x - 17 \geq 19 \Rightarrow$ _____

14) $x + 8 > -17 \Rightarrow$ _____

15) $x + 8 < -23 \Rightarrow$ _____

16) $16 \leq -5 + x \Rightarrow$ _____

17) $4x \leq 12 \Rightarrow$ _____

18) $28 \geq -7x \Rightarrow$ _____

19) $2x > -14 \Rightarrow$ _____

20) $13x \leq 39 \Rightarrow$ _____

21) $-8x > -16 \Rightarrow$ _____

22) $\frac{x}{2} < -6 \Rightarrow$ _____

23) $\frac{x}{6} > 6 \Rightarrow$ _____

24) $27 \leq \frac{x}{4} \Rightarrow$ _____

25) $\frac{x}{8} < -3 \Rightarrow$ _____

26) $6x \geq 18 \Rightarrow$ _____

27) $5x \geq -25 \Rightarrow$ _____

28) $3x > 45 \Rightarrow$ _____

29) $9x \leq 72 \Rightarrow$ _____

30) $-6x < -36 \Rightarrow$ _____

31) $70 > -10x \Rightarrow$ _____

Chapter 2: Equations and Inequalities

Graphing Linear Inequalities

✎ *Sketch the group of each linear inequality.*

1) $y < 2x - 1$

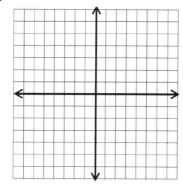

2) $y \geq x - 4$

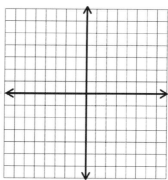

3) $y \geq -4x + 2$

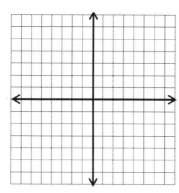

4) $y < -x - 3$

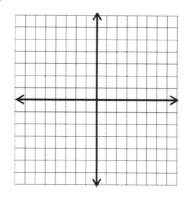

5) $y > -3x + 6$

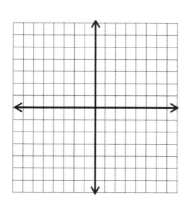

6) $y < 5x - 7$

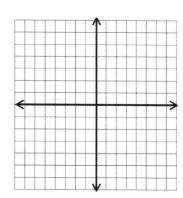

Chapter 2: Equations and Inequalities

Solving Compound Inequalities

✍ *Solve each inequality.*

1) $2x - 6 \leq 4 \rightarrow$ _____

2) $2 + 3x \geq 17 \rightarrow$ _____

3) $9 + 3x \geq 36 \rightarrow$ _____

4) $2x - 6 \leq 18 \rightarrow$ _____

5) $3x - 4 \leq 23 \rightarrow$ _____

6) $7x - 5 \leq 51 \rightarrow$ _____

7) $4x - 9 \leq 27 \rightarrow$ _____

8) $6x - 11 \leq 13 \rightarrow$ _____

9) $5x - 7 \leq 33 \rightarrow$ _____

10) $6 + 2x \geq 28 \rightarrow$ _____

11) $8 + 3x \geq 35 \rightarrow$ _____

12) $4 + 6x < 34 \rightarrow$ _____

13) $3 + 2x \geq 53 \rightarrow$ _____

14) $7 - 6x > 56 + x \rightarrow$ _____

15) $9 + 4x \geq 39 + 2x \rightarrow$ _____

16) $3 + 5x \geq 43 \rightarrow$ _____

17) $4 - 7x < 60 \rightarrow$ _____

18) $11 - 4x \geq 55 \rightarrow$ _____

19) $12 + x \geq 48 - 2x \rightarrow$ _____

20) $10 - 10x \leq -20 \rightarrow$ _____

21) $5 - 9x \geq -40 \rightarrow$ _____

22) $8 - 7x \geq 36 \rightarrow$ _____

23) $6 + 10x < 69 + 3x \rightarrow$ _____

24) $5 + 4x < 26 - 3x \rightarrow$ _____

25) $10 + 11x < 59 + 4x \rightarrow$ _____

26) $3 + 9x \geq 48 - 6x \rightarrow$ _____

27) $8 - 3x \geq 35 - 6x \rightarrow$ _____

28) $6x - 12 \geq 56 + 4x \rightarrow$ _____

29) $22 - 8x < 67 - 9x \rightarrow$ _____

30) $9x + 11 \geq 67 + 2x \rightarrow$ _____

Chapter 2: Equations and Inequalities

Solving Absolute Value Equations

✎ Solve each equation.

1) $|2x| = 8$

2) $|6x| = 4$

3) $|-3x| = 6$

4) $|9x| = 18$

5) $|-4x| = 24$

6) $|-5x| = 45$

7) $|-7x| = 49$

8) $\left|\dfrac{x}{4}\right| = 9$

9) $\left|\dfrac{x}{6}\right| = 3$

10) $|x + 1| = 4$

11) $\left|\dfrac{x}{6}\right| = 12$

12) $|x - 5| = 12$

13) $|x - 7| = 24$

14) $|x - 10| = 3$

15) $|x| + 2 = 11$

16) $|x| - 4 = 15$

17) $-10|x + 2| = -70$

18) $4|x + 8| = 56$

19) $|x + 12| = 45$

20) $|x - 11| = 22$

21) $|x + 9| = 67$

22) $|3 - x| = 5$

23) $|2 + 3x| = 14$

24) $|-2x - 1| = 11$

25) $|x + 8| - 5 = 2$

26) $6|1 - 5x| - 9 = 57$

Chapter 2: Equations and Inequalities

Solving Absolute Value Inequalities

✏️ **Solve each inequality.**

1) $|2x| > 14$

2) $|4x| < 16$

3) $|x - 2| \leq 6$

4) $|x + 3| > 12$

5) $|x - 9| \geq 32$

6) $|x| - 5 \geq 11$

7) $\left|\frac{x}{6}\right| < 4$

8) $\left|\frac{x-2}{3}\right| > 4$

9) $|x| - 4 < 17$

10) $6 + |x - 8| > 15$

11) $\left|\frac{x}{2} + 3\right| > 6$

12) $\left|\frac{x+5}{4}\right| < 7$

13) $|x| + 4 \geq 6$

14) $|x - 2| - 6 < 5$

15) $3 + |2 + x| < 5$

16) $|x + 7| - 9 < -6$

17) $|x| - 3 > 2$

18) $|x| - 2 > 0$

19) $|3x| \leq 15$

20) $|x + 4| \leq 8$

21) $|3x| \leq 24$

22) $|x - 8| - 10 < -6$

Chapter 2: Equations and Inequalities

Graphing Absolute Value Inequalities

✎ *Solve each inequality and graph its solution.*

1) $|2x - 2| \geq 10$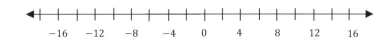

2) $|\frac{1}{3}x - 1| \leq 3$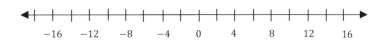

3) $|x| - 2 < 6$

4) $|x + 4| < 8$

5) $|2x - 2| \leq 14$

6) $|x| + 8 > 16$

7) $|2x + 8| \leq 24$

8) $|3x - 12| \leq 6$

9) $|x| - 6 > 2$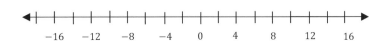

Chapter 2: Equations and Inequalities

Solving Systems of Equations

✍ *Solve each system of equations.*

1) $\begin{cases} x + 2y = 6 \\ 2x - y = 8 \end{cases}$ $x =$ $y =$

2) $\begin{cases} 2x + 4y = 6 \\ 4x - 2y = 8 \end{cases}$ $x =$ $y =$

3) $\begin{cases} -2x + 2y = -4 \\ 4x - 9y = 28 \end{cases}$ $x =$ $y =$

4) $\begin{cases} x + 8y = -5 \\ 2x + 6y = 0 \end{cases}$ $x =$ $y =$

5) $\begin{cases} 4x - 3y = -2 \\ x - y = 3 \end{cases}$ $x =$ $y =$

6) $\begin{cases} 2x + 9y = 17 \\ -3x + 8y = 39 \end{cases}$ $x =$ $y =$

7) $\begin{cases} -4x - 6y = 7 \\ 3x - 2y = 7 \end{cases}$ $x =$ $y =$

8) $\begin{cases} 3y = -6x + 12 \\ 8x - 9y = -10 \end{cases}$ $x =$ $y =$

9) $\begin{cases} 3x - 2y = 15 \\ 3x - 5y = 15 \end{cases}$ $x =$ $y =$

10) $\begin{cases} -5x + y = -3 \\ 3x - 7y = 21 \end{cases}$ $x =$ $y =$

11) $\begin{cases} x + 15y = 50 \\ x + 10y = 40 \end{cases}$ $x =$ $y =$

12) $\begin{cases} 3x - 6y = -12 \\ -x - 3y = -6 \end{cases}$ $x =$ $y =$

13) $\begin{cases} 3x + 6y = 18 \\ 6x - 3y = 24 \end{cases}$ $x =$ $y =$

14) $\begin{cases} 12x - 9y = -6 \\ 3x - 3y = 9 \end{cases}$ $x =$ $y =$

www.EffortlessMath.com

Chapter 2: Equations and Inequalities

Solving Special Systems

✎ *Determine whether the system given below has no solution, one solution, or infinitely many solutions.*

1) $\begin{cases} x + y = 7 \\ 4x + 4y = 12 \end{cases}$

2) $\begin{cases} 2x + y = 4 \\ 4x + 2y = 8 \end{cases}$

3) $\begin{cases} -3x + y = 1 \\ y = 3x - 4 \end{cases}$

4) $\begin{cases} -2x + y = 3 \\ -4x + 2y = 6 \end{cases}$

5) $\begin{cases} x - 5y = 1 \\ -2x + 10y = 3 \end{cases}$

6) $\begin{cases} 2x - 3y = 5 \\ 6x + y = 5 \end{cases}$

7) $\begin{cases} y = 2x3 \\ y = 5x - 18 \end{cases}$

8) $\begin{cases} 2x + y = 8 \\ 4x + 2y = -2 \end{cases}$

9) $\begin{cases} x - y = -2 \\ -x + y = 4 \end{cases}$

10) $\begin{cases} x + y = 3 \\ 2x + 2y = 6 \end{cases}$

11) $\begin{cases} x + y = 4 \\ 4x + 4y = 12 \end{cases}$

12) $\begin{cases} x = 3y - 7 \\ 2x - 6y = -14 \end{cases}$

13) $\begin{cases} x + y = 1 \\ x + y = 3 \end{cases}$

14) $\begin{cases} 2y = 2 + 6x \\ 2y - 6x = -8 \end{cases}$

Chapter 2: Equations and Inequalities

Systems of Equations Word Problems

✎ *Solve each word problems.*

1) The equations of two lines are $3x - y = 7$ and $2x + 3y = 1$. What is the value of x in the solution for this system of equations? _____

2) The perimeter of a rectangle is 100 feet. The rectangle's length is 10 feet less than 5 times its width. What are the length and width of the rectangle? _____

3) A theater sells tickets for a performance. Mr. Smith purchased 8 senior tickets and 5 child tickets for $136 for his friends and family. Mr. Jackson purchased 4 senior tickets and 6 child tickets for $96. What is the price of a senior ticket? $_____

4) The difference between two numbers is 6. Their sum is 14. What is the greater number? $_____

5) The sum of the digits of a certain two–digit number is 7. Reversing its digits increases the number by 9. What is the number? _____

6) The difference between two numbers is 18. Their sum is 66. What are the numbers? _____

24

www.EffortlessMath.com

Chapter 2: Equations and Inequalities

Answers – Chapter 2

Multi–Step Equations

1) $x = 5$
2) $x = -22$
3) $x = 24$
4) $x = -21$
5) $x = -1$
6) $x = 6$
7) $x = -17$
8) $x = -3$
9) $x = -8$
10) $x = 15$
11) $x = -4$
12) $x = 4$
13) $x = -13$
14) $x = 1$
15) $x = 9$
16) $x = -1$
17) $x = 10$
18) $x = -3$
19) $x = -4$
20) $x = 0$
21) $x = -4$
22) $x = -1$
23) $x = -3$
24) $x = -2$
25) $x = -4$
26) $x = 1$
27) $x = -5$
28) $x = -8$
29) $x = -4$
30) $x = -5$
31) $x = -2$
32) $x = -19$

Slope and Intercepts

1) 2
2) −6
3) −1
4) −2
5) 2
6) −8
7) −4
8) −9
9) −2
10) 9
11) $\frac{1}{2}$
12) $-\frac{2}{5}$
13) $\frac{1}{3}$
14) −1
15) $\frac{1}{3}$
16) $\frac{1}{3}$
17) 2
18) 1
19) −2
20) 2
21) −1
22) 2
23) 2
24) −3
25) 1
26) 1
27) 2
28) −1

Using Intercepts

1) x −intercept: $(-3, 0)$, y −intercept: $(0, -1)$
2) x −intercept: $(-2, 0)$, y −intercept: $(0, 10)$
3) x −intercepts: $(-4, 0)$, y −intercepts: $(0, -1)$
4) x −intercepts: $(8, 0)$, y −intercepts: $(0, -12)$
5) x −intercepts: $(5, 0)$, y −intercepts: $(0, -3)$
6) x −intercepts: $\left(\frac{5}{4}, 0\right)$, y −intercepts: $(0, -5)$
7) x −intercepts: $(\frac{18}{5}, 0)$, y −intercepts: $(0, -6)$
8) x −intercepts: $\left(\frac{8}{3}, 0\right)$, y −intercepts: $(0, -12)$
9) x −intercepts: $(-6, 0)$, y −intercepts: $(0, 12)$
10) x −intercepts: $(-5, 0)$, y −intercepts: $(0, -10)$

Transforming Linear Function

1)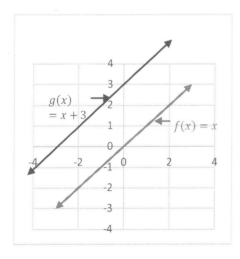

2)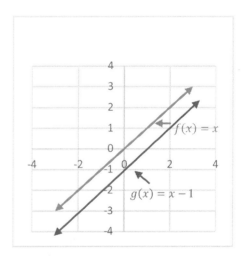

Chapter 2: Equations and Inequalities

3)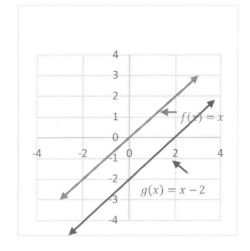

Solving Inequalities

1) $x < 29$
2) $20 \leq x$
3) $x > 40$
4) $x \geq 8$
5) $x > 41$
6) $x \geq -2$
7) $x < -2$
8) $x \leq -18$
9) $x \geq -27$
10) $x < -13$
11) $22 \leq x$

12) $x > 4$
13) $x \geq 36$
14) $x > -25$
15) $x < -31$
16) $21 \leq x$
17) $x \leq 3$
18) $-4 \leq x$
19) $x > -7$
20) $x \leq 3$
21) $x < 2$
22) $x < -12$

23) $x > 36$
24) $108 \leq x$
25) $x < -24$
26) $x \geq 3$
27) $x \geq -5$
28) $x > 15$
29) $x \leq 8$
30) $x > 6$
31) $-7 < x$

Graphing Linear Inequalities

1)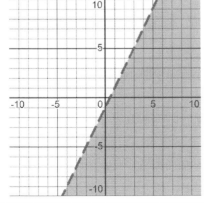

2)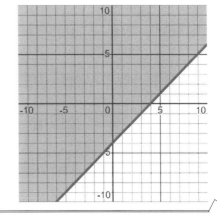

3)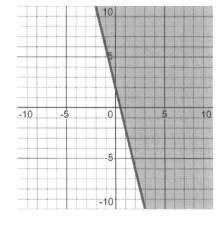
4)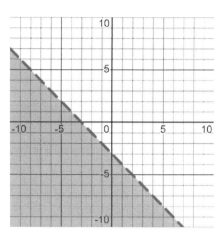
5)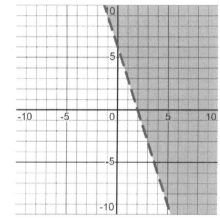
6)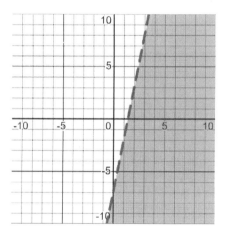

Solving Compound Inequalities

1) $x \leq 5$
2) $x \geq 5$
3) $x \geq 9$
4) $x \leq 12$
5) $x \leq 9$
6) $x \leq 8$
7) $x \leq 9$
8) $x \leq 4$
9) $x \leq 8$
10) $x \geq 11$
11) $x \geq 9$
12) $x < 5$
13) $x \geq 25$
14) $x < -7$
15) $x \geq 15$
16) $x \geq 8$
17) $x > -8$
18) $x \leq -11$
19) $x \geq 12$
20) $x \geq 3$
21) $x \leq 5$
22) $x \leq -4$
23) $x < 9$
24) $x < 3$
25) $x < 7$
26) $x \geq 3$
27) $x \geq 9$
28) $x \geq 34$
29) $x < 45$
30) $x \geq 8$

	Chapter 2: Equations and Inequalities

Solving Absolute Value Equations

1) $x = -4$ or 4
2) $x = -\frac{2}{3}$ or $\frac{2}{3}$
3) $x = -2$ or 2
4) $x = -2$ or 2
5) $x = -6$ or 6
6) $x = -9$ or 9
7) $x = -7$ or 7
8) $x = -36$ or 36
9) $x = -18$ or 18
10) $x = -5$ or 3
11) $x = -72$ or 72
12) $x = -7$ or 17
13) $x = -17$ or 31
14) $x = 7$ or 13
15) $x = -9$ or 9
16) $x = -19$ or 19
17) $x = -9$ or 5
18) $x = -22$ or 6
19) $x = -57$ or 33
20) $x = -11$ or 33
21) $x = -76$ or 58
22) $x = -2$ or 8
23) $x = -\frac{16}{3}$ or 4
24) $x = -6$ or 5
25) $x = -15$ or -1
26) $x = -2$ or $\frac{12}{5}$

Solving Absolute Value Inequalities

1) $x < -7$ or $x > 7$
2) $-4 < x < 4$
3) $-4 \leq x \leq 8$
4) $x < -15$ or $x > 9$
5) $x \leq -23$ or $x \geq 41$
6) $x \leq -16$ or $x \geq 16$
7) $-24 < x < 24$
8) $x < -10$ or $x > 14$
9) $-21 < x < 21$
10) $x > 17$ or $x < -1$
11) $x > 6$ or $x < -18$
12) $-33 < x < 23$
13) $x \geq 2$ or $x \leq -2$
14) $x < 13$ and $x > -9$
15) $x < 0$ and $x > -4$
16) $x < -4$ and $x > -10$
17) $x > 5$ or $x < -5$
18) $x > 2$ or $x < -2$
19) $x \leq 5$ and $x \geq -5$
20) $-12 \leq x \leq 4$
21) $x \leq 8$ and $x \geq -8$
22) $4 < x < 12$

Graphing Absolute Value Inequalities

1) $|2x - 2| \geq 10$

2) $|\frac{1}{3}x - 1| \leq 3$

3) $|x| - 2 < 6$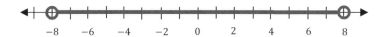

4) $|x + 4| < 8$

5) $|2x - 2| \leq 14$

6) $|x| + 8 > 16$

7) $|2x + 8| \leq 24$

8) $|3x - 12| \leq 6$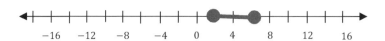

9) $|x| - 6 > 2$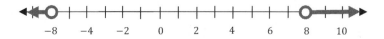

Chapter 2: Equations and Inequalities

Solving Systems of Equations

1) $x = \frac{22}{5}, y = \frac{4}{5}$
2) $x = \frac{11}{5}, y = \frac{2}{5}$
3) $x = -2, y = -4$
4) $x = 3, y = -1$
5) $x = -11, y = -14$
6) $x = -5, y = 3$
7) $x = \frac{14}{13}, y = -\frac{49}{26}$
8) $x = 1, y = 2$
9) $x = 5, y = 0$
10) $x = 0, y = -3$
11) $x = 20, y = 2$
12) $x = 0, y = 2$
13) $x = \frac{22}{5}, y = \frac{4}{5}$
14) $x = -11, y = -14$

Solving Special Systems

1) No solutions
2) Infinitely many solutions
3) No solutions
4) Infinitely many solutions
5) No solutions
6) One solution
7) One solution
8) No solutions
9) No solutions
10) Infinitely many solutions
11) No solutions
12) Infinitely many solutions
13) No solutions
14) No solutions

Systems of Equations Word Problems

1) $x = 2$
2) 10, 40
3) $12
4) 10
5) 34
6) 42, 24

Chapter 3: Quadratic Function

Math Topics that you'll learn in this Chapter:

- ✓ Solving a Quadratic Equation
- ✓ Graphing Quadratic Functions
- ✓ Axis of Symmetry of Quadratic Functions
- ✓ Solve a Quadratic Equation by Graphing
- ✓ Solving Quadratic Equations by Using Square Roots
- ✓ Build Quadratics from Roots
- ✓ Solving Quadratic Inequalities
- ✓ Graphing Quadratic Inequalities
- ✓ Factoring the Difference between Two Perfect Squares

Chapter 3: Quadratic Function

Solving a Quadratic Equations

✎ *Solve each equation by factoring or using the quadratic formula.*

1) $(x+2)(x-7) = 0$

2) $(x+3)(x+5) = 0$

3) $(x-9)(x+4) = 0$

4) $(x-7)(x-5) = 0$

5) $(x+4)(x+8) = 0$

6) $(5x+7)(x+4) = 0$

7) $(2x+5)(4x+3) = 0$

8) $(3x+4)(x+2) = 0$

9) $(6x+3)(2x+4) = 0$

10) $(9x+3)(x+6) = 0$

11) $x^2 = 2x$

12) $x^2 - 6 = x$

13) $2x^2 + 4 = 6x$

14) $-x^2 - 6 = 5x$

15) $x^2 + 8x = 9$

16) $x^2 + 10x = 24$

17) $x^2 + 7x = -10$

18) $x^2 + 12x = -32$

19) $x^2 + 11x = -28$

20) $x^2 + x - 20 = 2x$

21) $x^2 + 8x = -15$

22) $7x^2 - 14x = -7$

23) $10x^2 = 27x - 18$

24) $7x^2 - 6x + 3 = 3$

25) $2x^2 - 14 = -3x$

26) $10x^2 - 26x = -12$

27) $15x^2 + 80 = -80x$

28) $x^2 + 15x = -56$

29) $6x^2 - 18x - 18 = 6$

30) $2x^2 + 6x - 24 = 12$

31) $2x^2 - 22x + 38 = -10$

32) $-4x^2 - 8x - 3 = -3 - 5x^2$

www.EffortlessMath.com

Chapter 3: Quadratic Function

Graphing Quadratic Functions

✎ *Sketch the graph of each function. Identify the vertex and axis of symmetry.*

1) $y = 3(x + 1)^2 + 2$

2) $y = -(x - 2)^2 - 4$

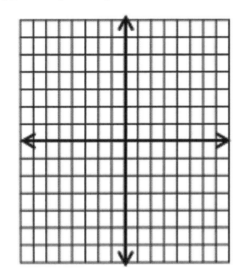
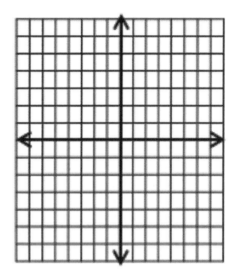

3) $y = 2(x - 3)^2 + 8$

4) $y = x^2 - 8x + 19$

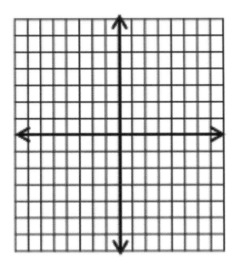
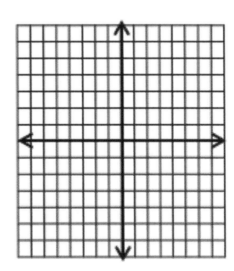

Chapter 3: Quadratic Function

Axis of Symmetry of Quadratic Functions

✎ *Graph the following quadratic equation, then find the axis of symmetry of the quadratic function.*

1) $y = x^2 - 4x + 6$

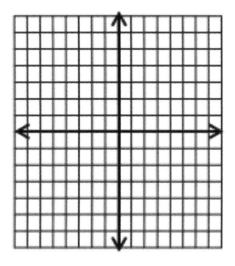

2) $y = x^2 + 8x + 12$

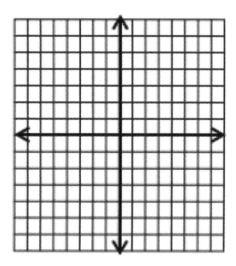

3) $y = x^2 + 6x + 12$

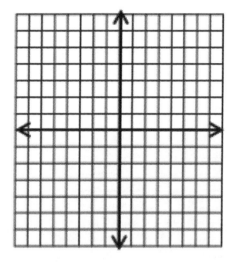

4) $y = x^2 + 4x - 32$

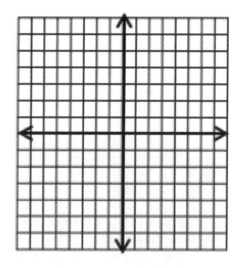

Chapter 3: Quadratic Function

Solve a Quadratic Equation by Graphing

✎ *Solve the following quadratic equation using graphing.*

1) $x^2 + 4x - 5 = 0$

2) $x^2 - 8x + 15 = 0$

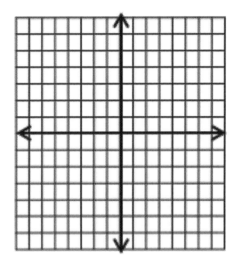
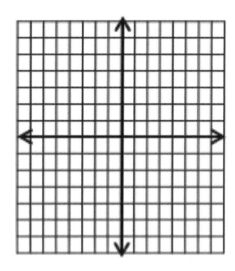

3) $x^2 + 3x - 28 = 0$

4) $x^2 - 3x - 18 = 0$

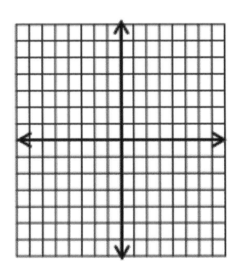
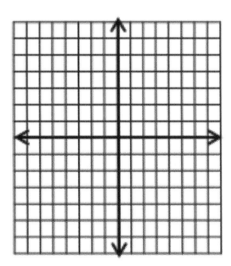

Chapter 3: Quadratic Function

Solving Quadratic Equations by Using Square Roots

✎ *Solving quadratic equations with square roots.*

1) $x^2 - 4 = 0$

2) $x^2 - 5 = 0$

3) $x^2 - 49 = 0$

4) $x^2 - 16 = 0$

5) $x^2 - 36 = 0$

6) $x^2 - 32 = 0$

7) $x^2 - 50 = 0$

8) $x^2 - 8 = 0$

9) $x^2 - 48 = 0$

10) $x^2 - 6 = -5$

11) $x^2 - 72 = 0$

12) $x^2 - 147 = 0$

13) $x^2 - 45 = 0$

14) $(x + 3)^2 = 16$

15) $x^2 + 6x = -9$

16) $7x^2 + 2 = 30$

17) $x^2 + 7 = 25$

18) $(x + 5)^2 - 32 = 0$

19) $2x^2 - 162 = 0$

20) $7x^2 - 448 = 0$

21) $(x - 2)^2 = 12$

22) $9x^2 + 10 = 91$

23) $8x^2 - 8 = 192$

24) $3x^2 - 108 = 0$

25) $3(x - 32)^2 - 54 = 0$

26) $4x^2 + 4x - 15 = 0$

Chapter 3: Quadratic Function

Build Quadratics from Roots

Build the quadratic equation.

1) $x = -2, x = -5$

2) $x = 3$

3) $x = 4, x = -2$

4) $x = -4, x = 3$

5) $x = -5, x = -4$

6) $x = -6, x = -3$

7) $x = -3, x = -2$

8) $x = 5, x = 4$

9) $x = -3, x = 2$

10) $x = 4, x = 2$

11) $x = 6, x = 3$

12) $x = -2, x = -3$

13) $x = 4, x = -5$

14) $x = -3, x = 7$

15) $x = 8, x = 4$

16) $x = 9, x = -2$

17) $x = -5, x = 6$

18) $x = -4, x = -7$

19) $x = 8, x = 7$

20) $x = 9, x = -6$

21) $x = -6, x = 8$

22) $x = 9, x = 8$

23) $x = -2, x = 12$

24) $x = -4, x = 6$

25) $x = 3, x = 11$

26) $x = 12, x = 2$

27) $x = 5, x = 10$

28) $x = 2, x = 15$

29) $x = -3, x = -9$

30) $x = -6, x = -12$

31) $x = 11, x = -7$

32) $x = 22, x = -3$

Chapter 3: Quadratic Function
Solving Quadratic Inequalities

✎ *Solve each quadratic inequality.*

1) $x^2 - 1 < 0$

2) $-x^2 - 5x + 6 > 0$

3) $x^2 - 5x - 6 < 0$

4) $x^2 + 4x - 5 > 0$

5) $x^2 - 2x - 3 \geq 0$

6) $x^2 > 5x + 6$

7) $-x^2 - 12x - 11 \leq 0$

8) $x^2 - 2x - 8 \geq 0$

9) $x^2 - 5x - 6 \geq 0$

10) $x^2 + 7x + 10 < 0$

11) $x^2 + 9x + 20 > 0$

12) $x^2 - 8x + 16 > 0$

13) $x^2 - 8x + 12 \leq 0$

14) $x^2 - 11x + 30 \leq 0$

15) $x^2 - 12x + 27 \geq 0$

16) $x^2 - 16x + 64 \geq 0$

17) $x^2 - 36 \leq 0$

18) $x^2 - 13x + 36 \geq 0$

19) $x^2 + 15x + 36 \leq 0$

20) $4x^2 - 6x - 9 > x^2$

21) $5x^2 - 15x + 10 < 0$

22) $3x^2 - 5x \geq 4x^2 + 6$

23) $4x^2 - 12 > 3x^2 + x$

24) $x^2 - 2x \geq x^2 - 6x + 12$

25) $2x^2 + 2x - 8 > x^2$

26) $4x^2 + 20x - 11 < 0$

27) $-9x^2 + 29x - 6 \geq 0$

28) $-8x^2 + 6x - 1 \leq 0$

29) $12x^2 + 10x - 12 > 0$

30) $18x^2 + 23x + 5 \leq 0$

31) $17x^2 + 15x - 2 \geq 0$

32) $3x^2 + 7x \leq 5x^2 + 3x - 6$

Chapter 3: Quadratic Function

Graphing Quadratic Inequalities

✎ *Sketch the graph of each quadratic inequality.*

1) $y > -2x^2$

2) $y < 3x^2$

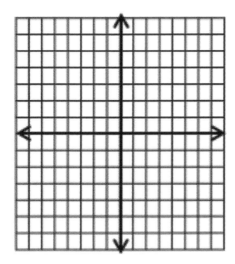
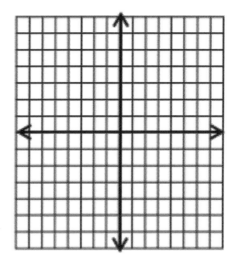

3) $y \geq -3x^2$

4) $y < x^2 + 4$

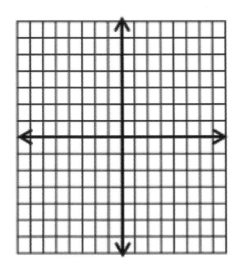
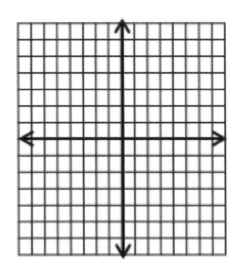

Chapter 3: Quadratic Function

Factoring the Difference between Two Perfect Squares

Factor each completely.

1) $1 - x^2 =$

2) $x^2 - 36 =$

3) $4x^2 - 16 =$

4) $25x^2 - 49 =$

5) $9x^2 - 64 =$

6) $4x^4 - 9 =$

7) $9x^4 - 36 =$

8) $36x^4 - 25 =$

9) $81x^4 - 121 =$

10) $25x^4 - 64 =$

11) $9x^4 - 49 =$

12) $25x^4 - 36 =$

13) $16x^4 - 81 =$

14) $9x^4 - 2 =$

15) $4x^4 - 12 =$

16) $49x^4 - 144 =$

17) $169x^4 - 121 =$

18) $81x^4 - 5 =$

19) $36x^2 - 121 =$

20) $49x^2 - 196 =$

21) $-36x^3 + 4x =$

22) $2x - 8x^3 =$

23) $3x - 48x^3 =$

24) $-36x^2 + 400 =$

25) $9x^2 - 54x + 81 =$

26) $49x^2 - 56x + 16 =$

27) $25x^2 - 80x + 64 =$

28) $81x^4 - 900x^2 =$

Chapter 3: Quadratic Function

Answers – Chapter 3

Solving a Quadratic Equation

1) $\{-2, 7\}$
2) $\{-3, -5\}$
3) $\{9, -4\}$
4) $\{7, 5\}$
5) $\{-4, -8\}$
6) $\{-\frac{7}{5}, -4\}$
7) $\{-\frac{5}{2}, -\frac{3}{4}\}$
8) $\{-\frac{4}{3}, -2\}$
9) $\{-\frac{1}{2}, -2\}$
10) $\{-\frac{1}{3}, -6\}$
11) $\{2, 0\}$
12) $\{3, -2\}$
13) $\{2, 1\}$
14) $\{-3, -2\}$
15) $\{1, -9\}$
16) $\{2, -12\}$
17) $\{-2, -5\}$
18) $\{-4, -8\}$
19) $\{-4, -7\}$
20) $\{5, -4\}$
21) $\{-5, -3\}$
22) $\{1\}$
23) $\{\frac{6}{5}, \frac{3}{2}\}$
24) $\{\frac{6}{7}, 0\}$
25) $\{-\frac{7}{2}, 2\}$
26) $\{\frac{3}{5}, 2\}$
27) $\{-\frac{4}{3}, -4\}$
28) $\{-8, -7\}$
29) $\{4, -1\}$
30) $\{3, -6\}$
31) $\{3, 8\}$
32) $\{8, 0\}$

Graphing Quadratic Functions

1) $(-1, 2), x = -1$

2) $(2, -4), x = 2$

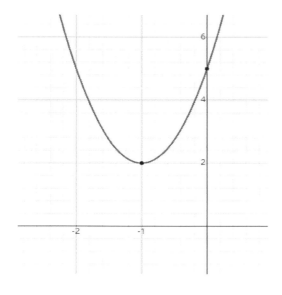

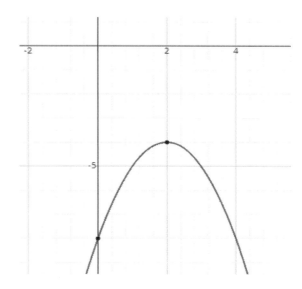

3) $(3, 8), x = 3$

4) $(4, 3), x = 4$

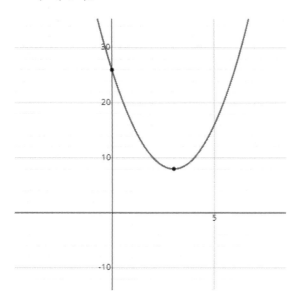
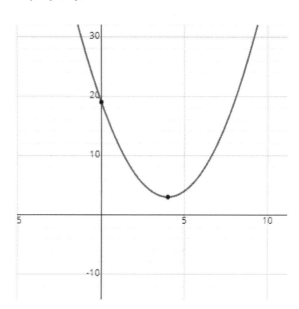

Axis of Symmetry of Quadratic Functions

1) $x = 2$

2) $x = -4$

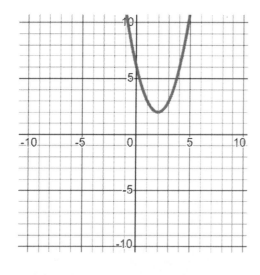
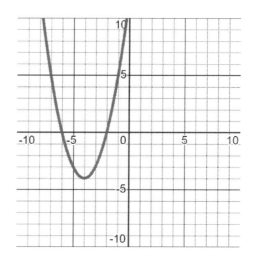

Chapter 3: Quadratic Function

3) $x = -3$

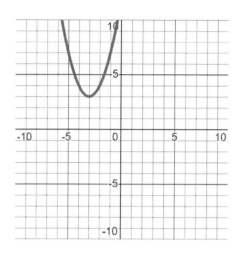

4) $x = -2$

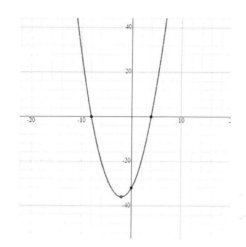

Solve a Quadratic Equation by Graphing

1) $x = 1, x = -5$

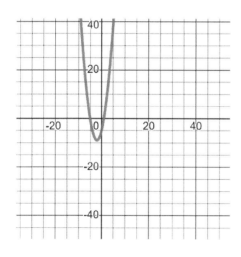

2) $x = 5, x = 3$

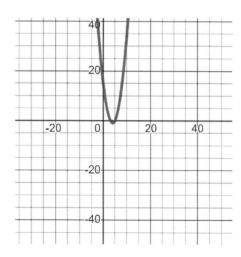

Chapter 3: Quadratic Function

3) $x = 4, x = -7$

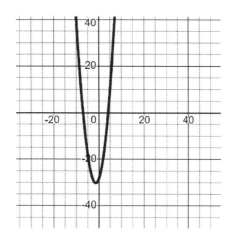

4) $x = 6, x = -3$

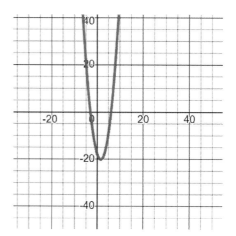

Solving Quadratic Equations by Using Square Roots

1) $x = \pm 2$
2) $x = \pm\sqrt{5}$
3) $x = \pm 7$
4) $x = \pm 4$
5) $x = \pm 6$
6) $x = \pm 4\sqrt{2}$
7) $x = \pm 5\sqrt{2}$
8) $x = \pm 2\sqrt{2}$
9) $x = \pm 4\sqrt{3}$
10) $x = \pm 1$
11) $x = \pm 6\sqrt{2}$
12) $x = \pm 7\sqrt{3}$
13) $x = \pm 3\sqrt{5}$
14) $x = 1, x = -7$
15) $x = -3$
16) $x = \pm 2$
17) $x = \pm 3\sqrt{2}$
18) $x = \pm 4\sqrt{2} - 5$
19) $x = \pm 9$
20) $x = \pm 8$
21) $x = \pm 2\sqrt{3} + 2$
22) $x = \pm 3$
23) $x = \pm 5$
24) $x = \pm 6$
25) $x = \pm 3\sqrt{2} + 32$
26) $x = \frac{3}{2}, x = -\frac{5}{2}$

Chapter 3: Quadratic Function

Build Quadratics from Roots

1) $x^2 + 7x + 10 = 0$
2) $x^2 - 6x + 9 = 0$
3) $x^2 - 2x - 8 = 0$
4) $x^2 + x - 12 = 0$
5) $x^2 + 9x + 20 = 0$
6) $x^2 + 9x + 18 = 0$
7) $x^2 + 5x + 6 = 0$
8) $x^2 - 9x + 20 = 0$
9) $x^2 + x - 6 = 0$
10) $x^2 - 6x + 8 = 0$
11) $x^2 - 9x + 18 = 0$
12) $x^2 + 5x + 6 = 0$
13) $x^2 + x - 20 = 0$
14) $x^2 - 4x - 21 = 0$
15) $x^2 - 12x + 32 = 0$
16) $x^2 - 7x - 18 = 0$
17) $x^2 - x - 30 = 0$
18) $x^2 + 11x + 28 = 0$
19) $x^2 - 15x + 56 = 0$
20) $x^2 - 3x - 54 = 0$
21) $x^2 - 2x - 48 = 0$
22) $x^2 - 17x + 72 = 0$
23) $x^2 - 10x - 24 = 0$
24) $x^2 - 2x - 24 = 0$
25) $x^2 - 14x + 33 = 0$
26) $x^2 - 14x + 24 = 0$
27) $x^2 - 15x + 50 = 0$
28) $x^2 - 17x + 30 = 0$
29) $x^2 + 12x + 27 = 0$
30) $x^2 + 18x + 72 = 0$
31) $x^2 - 4x - 77 = 0$
32) $x^2 - 19x - 66 = 0$

Solving Quadratic Inequalities

1) $-1 < x < 1$
2) $-6 < x < 1$
3) $-1 < x < 6$
4) $x < -5 \text{ or } x > 1$
5) $x \leq -1 \text{ or } x \geq 3$
6) $x < -1 \text{ or } x > 6$
7) $x \leq -11 \text{ or } x \geq -1$
8) $x \leq -2 \text{ or } x \geq 4$
9) $x \leq -1 \text{ or } x \geq 6$
10) $-5 < x < -2$
11) $x < -5 \text{ or } x > -4$
12) $x < 4 \text{ or } x > 4$
13) $2 \leq x \leq 6$
14) $5 \leq x \leq 6$
15) $x \leq 3 \text{ or } x \geq 9$
16) all real numbers
17) $-6 \leq x \leq 6$
18) $x \leq 4 \text{ or } x \geq 9$
19) $-12 \leq x \leq -3$
20) $x < -1 \text{ or } x > 3$
21) $1 < x < 2$
22) $-3 \leq x \leq -2$
23) $x < -3 \text{ or } x > 4$
24) $x \geq 3$
25) $x < -4 \text{ or } x > 2$
26) $-\frac{11}{2} < x < \frac{1}{2}$
27) $\frac{2}{9} \leq x \leq 3$
28) $x \leq \frac{1}{4} \text{ or } x \geq \frac{1}{2}$
29) $x < -1.5 \text{ or } x > \frac{2}{3}$
30) $-1 \leq x \leq -\frac{5}{18}$
31) $x \leq -1 \text{ or } x \geq \frac{2}{17}$
32) $x \leq -1 \text{ or } x \geq 3$

Graphing Quadratic Inequalities

1) $y > -2x^2$

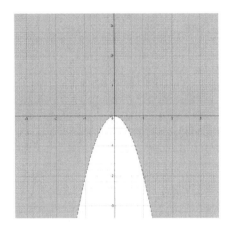

2) $y < 3x^2$

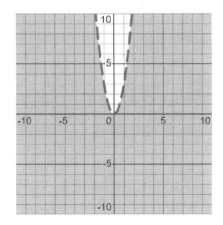

3) $y \geq -3x^2$

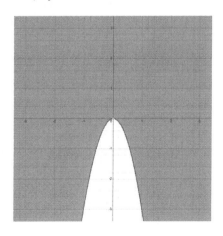

4) $y < x^2 + 4$

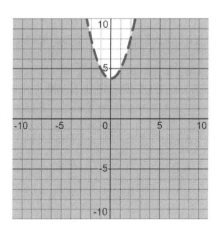

Chapter 3: Quadratic Function

Factoring the Difference between Two Perfect Squares

1) $(1 + x)(1 - x)$
2) $(x + 6)(x - 6)$
3) $(2x + 4)(2x - 4)$
4) $(5x + 7)(5x - 7)$
5) $(3x + 8)(3x - 8)$
6) $(2x^2 - 3)(2x^2 + 3)$
7) $(3x^2 - 6)(3x^2 + 6)$
8) $(6x^2 - 5)(6x^2 + 5)$
9) $(9x^2 - 11)(9x^2 + 11)$
10) $(5x^2 - 8)(5x^2 + 8)$
11) $(3x^2 - 7)(3x^2 + 7)$
12) $(5x^2 - 6)(5x^2 + 6)$
13) $(4x^2 - 9)(4x^2 + 9)$
14) $(3x^2 - \sqrt{2})(3x^2 + \sqrt{2})$
15) $(2x^2 - 2\sqrt{3})(2x^2 + 2\sqrt{3})$
16) $(7x^2 - 12)(7x^2 + 12)$
17) $(13x^2 - 11)(13x^2 + 11)$
18) $(9x^2 - \sqrt{5})(9x^2 + \sqrt{5})$
19) $(6x - 11)(6x + 11)$
20) $(7x - 14)(7x + 14)$
21) $4x(1 - 3x)(1 + 3x)$
22) $2x(1 - 2x)(1 + 2x)$
23) $3x(1 - 4x)(1 + 4x)$
24) $-4(3x + 10)(3x - 10)$
25) $(3x - 9)^2$
26) $(7x - 4)^2$
27) $(5x - 8)^2$
28) $9x^2(3x + 10)(3x - 10)$

Chapter 4: Complex Numbers

Math Topics that you'll learn in this Chapter:

- ✓ Adding and Subtracting Complex Numbers
- ✓ Multiplying and Dividing Complex Numbers
- ✓ Rationalizing Imaginary Denominators

Chapter 4: Complex Numbers

Adding and Subtracting Complex Numbers

✎ **Simplify.**

1) $(2i) - (i) =$

2) $(2i) + (2i) =$

3) $(i) + (3i) =$

4) $(-2i) - (6i) =$

5) $(5i) + (4i) =$

6) $(3i) - (-7i) =$

7) $(-6i) + (-9i) =$

8) $(15i) - (7i) =$

9) $(-12i) - (5i) =$

10) $(2i) + (2 + 3i) =$

11) $(2 - 4i) + (-i) =$

12) $(-3i) + (3 + 5i) =$

13) $3 + (2 - 4i) =$

14) $(-5i) - (-5 + 2i) =$

15) $(5 + 3i) - (-4i) =$

16) $(8 + 5i) + (-7i) =$

17) $(9i) - (-6i + 10) =$

18) $(12i + 8) + (-7i) =$

19) $(13i) - (17 + 3i) =$

20) $(3 + 5i) + (8 + 3i) =$

21) $(8 - 3i) + (4 + i) =$

22) $(10 + 9i) + (6 + 8i) =$

23) $(-3 + 6i) - (-9 - i) =$

24) $(-5 + 15i) - (-3 + 3i) =$

25) $(-14 + i) - (-12 - 11i) =$

26) $(-18 - 3i) + (11 + 5i) =$

27) $(-11 - 9i) - (-9 - 3i) =$

28) $-8 + (2i) + (-8 + 6i) =$

29) $12 - (5i) + (4 - 14i) =$

30) $-2 + (-8 - 7i) - 9 =$

31) $(-12i) + (2 - 6i) + 10 =$

32) $(-8i) - (8 - 5i) + 6i =$

Chapter 4: Complex Numbers

Multiplying and Dividing Complex Numbers

✏️ **Simplify.**

1) $(5i)(-i) =$

2) $(-4i)(5i) =$

3) $(i)(7i)(-i) =$

4) $(3i)(-4i) =$

5) $(-2-i)(4+i) =$

6) $(2-2i)^2 =$

7) $(4-3i)(6-6i) =$

8) $(5+4i)^2 =$

9) $(4i)(-i)(2-5i) =$

10) $(2-8i)(3-5i) =$

11) $(-5+9i)(3+5i) =$

12) $(7+3i)(7+8i) =$

13) $2(3i) - (5i)(-8+5i) =$

14) $\dfrac{5}{-10i} =$

15) $\dfrac{4-3i}{-4i} =$

16) $\dfrac{5+9i}{i} =$

17) $\dfrac{12i}{-9+3i} =$

18) $\dfrac{-3-10i}{5i} =$

19) $\dfrac{9i}{3-i} =$

20) $\dfrac{2+4i}{14+4i} =$

21) $\dfrac{5+6i}{-1+8i} =$

22) $\dfrac{-8-i}{-4-6i} =$

23) $\dfrac{-1+5i}{-8-7i} =$

Chapter 4: Complex Numbers

Rationalizing Imaginary Denominators

✎ Simplify.

1) $\dfrac{-2}{-2i} =$

2) $\dfrac{-1}{-9i} =$

3) $\dfrac{-8}{-5i} =$

4) $\dfrac{-5}{-i} =$

5) $\dfrac{3}{5i} =$

6) $\dfrac{6}{-4i} =$

7) $\dfrac{6}{-7i} =$

8) $\dfrac{-10}{3i} =$

9) $\dfrac{a}{bi} =$

10) $\dfrac{10-10i}{-5i} =$

11) $\dfrac{4-9i}{-6i} =$

12) $\dfrac{6+8i}{9i} =$

13) $\dfrac{8i}{-1+3i} =$

14) $\dfrac{5i}{-2-6i} =$

15) $\dfrac{-10-5i}{-6+6i} =$

16) $\dfrac{-5-9i}{9+8i} =$

17) $\dfrac{-5-3i}{7-10i} =$

18) $\dfrac{-1+i}{-5i} =$

19) $\dfrac{-6-i}{i} =$

20) $\dfrac{-4-i}{9+5i} =$

21) $\dfrac{-3+i}{-2i} =$

22) $\dfrac{-6-i}{-1+6i} =$

23) $\dfrac{-9-3i}{-3+3i} =$

24) $\dfrac{4i+1}{-1+3i} =$

Chapter 4: Complex Numbers

Answers – Chapter 4

Adding and Subtracting Complex Numbers

1) i
2) $4i$
3) $4i$
4) $-8i$
5) $9i$
6) $10i$
7) $-15i$
8) $8i$
9) $-17i$
10) $2 + 5i$
11) $2 - 5i$
12) $3 + 2i$
13) $5 - 4i$
14) $5 - 7i$
15) $5 + 7i$
16) $8 - 2i$
17) $-10 + 15i$
18) $8 + 5i$
19) $-17 + 10i$
20) $11 + 8i$
21) $12 - 2i$
22) $16 + 17i$
23) $6 + 7i$
24) $-2 + 12i$
25) $-2 + 12i$
26) $-7 + 2i$
27) $-2 - 6i$
28) $-16 + 8i$
29) $16 - 19i$
30) $-19 - 7i$
31) $12 - 18i$
32) $-8 + 3i$

Multiplying and Dividing Complex Numbers

1) 5
2) 20
3) $7i$
4) 12
5) $-7 - 6i$
6) $-8i$
7) $6 - 42i$
8) $9 + 40i$
9) $8 - 20i$
10) $-34 - 34i$
11) $-60 + 2i$
12) $25 + 77i$
13) $25 + 46i$
14) $\frac{i}{2}$
15) $\frac{3}{4} + i$
16) $9 - 5i$
17) $\frac{2}{5} - \frac{6}{5}i$
18) $-2 + \frac{3}{5}i$
19) $-\frac{9}{10} + \frac{27}{10}i$
20) $\frac{11}{53} + \frac{12}{53}i$
21) $\frac{43}{65} - \frac{46}{65}i$
22) $\frac{19}{26} - \frac{11}{13}i$
23) $-\frac{27}{113} - \frac{47}{113}i$

Chapter 4: Complex Numbers

Rationalizing Imaginary Denominators

1) $-i$

2) $-\frac{1}{9}i$

3) $\frac{-8}{5}i$

4) $-5i$

5) $-\frac{3}{5}i$

6) $\frac{3}{2}i$

7) $\frac{6}{7}i$

8) $\frac{10}{3}i$

9) $-\frac{a}{b}i$

10) $2 + 2i$

11) $\frac{3}{2} + \frac{2}{3}i$

12) $\frac{8}{9} - \frac{2}{3}i$

13) $\frac{12}{5} - \frac{4}{5}i$

14) $-\frac{3}{4} - \frac{1}{4}i$

15) $\frac{5}{12} + \frac{5}{4}i$

16) $-\frac{117}{145} - \frac{41}{145}i$

17) $-\frac{5}{149} - \frac{71}{149}i$

18) $-\frac{1}{5} - \frac{1}{5}i$

19) $-1 + 6i$

20) $-\frac{41}{106} + \frac{11}{106}i$

21) $-\frac{1}{2} - \frac{3}{2}i$

22) i

23) $1 + 2i$

24) $\frac{11}{10} - \frac{7}{10}i$

Chapter 5: Matrices

Math Topics that you'll learn in this Chapter:

- ✓ Using Matrices to Represent Data
- ✓ Adding and Subtracting Matrices
- ✓ Matrix Multiplications
- ✓ The Inverse of a Matrix
- ✓ Solving Systems with Matrix Equations
- ✓ Finding Determinants of a Matrix

Chapter 5: Matrices

Using Matrices to Represent Data

✏️ *Write each equation as a matrix.*

1) $\begin{cases} 2x + 9y = 17 \\ -3x + 8y = 39 \end{cases}$

2) $\begin{cases} 2x - y = 12 \\ x - 2y = 48 \end{cases}$

3) $\begin{cases} 3x - y = 23 \\ 4x + 3y = 48 \end{cases}$

4) $\begin{cases} 3x + 2y = 16 \\ 7x + y = 19 \end{cases}$

5) $\begin{cases} 4x + 3y = -2 \\ 8x - 2y = 12 \end{cases}$

6) $\begin{cases} x + y = 6 \\ -3x + y = 2 \end{cases}$

7) $\begin{cases} 2z - y = 4 \\ 6z - 3y = 3 \end{cases}$

8) $\begin{cases} x + y + z = 6 \\ 2x + 5y - z = 27 \end{cases}$

9) $\begin{cases} 3y = -6x + 10 \\ 12x - 8y = -6 \end{cases}$

10) $\begin{cases} 7x - 14y = -28 \\ -5x = -7y + 8 \end{cases}$

11) $\begin{cases} 2x + 5y = 10 \\ 3x + 4y = 24 \end{cases}$

12) $\begin{cases} 4x + 6y = 16 \\ 10x + 4y = 4 \end{cases}$

13) $\begin{cases} 6x - 4y = 8 \\ 2x + 10y = -6 \\ -8x - 2y + 6z = 0 \end{cases}$

14) $\begin{cases} 2x - 4y - 2z = 4 \\ 4x - 2y + 2z = 8 \\ -2x - 2y - 4z = -8 \end{cases}$

15) $\begin{cases} x - 3z = -2 \\ 2x + 2y + z = 4 \\ 3x + y - 2z = 5 \end{cases}$

Chapter 5: Matrices

Adding and Subtracting Matrices

✏️ **Solve.**

1) $[2 \quad -5 \quad -3] + [1 \quad -2 \quad -3] =$

2) $\begin{bmatrix} 3 & -6 \\ -1 & -3 \\ -5 & -1 \end{bmatrix} + \begin{bmatrix} 0 & -1 \\ 6 & 3 \\ 2 & 3 \end{bmatrix} =$

3) $\begin{bmatrix} -5 & 2 & -2 \\ 4 & -2 & 0 \end{bmatrix} - \begin{bmatrix} 6 & -5 & -6 \\ 1 & 3 & -3 \end{bmatrix} =$

4) $\begin{bmatrix} 2 & 1 \\ -1 & 3 \end{bmatrix} - \begin{bmatrix} 2 & 5 \\ -7 & -2 \end{bmatrix} =$

5) $\begin{bmatrix} 6 & 4 \\ -9 & 7 \end{bmatrix} + \begin{bmatrix} 5 & 3 \\ -4 & 1 \end{bmatrix} =$

6) $\begin{bmatrix} 2 & 0 \\ -1 & 1 \end{bmatrix} - \begin{bmatrix} 4 & -2 \\ 2 & 1 \end{bmatrix} =$

7) $\begin{bmatrix} 6 & -7 \\ -3 & 11 \end{bmatrix} + \begin{bmatrix} 10 & -11 \\ 12 & 18 \end{bmatrix} =$

8) $\begin{bmatrix} -1 & 2 & -1 \\ 2 & -1 & 0 \end{bmatrix} - \begin{bmatrix} 2 & -5 & -4 \\ 1 & 1 & -3 \end{bmatrix} =$

9) $\begin{bmatrix} 8 & 12 \\ 14 & 21 \end{bmatrix} + \begin{bmatrix} 8 & -15 \\ 10 & -7 \end{bmatrix} =$

10) $\begin{bmatrix} 12 \\ 9 \\ 5 \end{bmatrix} + \begin{bmatrix} 18 \\ -14 \\ 19 \end{bmatrix} =$

11) $\begin{bmatrix} 14 \\ -16 \\ 13 \\ 21 \end{bmatrix} + \begin{bmatrix} -16 \\ 8 \\ -5 \\ -18 \end{bmatrix} =$

12) $\begin{bmatrix} 2 & -5 & -9 \\ 4 & -7 & 11 \\ -6 & 3 & -17 \end{bmatrix} + \begin{bmatrix} 3 & 4 & -5 \\ 13 & 2 & 5 \\ 4 & -8 & 1 \end{bmatrix} =$

13) $\begin{bmatrix} 1 & -7 & 5 \\ 31 & 3 & 18 \\ 22 & 6 & 4 \end{bmatrix} + \begin{bmatrix} 13 & 17 & 5 \\ 3 & 8 & -1 \\ -9 & 2 & 12 \end{bmatrix} =$

14) $\begin{bmatrix} 2 & 4 & 6 \\ 1 & 3 & 5 \end{bmatrix} - \begin{bmatrix} 1 & 2 & -1 \\ 3 & -1 & 4 \end{bmatrix} =$

15) $\begin{bmatrix} 2 & 1 \\ -1 & 3 \\ 6 & -2 \end{bmatrix} + \begin{bmatrix} -1 & 5 \\ 7 & -2 \\ 3 & 5 \end{bmatrix} =$

16) $\begin{bmatrix} -1 & -2 \\ 4 & 6 \\ 3 & -1 \end{bmatrix} + \begin{bmatrix} 4 & 6 \\ 8 & 1 \\ 1 & -3 \end{bmatrix} =$

Chapter 5: Matrices

Matrix Multiplications

Solve.

1) $\begin{bmatrix} 5 \\ 6 \\ 0 \end{bmatrix} \begin{bmatrix} 3 & -1 \end{bmatrix} =$

2) $\begin{bmatrix} -5 & -5 \\ -1 & 2 \end{bmatrix} \begin{bmatrix} -2 & -3 \\ 3 & 5 \end{bmatrix} =$

3) $\begin{bmatrix} 0 & 5 \\ -3 & 1 \\ -5 & 1 \end{bmatrix} \begin{bmatrix} -4 & 4 \\ -2 & -4 \end{bmatrix} =$

4) $\begin{bmatrix} 5 & 3 & 5 \\ 1 & 5 & 0 \end{bmatrix} \begin{bmatrix} -4 & 2 \\ -3 & 4 \\ 3 & -5 \end{bmatrix} =$

5) $\begin{bmatrix} 3 & -1 \\ -3 & 6 \\ -6 & -6 \end{bmatrix} \begin{bmatrix} -1 & 6 \\ 5 & 4 \end{bmatrix} =$

6) $\begin{bmatrix} -2 & -6 \\ -4 & 3 \\ 5 & 0 \\ 4 & -6 \end{bmatrix} \begin{bmatrix} 2 & -2 & 2 \\ -2 & 0 & -3 \end{bmatrix} =$

7) $\begin{bmatrix} -1 & 0 & 3 \end{bmatrix} \begin{bmatrix} 1 \\ 2 \\ -1 \end{bmatrix} =$

8) $\begin{bmatrix} -1 \\ 6 \\ -6 \end{bmatrix} \begin{bmatrix} 8 & 5 & 4 \end{bmatrix} =$

9) $\begin{bmatrix} 0 & 2 \\ 2 & -1 \end{bmatrix} \begin{bmatrix} -2 & 1 \\ 1 & 4 \end{bmatrix} =$

10) $\begin{bmatrix} 2 & 4 & 3 \\ 4 & 3 & 2 \end{bmatrix} \begin{bmatrix} 4 & 3 \\ 5 & 5 \\ 2 & 5 \end{bmatrix} =$

11) $\begin{bmatrix} 2 & 5 \\ -4 & -3 \end{bmatrix} \begin{bmatrix} 1 & -5 \\ 3 & 2 \end{bmatrix} =$

12) $\begin{bmatrix} 1 & -2 \\ -4 & 5 \end{bmatrix} \begin{bmatrix} 4 & 3 \\ 4 & 0 \end{bmatrix} =$

13) $\begin{bmatrix} 3 & 1 & 2 \\ -5 & 6 & 5 \end{bmatrix} \begin{bmatrix} 3 \\ 5 \\ 2 \end{bmatrix} =$

14) $\begin{bmatrix} -1 & 2 & 5 \\ 0 & -2 & -1 \end{bmatrix} \begin{bmatrix} 5 & 1 \\ 2 & -2 \\ 0 & 1 \end{bmatrix} =$

15) $\begin{bmatrix} 2 & 3 \\ 5 & 7 \\ -2 & -1 \end{bmatrix} \begin{bmatrix} 2 & 4 \\ 5 & 3 \end{bmatrix} =$

16) $\begin{bmatrix} -3 & 5 \\ 9 & 1 \\ 3 & 2 \end{bmatrix} \begin{bmatrix} -2 & 1 & 5 \\ 8 & 2 & -6 \end{bmatrix} =$

Chapter 5: Matrices

The Inverse of a Matrix

✏️ *Find the inverse of the matrix.*

1) $C = \begin{bmatrix} 3 & -2 \\ -4 & 6 \end{bmatrix}$

2) $C = \begin{bmatrix} 5 & -8 \\ 6 & -9 \end{bmatrix}$

3) $C = \begin{bmatrix} 2 & -10 \\ -11 & 8 \end{bmatrix}$

4) $C = \begin{bmatrix} -9 & -6 \\ -5 & -4 \end{bmatrix}$

5) $C = \begin{bmatrix} -3 & 3 \\ 8 & 7 \end{bmatrix}$

6) $C = \begin{bmatrix} -2 & 2 \\ -9 & 8 \end{bmatrix}$

7) $C = \begin{bmatrix} 3 & -2 \\ -4 & 6 \end{bmatrix}$

8) $C = \begin{bmatrix} -6 & 11 \\ -4 & 7 \end{bmatrix}$

9) $C = \begin{bmatrix} -1 & 7 \\ -1 & 7 \end{bmatrix}$

10) $C = \begin{bmatrix} 1 & -1 \\ -6 & -3 \end{bmatrix}$

11) $C = \begin{bmatrix} 11 & -5 \\ 2 & -1 \end{bmatrix}$

12) $C = \begin{bmatrix} 0 & -2 \\ -1 & -9 \end{bmatrix}$

13) $C = \begin{bmatrix} 0 & 0 \\ -6 & 4 \end{bmatrix}$

14) $C = \begin{bmatrix} -9 & -9 \\ -2 & -2 \end{bmatrix}$

15) $C = \begin{bmatrix} -1 & -4 \\ 0 & -2 \end{bmatrix}$

16) $C = \begin{bmatrix} 2 & 3 & -4 \\ 0 & -1 & -2 \\ 2 & 4 & 0 \end{bmatrix}$

17) $C = \begin{bmatrix} -2 & 1 \\ 4 & 2 \end{bmatrix}$

18) $C = \begin{bmatrix} -2 & 1 & -1 \\ 0 & 4 & -4 \\ 0 & 2 & -4 \end{bmatrix}$

19) $C = \begin{bmatrix} 2 & 1 & -3 & 1 \\ -1 & 3 & 4 & 5 \\ -2 & -1 & 2 & 3 \\ 6 & 7 & -4 & 1 \end{bmatrix}$

Chapter 5: Matrices

Solving Systems with Matrix Equations

✎ **What is the value of x and y in the following system of equations?**

1) $2x - y = -2$

   $2x + 3y = 6$

   $x = \underline{}, y = \underline{}$

2) $3x + 4y = 5$

   $x + 2y = 1$

   $x = \underline{}, y = \underline{}$

3) $2x + 2y = 14$

   $-10x - 2y = -54$

   $x = \underline{}, y = \underline{}$

4) $-2x + 8y = -6$

   $-2x + 4y = -6$

   $x = \underline{}, y = \underline{}$

5) $-2x + 2y = 4$

   $-2x + y = 3$

   $x = \underline{}, y = \underline{}$

6) $-10x + 2y = -6$

   $6x - 16y = 48$

   $x = \underline{}, y = \underline{}$

7) $2y = -6x + 10$

   $10x - 8y = -6$

   $x = \underline{}, y = \underline{}$

8) $10x - 9y = -13$

   $-5x + 3y = 11$

   $x = \underline{}, y = \underline{}$

9) $-3x - 4y = 5$

   $x - 2y = 5$

   $x = \underline{}, y = \underline{}$

10) $5x - 14y = -23$

    $-6x + 7y = 8$

    $x = \underline{}, y = \underline{}$

Chapter 5: Matrices

Finding Determinants of a Matrix

✎ *Evaluate the determinant of each matrix.*

1) $\begin{bmatrix} 2 & 5 \\ 3 & 8 \end{bmatrix} =$

2) $\begin{bmatrix} 8 & -6 \\ -10 & 9 \end{bmatrix} =$

3) $\begin{bmatrix} 2 & -2 \\ 7 & -7 \end{bmatrix} =$

4) $\begin{bmatrix} -5 & 0 \\ 3 & 10 \end{bmatrix} =$

5) $\begin{bmatrix} 0 & 6 \\ -6 & 0 \end{bmatrix} =$

6) $\begin{bmatrix} 3 & 4 \\ 2 & -6 \end{bmatrix} =$

7) $\begin{bmatrix} 8 & 5 \\ -4 & -6 \end{bmatrix} =$

8) $\begin{bmatrix} 0 & 4 \\ 6 & 5 \end{bmatrix} =$

9) $\begin{bmatrix} 6 & 1 & 7 \\ 2 & -3 & 3 \\ 4 & -1 & 2 \end{bmatrix} =$

10) $\begin{bmatrix} -2 & 5 & -4 \\ 0 & -3 & 5 \\ -5 & 5 & -6 \end{bmatrix} = 0$

11) $\begin{bmatrix} -3 & 1 & 8 \\ -9 & -1 & 7 \\ 0 & 2 & 1 \end{bmatrix} =$

12) $\begin{bmatrix} 5 & 3 & 3 \\ -4 & -5 & 1 \\ 5 & 3 & 0 \end{bmatrix} =$

13) $\begin{bmatrix} 6 & 2 & -1 \\ -5 & -4 & -5 \\ 3 & -3 & 1 \end{bmatrix} =$

14) $\begin{bmatrix} 6 & 5 & -3 \\ -5 & 4 & -2 \\ 1 & -4 & 5 \end{bmatrix} =$

15) $\begin{bmatrix} -2 & -1 & 3 \\ 5 & 11 & -2 \\ -1 & 5 & 1 \end{bmatrix} =$

16) $\begin{bmatrix} 3 & 9 & 1 \\ 2 & -10 & 1 \\ 5 & 3 & 8 \end{bmatrix} =$

17) $\begin{bmatrix} 6 & 4 & 2 \\ 3 & -7 & 1 \\ 5 & 5 & 3 \end{bmatrix} =$

18) $\begin{bmatrix} -1 & -8 & 9 \\ 4 & 12 & -7 \\ -10 & 3 & 2 \end{bmatrix} =$

19) $\begin{bmatrix} 5 & 4 & 7 \\ 3 & -6 & 5 \\ 4 & 2 & -3 \end{bmatrix} =$

20) $\begin{bmatrix} 3 & 4 & 1 \\ 2 & 5 & -2 \\ -1 & 6 & -3 \end{bmatrix} =$

Effortless Math Education

Chapter 5: Matrices

Answers – Chapter 5

Using Matrices to Represent Data

1) $\begin{bmatrix} 2 & 9 \\ -3 & 8 \end{bmatrix} \begin{bmatrix} x \\ y \end{bmatrix} = \begin{bmatrix} 17 \\ 39 \end{bmatrix}$

2) $\begin{bmatrix} 2 & -1 \\ 1 & -2 \end{bmatrix} \begin{bmatrix} x \\ y \end{bmatrix} = \begin{bmatrix} 12 \\ 48 \end{bmatrix}$

3) $\begin{bmatrix} 3 & -1 \\ 4 & 3 \end{bmatrix} \begin{bmatrix} x \\ y \end{bmatrix} = \begin{bmatrix} 23 \\ 48 \end{bmatrix}$

4) $\begin{bmatrix} 3 & 2 \\ 7 & 1 \end{bmatrix} \begin{bmatrix} x \\ y \end{bmatrix} = \begin{bmatrix} 16 \\ 19 \end{bmatrix}$

5) $\begin{bmatrix} 4 & 3 \\ 8 & -2 \end{bmatrix} \begin{bmatrix} x \\ y \end{bmatrix} = \begin{bmatrix} -2 \\ 12 \end{bmatrix}$

6) $\begin{bmatrix} 1 & 1 \\ -3 & 1 \end{bmatrix} \begin{bmatrix} x \\ y \end{bmatrix} = \begin{bmatrix} 6 \\ 2 \end{bmatrix}$

7) $\begin{bmatrix} 2 & -1 \\ 6 & -3 \end{bmatrix} \begin{bmatrix} z \\ y \end{bmatrix} = \begin{bmatrix} 4 \\ 3 \end{bmatrix}$

8) $\begin{bmatrix} 1 & 1 & 1 \\ 2 & 5 & -1 \end{bmatrix} \begin{bmatrix} x \\ y \\ z \end{bmatrix} = \begin{bmatrix} 6 \\ 27 \end{bmatrix}$

9) $\begin{bmatrix} 6 & 3 \\ 12 & -8 \end{bmatrix} \begin{bmatrix} x \\ y \end{bmatrix} = \begin{bmatrix} 10 \\ -6 \end{bmatrix}$

10) $\begin{bmatrix} 7 & -14 \\ -5 & 7 \end{bmatrix} \begin{bmatrix} x \\ y \end{bmatrix} = \begin{bmatrix} -28 \\ 8 \end{bmatrix}$

11) $\begin{bmatrix} 2 & 5 \\ 3 & 4 \end{bmatrix} \begin{bmatrix} x \\ y \end{bmatrix} = \begin{bmatrix} 10 \\ 24 \end{bmatrix}$

12) $\begin{bmatrix} 4 & 6 \\ 10 & 4 \end{bmatrix} \begin{bmatrix} x \\ y \end{bmatrix} = \begin{bmatrix} 16 \\ 4 \end{bmatrix}$

13) $\begin{bmatrix} 6 & -4 & 0 \\ 2 & 10 & 0 \\ -8 & -2 & 6 \end{bmatrix} \begin{bmatrix} x \\ y \\ z \end{bmatrix} = \begin{bmatrix} 8 \\ -6 \\ 0 \end{bmatrix}$

14) $\begin{bmatrix} 2 & -4 & -2 \\ 4 & -2 & 2 \\ -2 & -2 & -4 \end{bmatrix} \begin{bmatrix} x \\ y \\ z \end{bmatrix} = \begin{bmatrix} 4 \\ 8 \\ -8 \end{bmatrix}$

15) $\begin{bmatrix} 1 & 0 & -3 \\ 2 & 2 & 1 \\ 3 & 1 & -2 \end{bmatrix} \begin{bmatrix} x \\ y \\ z \end{bmatrix} = \begin{bmatrix} -2 \\ 4 \\ 5 \end{bmatrix}$

Adding and Subtracting Matrices

1) $[3 \ -7 \ -6]$

2) $\begin{bmatrix} 3 & -7 \\ 5 & 0 \\ -3 & 2 \end{bmatrix}$

3) $\begin{bmatrix} -11 & 7 & 4 \\ 3 & -5 & 3 \end{bmatrix}$

4) $\begin{bmatrix} 0 & -4 \\ 6 & 5 \end{bmatrix}$

5) $\begin{bmatrix} 11 & 7 \\ -13 & 8 \end{bmatrix}$

6) $\begin{bmatrix} -2 & 2 \\ -3 & 0 \end{bmatrix}$

7) $\begin{bmatrix} 16 & -18 \\ 9 & 29 \end{bmatrix}$

8) $\begin{bmatrix} -3 & 7 & 3 \\ 1 & -2 & 3 \end{bmatrix}$

9) $\begin{bmatrix} 16 & -3 \\ 24 & 14 \end{bmatrix}$

10) $\begin{bmatrix} 30 \\ -5 \\ 24 \end{bmatrix}$

11) $\begin{bmatrix} -2 \\ -8 \\ 8 \\ 3 \end{bmatrix}$

12) $\begin{bmatrix} 5 & -1 & -14 \\ 17 & -5 & 16 \\ -2 & -5 & -16 \end{bmatrix}$

13) $\begin{bmatrix} 14 & 10 & 10 \\ 34 & 11 & 17 \\ 13 & 8 & 16 \end{bmatrix}$

14) $\begin{bmatrix} 1 & 2 & 7 \\ -2 & 4 & 1 \end{bmatrix}$

15) $\begin{bmatrix} 1 & 6 \\ 6 & 1 \\ 9 & 3 \end{bmatrix}$

16) $\begin{bmatrix} 3 & 4 \\ 12 & 7 \\ 4 & -4 \end{bmatrix}$

Effortless Math Education

Chapter 5: Matrices

Matrix Multiplications

1) $\begin{bmatrix} 15 & -5 \\ 18 & -6 \\ 0 & 0 \end{bmatrix}$

2) $\begin{bmatrix} -5 & -10 \\ 8 & 13 \end{bmatrix}$

3) $\begin{bmatrix} -10 & -20 \\ 10 & -16 \\ 18 & -24 \end{bmatrix}$

4) $\begin{bmatrix} -14 & -3 \\ -19 & 22 \end{bmatrix}$

5) $\begin{bmatrix} -8 & 14 \\ 33 & 6 \\ -24 & -60 \end{bmatrix}$

6) $\begin{bmatrix} 8 & 4 & 14 \\ -14 & 8 & -17 \\ 10 & -10 & 10 \\ 20 & -8 & 26 \end{bmatrix}$

7) $[-4]$

8) $\begin{bmatrix} -8 & -5 & -4 \\ 48 & 30 & 24 \\ -48 & -30 & -24 \end{bmatrix}$

9) $\begin{bmatrix} 2 & 8 \\ -5 & -2 \end{bmatrix}$

10) $\begin{bmatrix} 34 & 41 \\ 35 & 37 \end{bmatrix}$

11) $\begin{bmatrix} 17 & 0 \\ -13 & 14 \end{bmatrix}$

12) $\begin{bmatrix} -4 & 3 \\ 4 & -12 \end{bmatrix}$

13) $\begin{bmatrix} 18 \\ 25 \end{bmatrix}$

14) $\begin{bmatrix} -1 & 0 \\ -4 & 3 \end{bmatrix}$

15) $\begin{bmatrix} 19 & 17 \\ 45 & 41 \\ -9 & -11 \end{bmatrix}$

16) $\begin{bmatrix} 46 & 7 & -45 \\ -10 & 11 & 39 \\ 10 & 7 & 3 \end{bmatrix}$

The Inverse of a Matrix

1) $C^{-1} = \begin{bmatrix} \frac{3}{5} & \frac{1}{5} \\ \frac{2}{5} & \frac{3}{10} \end{bmatrix}$

2) $C^{-1} = \begin{bmatrix} -3 & \frac{8}{3} \\ -2 & \frac{5}{3} \end{bmatrix}$

3) $C^{-1} = \begin{bmatrix} -\frac{4}{47} & -\frac{5}{47} \\ -\frac{11}{94} & -\frac{1}{47} \end{bmatrix}$

4) $C^{-1} = \begin{bmatrix} -\frac{2}{3} & 1 \\ \frac{5}{6} & -\frac{3}{2} \end{bmatrix}$

5) $C^{-1} = \begin{bmatrix} -\frac{7}{45} & \frac{1}{15} \\ \frac{8}{45} & \frac{1}{15} \end{bmatrix}$

6) $C^{-1} = \begin{bmatrix} 4 & -1 \\ \frac{9}{2} & -1 \end{bmatrix}$

7) $C^{-1} = \begin{bmatrix} \frac{3}{5} & \frac{1}{5} \\ \frac{2}{5} & \frac{3}{10} \end{bmatrix}$

8) $C^{-1} = \begin{bmatrix} \frac{7}{2} & -\frac{11}{2} \\ 2 & -3 \end{bmatrix}$

9) No inverse exists

10) $C^{-1} = \begin{bmatrix} \frac{1}{3} & -\frac{1}{9} \\ -\frac{2}{3} & -\frac{1}{9} \end{bmatrix}$

11) $C^{-1} = \begin{bmatrix} 1 & -5 \\ 2 & -11 \end{bmatrix}$

12) $C^{-1} = \begin{bmatrix} \frac{9}{2} & -1 \\ -\frac{1}{2} & 0 \end{bmatrix}$

13) No inverse exists

14) No inverse exists

Chapter 5: Matrices

15) $C^{-1} = \begin{bmatrix} -1 & 2 \\ 0 & -\frac{1}{2} \end{bmatrix}$

16) $C^{-1} = \begin{bmatrix} -2 & 4 & \frac{5}{2} \\ 1 & -2 & -1 \\ -\frac{1}{2} & \frac{1}{2} & \frac{1}{2} \end{bmatrix}$

17) $C^{-1} = \begin{bmatrix} -\frac{1}{4} & \frac{1}{8} \\ \frac{1}{2} & \frac{1}{4} \end{bmatrix}$

18) $C^{-1} = \begin{bmatrix} -\frac{1}{2} & \frac{1}{8} & 0 \\ 0 & \frac{1}{2} & -\frac{1}{2} \\ 0 & \frac{1}{4} & -\frac{1}{2} \end{bmatrix}$

19) $C^{-1} = \begin{bmatrix} -40 & -31 & 56 & 27 \\ 23 & 18 & -\frac{65}{2} & -\frac{31}{2} \\ -21 & -16 & 29 & 14 \\ -5 & -4 & \frac{15}{2} & \frac{7}{2} \end{bmatrix}$

Solving Systems with Matrix Equations

1) $x = 0, y = 2$
2) $x = 3, y = -1$
3) $x = 5, y = 2$
4) $x = 3, y = 0$
5) $x = -1, y = 1$
6) $x = 0, y = -3$
7) $x = 1, y = 2$
8) $x = -4, y = -3$
9) $x = 1, y = -2$
10) $x = 1, y = 2$

Finding Determinants of a Matrix

1) 1
2) 12
3) 0
4) −50
5) 36
6) −26
7) −28
8) −24
9) 60
10) −51
11) −90
12) 39
13) −161
14) 139
15) 69
16) −292
17) −72
18) 647
19) 366
20) 40

Chapter 6: Polynomial Operations

Math Topics that you'll learn in this Chapter:

- Writing Polynomials in Standard Form
- Simplifying Polynomials
- Adding and Subtracting Polynomials
- Multiplying and Dividing Monomials
- Multiplying a Polynomial and a Monomial
- Multiplying Binomials
- Factoring Trinomials
- Choosing a Factoring Method for Polynomials
- Factors and Greatest Common Factors
- Operations with Polynomials
- Even and Odd Functions
- End Behavior of Polynomial Functions
- Remainder and Factor Theorems
- Polynomial Division (Long Division)
- Polynomial Division (Synthetic Division)
- Finding Zeros of Polynomials
- Polynomial Identities

Chapter 6: Polynomial Operations

Writing Polynomials in Standard Form

Write polynomials in standard form.

1) $10x - 7x =$

2) $-3 + 12x - 12x =$

3) $3x^2 - 4x^3 =$

4) $6 + 4x^3 - 6 =$

5) $2x^2 + 1x - 7x^3 =$

6) $-x^2 + 4x^3 =$

7) $2x + 4x^3 - 2x^2 =$

8) $-2x^2 + 4x - 6x^3 =$

9) $2x^2 + 2 - 5x =$

10) $12 - 7x + 9x^4 =$

11) $5x^2 + 13x - 2x^3 =$

12) $10 + 6x^2 - x^3 =$

13) $12x^2 - 7x + 9x^3 =$

14) $5x^4 - 3x^2 - 2x^3 =$

15) $-12 + 3x^2 - 6x^4 =$

16) $5x^2 - 9x^5 + 8x^3 - 11 =$

17) $4x^2 - 2x^5 + 14 - 7x^4 =$

18) $-x^2 + 2x - 5x^3 - 4x =$

19) $8x^5 + 11x^3 - 6x^5 - 8x^2 =$

20) $5x^2 - 12x^4 + 4x^2 + 5x^3 =$

21) $7x^3 - 6x^4 - 3x^2 + 22x^3 =$

22) $9x^2 + x^4 + 12x^3 - 5x^4 =$

23) $3x(2x + 5 - 2x^2) =$

24) $11x(x^5 + 2x^3) =$

25) $5x(3x^2 + 2x + 1) =$

26) $7x(3 - x + 6x^3) =$

27) $2x(3x^2 - 4x^4 + 3) =$

28) $6x(4x^5 + 7x^3 - 2) =$

29) $-4x(5x^2 - 6x + 3x^3) =$

30) $9x(-2x^3 + 3 - 6x) =$

31) $2x^2(3x - 16 + 2x^2) =$

32) $-3x^2(-2x^3 + 2x^2 + 28) =$

Chapter 6: Polynomial Operations

Simplifying Polynomials

✏️ *Simplify each expression.*

1) $4(2x - 10) =$

2) $2x(3x - 2) =$

3) $3x(5x - 3) =$

4) $2x(7x + 3) =$

5) $4x(8x - 4) =$

6) $5x(6x + 4) =$

7) $(2x - 3)(x - 4) =$

8) $(x - 5)(3x + 4) =$

9) $(x - 5)(x - 3) =$

10) $(3x + 8)(3x - 8) =$

11) $(3x - 8)(3x - 4) =$

12) $3x^2 + 3x^2 - 2x^3 =$

13) $2x - x^2 + 6x^3 + 4 =$

14) $5x + 2x^2 - 9x^3 =$

15) $8x^2 - 3x^3 - 9x =$

16) $5x^3 + 2x^4 - 7x^2 =$

17) $-4x^5 - 6x^2 + 2x^4 =$

18) $2x^4 + 3x^2 - 3x^3 - 2x =$

19) $7x^2 + 5x^4 - 2x^3 =$

20) $-3x^2 + 5x^3 + 6x^4 =$

21) $-8x^2 + 2x^3 - 10x^4 + 5x =$

22) $11 - 6x^2 + 5x^2 - 12x^3 + 22 =$

23) $2x^2 - 2x + 3x^3 + 12x - 22x =$

24) $11 - 4x^2 + 3x^2 - 7x^3 + 3 =$

25) $2x^5 - x^3 + 8x^2 - 2x^5 =$

26) $(2x^3 - 1) + (3x^3 - 2x^3) =$

27) $3(4x^4 - 4x^3 - 5x^4) =$

28) $-5(x^6 + 10) - 8(14 - x^6) =$

29) $3x^2 - 5x^3 - x + 10 - 2x^2 =$

30) $11 - 3x^2 + 2x^2 - 5x^3 + 7 =$

31) $(8x^2 - 3x) - (5x - 5 - 8x^2) =$

32) $3x^2 - 5x^3 - x(2x^2 + 4x) =$

Chapter 6: Polynomial Operations

Adding and Subtracting Polynomials

✍ *Add or subtract expressions.*

1) $(x^2 - 5) + (x^2 + 6) =$ _____

2) $(2x^2 - 6) - (3 - 2x^2) =$ _____

3) $(x^3 + 3x^2) - (x^3 + 6) =$ _____

4) $(4x^3 - x^2) + (6x^2 - 8x) =$ _____

5) $(2x^3 + 3x) - (5x^3 + 2) =$ _____

6) $(5x^3 - 2) + (2x^3 + 10) =$ _____

7) $(7x^3 + 5) - (9 - 4x^3) =$ _____

8) $(5x^2 + 3x^3) - (2x^3 + 6) =$ _____

9) $(8x^2 - x) + (4x - 8x^2) =$ _____

10) $(6x + 9x^2) - (5x + 2) =$ _____

11) $(7x^4 - 2x) - (6x - 2x^4) =$ _____

12) $(2x - 4x^3) - (9x^3 + 6x) =$ _____

13) $(8x^3 - 8x^2) - (6x^2 - 3x) =$ _____

14) $(9x^2 - 6) + (5x^2 - 4x^3) =$ _____

15) $(8x^3 + 3x^4) - (x^4 - 3x^3) =$ _____

16) $(-4x^3 - 2x) + (5x - 2x^3) =$ _____

17) $(9x - 5x^4) - (8x^4 + 4x) =$ _____

18) $(8x - 3x^2) - (7x^4 - 3x^2) =$ _____

19) $(9x^3 - 7) + (5x^3 - 4x^2) =$ _____

20) $(7x^3 + x^4) - (6x^4 - 5x^3) =$ _____

Chapter 6: Polynomial Operations

Multiplying and Dividing Monomials

✏️ *Simplify each expression.*

1) $(3x^5)(2x^2) =$

2) $(6x^5)(2x^4) =$

3) $(-7x^9)(2x^5) =$

4) $(7x^7y^9)(-5x^6y^6) =$

5) $(8x^5y^6)(3x^2y^5) =$

6) $(8yx^2)(7y^5x^3) =$

7) $(4x^2y)(2x^2y^3) =$

8) $(-2x^9y^4)(-9x^6y^8) =$

9) $(-5x^8y^2)(-6x^4y^5) =$

10) $(8x^8y)(-7x^4y^3) =$

11) $(9x^6y^2)(6x^7y^4) =$

12) $(8x^9y^5)(6x^5y^4) =$

13) $(-5x^8y^9)(7x^7y^8) =$

14) $(6x^2y^5)(5x^3y^2) =$

15) $(9x^5y^{12})(4x^7y^9) =$

16) $(-10x^{14}y^8)(2x^7y^5) =$

17) $\dfrac{6x^5y^7}{xy^6} =$

18) $\dfrac{9x^6y^6}{3x^4y} =$

19) $\dfrac{16x^4y^6}{4xy} =$

71

Chapter 6: Polynomial Operations

Multiplying a Polynomial and a Monomial

✍ *Find each product.*

1) $x(x-5) =$

2) $2(3+x) =$

3) $x(x-7) =$

4) $x(x+9) =$

5) $2x(x-2) =$

6) $5(4x+3) =$

7) $4x(3x-4) =$

8) $x(5x+2y) =$

9) $3x(x-2y) =$

10) $6x(3x-4y) =$

11) $2x(3x-8) =$

12) $6x(4x-6y) =$

13) $3x(4x-2y) =$

14) $2x(2x-6y) =$

15) $5x(x^2+y^2) =$

16) $3x(2x^2-y^2) =$

17) $6(9x^2+3y^2) =$

18) $4x(-3x^2y+2y) =$

19) $-3(6x^2-5xy+3) =$

20) $6(x^2-4xy-3) =$

Chapter 6: Polynomial Operations

Multiplying Binomials

✎ *Find each product.*

1) $(x-3)(x+4) =$

2) $(x+3)(x+5) =$

3) $(x-6)(x-7) =$

4) $(x-9)(x-4) =$

5) $(x-7)(x-5) =$

6) $(x+6)(x+2) =$

7) $(x-9)(x+3) =$

8) $(x-8)(x-5) =$

9) $(x+3)(x+7) =$

10) $(x-9)(x+4) =$

11) $(x+6)(x+6) =$

12) $(x+7)(x+7) =$

13) $(x-8)(x+7) =$

14) $(x+9)(x+9) =$

15) $(x-8)(x-8) =$

16) $(x-9)(x+5) =$

17) $(2x-5)(x+4) =$

18) $(2x+6)(x+3) =$

19) $(2x+4)(x+5) =$

20) $(2x-3)(2x+2) =$

73

www.EffortlessMath.com

Chapter 6: Polynomial Operations

Factoring Trinomials

Factor each trinomial.

1) $x^2 + 5x + 4 =$

2) $x^2 + 5x + 6 =$

3) $x^2 - 4x + 3 =$

4) $x^2 - 10x + 25 =$

5) $x^2 - 13x + 40 =$

6) $x^2 + 8x + 12 =$

7) $x^2 - 6x - 27 =$

8) $x^2 - 14x + 48 =$

9) $x^2 + 15x + 56 =$

10) $x^2 - 5x - 36 =$

11) $x^2 + 12x + 36 =$

12) $x^2 + 16x + 63 =$

13) $x^2 + x - 72 =$

14) $x^2 + 18x + 81 =$

15) $x^2 - 16x + 64 =$

16) $x^2 - 18x + 81 =$

17) $2x^2 + 10x + 8 =$

18) $2x^2 + 4x - 6 =$

19) $2x^2 + 9x + 4 =$

20) $4x^2 + 4x - 24 =$

Chapter 6: Polynomial Operations

Choosing a Factoring Method for Polynomials

✎ Factor the polynomials expression completely.

1) $xy^2 - 4xy + 4x =$

2) $xy^2 - 8xy + 16x =$

3) $xy^2 + 6xy + 9x =$

4) $xy^2 - 8xy + 16x =$

5) $4xy^2 + 36xy + 81x =$

6) $16xy^2 - 40xy + 25x =$

7) $xy^2 + 12xy + 36x =$

8) $4xy^2 + 20xy + 25x =$

9) $9xy^2 - 42xy + 49x =$

10) $16xy^2 - 24xy + 9x =$

11) $4xy^2 + 32xy + 64x =$

12) $18xy^2 - 60xy + 50x =$

13) $2xy^2 + 20xy + 50x =$

14) $3xy^2 - 36xy + 108x =$

15) $4xy^2 + 24xy + 36x =$

16) $7xy^2 + 56xy + 112x =$

17) $5xy^2 - 90xy + 405x =$

18) $4xy^2 - 56xy + 196x =$

19) $4xy^2 - 20xy + 25x =$

20) $8xy^2 + 48xy + 72x =$

21) $9xy^2 - 24xy + 16x =$

22) $27xy^2 + 36xy + 12x =$

23) $18xy^2 - 24xy + 8x =$

24) $32xy^2 - 96xy + 72x =$

25) $20xy^2 - 140xy + 245x =$

26) $64xy^2 + 160xy + 100x =$

www.EffortlessMath.com

Chapter 6: Polynomial Operations

Factors and Greatest Common Factors

✎ Find the GCF.

1) 5, 10 and 40
GCF = _____

2) 8, 14 and 64
GCF = _____

3) 26, 32 and 58
GCF = _____

4) 7, 10 and 81
GCF = _____

5) $18t, 48t^4$
GCF = _____

6) $18ab, 9ab$
GCF = _____

7) $39x, 30xy$
GCF = _____

8) $60a, 56a^2$
GCF = _____

9) $18x^2, 54x^2$
GCF = _____

10) $36x^2, 21x^3$
GCF = _____

11) $54x^3, 36x^3$
GCF = _____

12) $16x^3y, 8x^2$
GCF = _____

13) $6x^4, 12x^4$ and $24x^4$
GCF = _____

14) $14x^3, 22x^6$ and $28x^5$
GCF = _____

15) $36x^5, 48x^4$ and $62x^6$
GCF = _____

16) $78x^3, 54x^4$ and $92x^4$
GCF = _____

17) $8x^3, 24x^3$ and $36x^6$
GCF = _____

18) $15m^2n, 25m^2n^2$
GCF = _____

19) $12x^2yz, 3xy^2$
GCF = _____

20) $22m^5n^2, 11m^2n^4$
GCF = _____

21) $x^3yz^2, 2x^3yz^3$
GCF = _____

22) $140x, 140y^2$ and $80y^2$
GCF = _____

23) $24a, 36a$ and $24ab^2$
GCF = _____

24) $10x^3, 45x^3$ and $35x$
GCF = _____

Chapter 6: Polynomial Operations

Operations with Polynomials

✏️ *Find each product.*

1) $2(3x + 2) =$

2) $-3(2x + 5) =$

3) $4(7x - 3) =$

4) $5(2x - 4) =$

5) $3x(2x - 7) =$

6) $-2x(3x + 4) =$

7) $4x(4x - 6) =$

8) $x^2(3x + 4) =$

9) $x^3(x + 5) =$

10) $x^4(5x - 3) =$

11) $9(6x + 2) =$

12) $8(3x + 7) =$

13) $5(6x - 1) =$

14) $-3(8x - 3) =$

15) $3x^2(6x - 5) =$

16) $5x^2(7x - 2) =$

17) $6x^3(-3x + 4) =$

18) $-7x^4(2x - 4) =$

19) $8(x^2 + 2x - 3) =$

20) $4(4x^2 - 2x + 1) =$

21) $2(3x^2 + 2x - 2) =$

22) $8x(5x^2 + 3x + 8) =$

23) $(9x + 1)(3x - 1) =$

24) $(4x + 5)(6x - 5) =$

25) $(7x + 3)(5x - 6) =$

26) $(3x - 4)(3x + 8) =$

Chapter 6: Polynomial Operations

Even and Odd Functions

✎ *Identify whether the following functions is even, odd, or neither.*

1) $f(x) = -x^2 + 8$

2) $f(x) = x^3 + 6x$

3) $f(x) = -x^3 + 4x - 2$

4) $f(x) = x^2 + 6$

5) $f(x) = x^3 - 4x$

6) $f(x) = -x^2 - 8$

7) $f(x) = 4x^4 + 2$

8) $f(x) = 2x^3 - 2x + 2$

9) $f(x) = x^4 - 4x^2 + 4$

10) $f(x) = 2x^3 + 5x$

11) $f(x) = x^2 - 3x$

12) $f(x) = \frac{1}{x^2+3}$

13) $f(x) = \frac{x}{x^2-2}$

14) $f(x) = 2x^5 + 2x^3$

15) $f(x) = \frac{3+x^2}{2+x^4}$

16) $f(x) = -x^4 - 6x^2$

17) $f(x) = \frac{x}{5+x^2}$

18) $f(x) = x^4 + 2x^2$

19) $f(x) = x^3 + 2x$

20) $f(x) = \frac{x^5 - 3x^3 - x}{x^2 + 1}$

21) $f(x) = 2x^4 + 3x^2 + 6$

22) $f(x) = -x^3 - 4x$

23) $f(x) = \frac{x^5 + 4x^3}{x^2 + 4}$

Chapter 6: Polynomial Operations

End Behavior of Polynomial Functions

✎ **Find the end behavior of the functions.**

1) $f(x) = x^2 - 3x + 5$

   $f(x) \to$ ___, as $x \to$ ___
   $f(x) \to$ ___, as $x \to$ ___

2) $f(x) = -x^2 - 3x$

   $f(x) \to$ ___, as $x \to$ ___
   $f(x) \to$ ___, as $x \to$ ___

3) $f(x) = x^3 - 4x + 2$

   $f(x) \to$ ___, as $x \to$ ___
   $f(x) \to$ ___, as $x \to$ ___

4) $f(x) = -x^3 + 3x^2$

   $f(x) \to$ ___, as $x \to$ ___
   $f(x) \to$ ___, as $x \to$ ___

5) $f(x) = x^2 - 6x + 12$

   $f(x) \to$ ___, as $x \to$ ___
   $f(x) \to$ ___, as $x \to$ ___

6) $f(x) = x^3 + 8x + 16$

   $f(x) \to$ ___, as $x \to$ ___
   $f(x) \to$ ___, as $x \to$ ___

7) $f(x) = x^5 - 4x^3 + 4x + 2$

   $f(x) \to$ ___, as $x \to$ ___
   $f(x) \to$ ___, as $x \to$ ___

8) $f(x) = -x^4 + x^2 + 6$

   $f(x) \to$ ___, as $x \to$ ___
   $f(x) \to$ ___, as $x \to$ ___

9) $f(x) = -x^3 + 2x^2 + 8$

   $f(x) \to$ ___, as $x \to$ ___
   $f(x) \to$ ___, as $x \to$ ___

10) $f(x) = x^4 - x^2 - 3$

    $f(x) \to$ ___, as $x \to$ ___
    $f(x) \to$ ___, as $x \to$ ___

11) $f(x) = -x^2 - 7x - 12$

    $f(x) \to$ ___, as $x \to$ ___
    $f(x) \to$ ___, as $x \to$ ___

12) $f(x) = -x^2 + 8x$

    $f(x) \to$ ___, as $x \to$ ___
    $f(x) \to$ ___, as $x \to$ ___

13) $f(x) = -x^5 + 4x^3 - 2x - 4$

    $f(x) \to$ ___, as $x \to$ ___
    $f(x) \to$ ___, as $x \to$ ___

14) $f(x) = x^3 + 10x^2 + 22x + 4$

    $f(x) \to$ ___, as $x \to$ ___
    $f(x) \to$ ___, as $x \to$ ___

Chapter 6: Polynomial Operations

Remainder and Factor Theorems

✎ *Evaluate each function at the given value.*

1) $f(x) = x^2 - 6x + 12$ by $x = 1$ _____

2) $f(x) = 4x^2 + 8x - 10$ by $x = 2$ _____

3) $f(x) = 3x^2 - 6x + 8$ by $x = -2$ _____

4) $f(x) = 2x^3 - 4x^2 + 1$ by $x = 2$ _____

5) $g(x) = x^3 + 5x^2 + 10x + 12$ by $x = -2$ _____

6) $k(x) = x^4 + 2x^3 - 15x^2 + 5$ by $x = 3$ _____

7) $t(x) = 3x^3 - 2x^2 - 12x + 8$ by $x = 4$ _____

8) $f(x) = -x^4 - 3x^3 + 4x$ by $x = -3$ _____

9) $k(x) = 3x^3 + 7x^2 - 3x^2 - 6$ by $x = 2$ _____

10) $k(x) = 4x^4 - 8x^3 + 2x^2 + 4$ by $x = -2$ _____

11) $f(x) = -3x^3 + 5x^2 - 3x + 12$ by $x = -4$ _____

12) $k(x) = 2x^4 - 3x^3 + 8x^2 + 6$ by $x = 2$ _____

Chapter 6: Polynomial Operations

Polynomial Division (Long Division)

✎ **Evaluate.**

1) $(x^2 - 3x + 4) \div (x - 1) =$

2) $(x^2 + 6x + 8) \div (x - 2) =$

3) $(x^2 + 6x - 5) \div (x + 3) =$

4) $(x^2 - 4x + 12) \div (x - 2) =$

5) $(x^2 + 2x - 36) \div (x - 5) =$

6) $(x^2 + 32) \div (x + 2) =$

7) $(2x^2 - x - 6) \div (x - 3) =$

8) $(x^2 + x - 79) \div (x + 9) =$

9) $(x^2 - x - 29) \div (x - 6) =$

10) $(x^2 - 3x - 21) \div (x - 7) =$

11) $(x^2 - 28) \div (x - 5) =$

12) $(2x^2 - 15x - 36) \div (2x + 3) =$

13) $(x^2 + 14x + 38) \div (x + 8) =$

14) $(x^2 - 3x - 21) \div (x - 7) =$

15) $(x^3 + 2x - 7x - 12) \div (x + 3) =$

16) $(x^3 + 5x^2 + 10x + 6) \div (x + 1) =$

17) $(x^3 + x^2 - 36x + 42) \div (x + 7) =$

18) $(x^3 + 13x^2 + 42x + 54) \div (x + 9) =$

19) $(x^5 - 5x^4 + 10x^2 - 42) \div (x - 5) =$

20) $(x^3 - 2x^2 - 14x - 5) \div (x + 3) =$

21) $(x^4 - 20x^3 + 93x + 71x) \div (x - 4) =$

22) $(-x^4 + 4x^3 - 14x^3 + 14) \div (x - 2) =$

Chapter 6: Polynomial Operations

Polynomial Division (Synthetic Division)

✎ *Evaluate.*

1) $(x^2 + 12) \div (x + 2) =$

2) $(x^2 + 5x + 15) \div (x + 5) =$

3) $(x^3 - 3x^2 - 9x) \div (x - 3) =$

4) $(3x^2 + 5x + 2) \div (x + 2) =$

5) $(7x^2 - 3x + 6) \div (x + 3) =$

6) $(4x^3 - 2x^2) \div (x + 2) =$

7) $(4x^2 + x + 1) \div (x - 1) =$

8) $(3x^2 - 4x + 2) \div (x - 2) =$

9) $(x^2 + 4x + 12) \div (x + 2) =$

10) $(x^3 - 20) \div (x - 3) =$

11) $(x^2 + 5x + 6) \div (x + 2) =$

12) $(x^3 - 3x^2 - 9x + 6) \div (x - 3) =$

13) $(3x^3 + 4x^2 - 2x - 4) \div (x + 2) =$

14) $(x^4 + 5x^3 - 6x + 3) \div (x + 3) =$

15) $(2x^3 - 5x^2 - 33x - 37) \div (x - 9) =$

16) $(x^4 + 2x^3 - 8x^2 - 9x) \div (x - 2) =$

17) $(5x^4 + 2x^2 - 15x + 12) \div (x + 2) =$

18) $(4x^3 - 49x^2 - 45x - 36) \div (x - 2) =$

19) $(x^3 - 13x^2 - 77x + 60) \div (x - 5) =$

20) $(x^3 - 13x^2 + 25x + 50) \div (x - 3) =$

21) $(x^3 - 11x^2 + 26x + 20) \div (x - 5) =$

22) $(x^3 + 15x^2 + 47x - 38) \div (x + 3) =$

23) $(x^3 - 3x^2 - 3x - 2) \div (x - 2) =$

24) $(x^4 - 6x^2 + 8x - 42) \div (x - 4) =$

Chapter 6: Polynomial Operations

Finding Zeros of Polynomials

✎ *Find the zeros of the Polynomials.*

1) $16x^2 - 4$

2) $25x^2 - 9$

3) $3x^2 + x - 5$

4) $x^2 - 2x - 6$

5) $3x^2 - 2x + 4$

6) $6x^2 + 13x - 15$

7) $5x^2 + 14x - 24$

8) $4x^2 - 8x - 16$

9) $x^3 + 5x^2 + 4x$

10) $x^3 - 2x^2 - 3x$

11) $x^3 + 5x^2 + 6x$

12) $x^3 + 8x^2 + 12x$

13) $x^3 - 4x$

14) $x^3 - 2x^2 - 3x + 6$

15) $x^3 + 3x^2 - x - 3$

16) $x^3 + x^2 - 8x - 6$

17) $x^3 - 3x^2 - 4x + 12$

18) $x^3 + 3x^2 - 10x$

19) $x^3 + 2x^2 - 5x - 6$

20) $x^3 - 4x^2 - 5x$

21) $x^4 - x^3 - 20x^2$

22) $x^3 + 4x^2 - 3x$

23) $x^4 - 14x^2 + 45$

24) $x^3 + 3x^2 - 14x - 20$

25) $x^4 - 10x^2 + 21$

26) $x^4 - 2x^2 - 2x - 4$

Chapter 6: Polynomial Operations

Polynomial Identities

✎ *Factorize the following expressions.*

1) $x^2 + 5xy + 4y^2$

2) $x^2 - xy - 6y^2$

3) $8x^2 - 10xy + 2y^2$

4) $3x^2 - 10xy - 8y^2$

5) $10x^2 - 13xy - 3y^2$

6) $18x^2 - 6xy - 4y^2$

7) $8x^3 + 12x^2 + 6x + 1$

8) $20x^2 + xy - 12y^2$

9) $2x^2 + 3xy - 2y^2$

10) $4x^2 - 10xy - 6y^2$

11) $8x^3 + 60x^2 + 150x + 125$

12) $8x^3 - 36x^2 + 54x - 27$

13) $27x^3 + 108x^2 + 144x + 64$

14) $-27x^3 - 54x^2 - 36x - 8$

15) $9x^2 + y^2 + 6xy + 2y + 6x + 1$

16) $-64x^3 + 96x^2 - 48x + 8$

17) $27x^3 + 27x^2 + 9x + 1$

18) $4x^2 + 4xy + 12x + y^2 + 6y + 9$

19) $125x^3 + 150x^2 + 60x + 8$

20) $8x^3 + 96x^2 + 384x + 512$

21) $64x^3 + 144x^2 + 108x + 27$

22) $9x^2 + 6xy + 6x + y^2 + 2y + 1$

23) $8x^3 + 12x^2y + 6xy^2 + y^3$

24) $27x^3 + 54x^2y + 36xy^2 + 8y^3$

25) $64x^3 - 144x^2y + 108xy^2 - 27y^3$

26) $4x^2 + 12xy + 9y^2 + 8x + 12y + 4$

Chapter 6: Polynomial Operations

Answers – Chapter 6

Writing Polynomials in Standard Form

1) $3x$
2) -3
3) $-4x^3 + 3x^2$
4) $4x^3$
5) $-7x^3 + 2x^2 + x$
6) $4x^3 - x^2$
7) $4x^3 - 2x^2 + 2x$
8) $-6x^3 - 2x^2 + 4x$
9) $2x^2 - 5x + 2$
10) $9x^4 - 7x + 12$
11) $-2x^3 + 5x^2 + 13x$
12) $-x^3 + 6x^2 + 10$
13) $9x^3 + 12x^2 - 7x$
14) $5x^4 - 2x^3 - 3x^2$
15) $-6x^4 + 3x^2 - 12$
16) $-9x^5 + 8x^3 + 5x^2 - 11$
17) $-2x^5 - 7x^4 + 4x^2 + 14$
18) $-5x^3 - x^2 - 2x$
19) $2x^5 + 11x^3 - 8x^2$
20) $-12x^4 + 5x^3 + 9x^2$
21) $-6x^4 + 29x^3 - 3x^2$
22) $-4x^4 + 12x^3 + 9x^2$
23) $-6x^3 + 6x^2 + 15x$
24) $11x^6 + 22x^4$
25) $15x^3 + 10x^2 + 5x$
26) $42x^4 - 7x^2 + 21x$
27) $-8x^5 + 6x^3 + 6x$
28) $24x^6 + 42x^4 - 12x$
29) $-12x^4 - 20x^3 + 24x^2$
30) $-18x^4 - 54x^2 + 27x$
31) $4x^4 + 6x^3 - 32x^2$
32) $6x^5 - 6x^4 - 84x^2$

Simplifying Polynomials

1) $8x - 40$
2) $6x^2 - 4x$
3) $15x^2 - 9x$
4) $14x^2 + 6x$
5) $32x^2 - 16x$
6) $30x^2 + 20x$
7) $2x^2 - 11x + 12$
8) $3x^2 - 11x - 20$
9) $x^2 - 8x + 15$
10) $9x^2 - 64$
11) $9x^2 - 36x + 32$
12) $-2x^3 + 6x^2$
13) $6x^3 - x^2 + 2x + 4$
14) $-9x^3 + 2x^2 + 5x$
15) $-3x^3 + 8x^2 - 9$
16) $2x^4 + 5x^3 - 7x^2$

Effortless Math Education

Chapter 6: Polynomial Operations

17) $-4x^5 + 2x^4 - 6x^2$
18) $2x^4 - 3x^3 + 3x^2 - 2x$
19) $5x^4 - 2x^3 + 7x^2$
20) $6x^4 + 5x^3 - 3x^2$
21) $-10x^4 + 2x^3 - 8x^2 + 5x$
22) $-12x^3 - x^2 + 33$
23) $3x^3 + 2x^2 - 12x$
24) $-7x^3 - x^2 + 14$

25) $-x^3 + 8x^2$
26) $3x^3 - 1$
27) $-3x^4 - 12x^3$
28) $3x^6 - 162$
29) $-5x^3 + x^2 - x + 10$
30) $-5x^3 - x^2 + 18$
31) $16x^2 - 8x + 5$
32) $-7x^3 - x^2$

Adding and Subtracting Polynomials

1) $2x^2 + 1$
2) $4x^2 - 9$
3) $3x^2 - 6$
4) $4x^3 + 5x^2 - 8x$
5) $-3x^3 + 3x - 2$
6) $7x^3 + 8$
7) $11x^3 - 4$
8) $x^3 + 5x^2 - 6$
9) $3x$
10) $9x^2 + x - 2$
11) $9x^4 - 8x$
12) $-13x^3 - 4x$
13) $8x^3 - 14x^2 + 3x$
14) $-4x^3 + 14x^2 - 6$
15) $2x^4 + 11x^3$
16) $-6x^3 + 3x$
17) $-13x^4 + 5x$
18) $-7x^4 + 8x$
19) $14x^3 - 4x^2 - 7$
20) $-5x^4 + 12x^3$

Multiplying and Dividing Monomials

1) $6x^7$
2) $12x^9$
3) $-14x^{14}$
4) $-35x^{13}y^{15}$
5) $24x^7y^{11}$
6) $56y^6x^5$
7) $8x^4y^4$
8) $18x^{15}y^{12}$
9) $30x^{12}y^7$
10) $-56x^{12}y^4$
11) $54x^{13}y^6$
12) $48x^{14}y^9$
13) $-35x^{15}y^{17}$
14) $30x^5y^7$
15) $36x^{12}y^{21}$
16) $-20x^{21}y^{13}$
17) $6x^4y$
18) $3x^2y^5$
19) $4x^3y^5$

Chapter 6: Polynomial Operations

Multiplying a Polynomial and a Monomial

1) $x^2 - 5x$
2) $2x + 6$
3) $x^2 - 7x$
4) $x^2 + 9x$
5) $2x^2 - 4x$
6) $20x + 15$
7) $12x^2 - 16x$
8) $5x^2 + 2xy$
9) $3x^2 - 6xy$
10) $18x^2 - 24xy$
11) $6x^2 - 16x$
12) $24x^2 - 36xy$
13) $12x^2 - 6xy$
14) $4x^2 - 12xy$
15) $5x^3 + 5xy^2$
16) $6x^3 - 3xy^2$
17) $54x^2 + 18y^2$
18) $-12x^3y + 8xy$
19) $-18x^2 + 15xy - 9$
20) $6x^2 - 24xy - 18$

Multiplying Binomials

1) $x^2 + x - 12$
2) $x^2 + 8x + 15$
3) $x^2 - 13x + 42$
4) $x^2 - 13x + 36$
5) $x^2 - 12x + 35$
6) $x^2 + 8x + 12$
7) $x^2 - 6x - 27$
8) $x^2 - 13x + 40$
9) $x^2 + 10x + 21$
10) $x^2 - 5x - 36$
11) $x^2 + 12x + 36$
12) $x^2 + 14x + 49$
13) $x^2 - x - 56$
14) $x^2 + 18x + 81$
15) $x^2 - 16x + 64$
16) $x^2 - 4x - 45$
17) $2x^2 + 3x - 20$
18) $2x^2 + 12x + 18$
19) $2x^2 + 14x + 20$
20) $4x^2 - 2x - 6$

Factoring Trinomials

1) $(x + 4)(x + 1)$
2) $(x + 3)(x + 2)$
3) $(x - 1)(x - 3)$
4) $(x - 5)(x - 5)$
5) $(x - 8)(x - 5)$
6) $(x + 6)(x + 2)$
7) $(x - 9)(x + 3)$
8) $(x - 8)(x - 6)$
9) $(x + 8)(x + 7)$
10) $(x - 9)(x + 4)$
11) $(x + 6)(x + 6)$
12) $(x + 7)(x + 9)$
13) $(x - 8)(x + 9)$
14) $(x + 9)(x + 9)$
15) $(x - 8)(x - 8)$
16) $(x - 9)(x - 9)$
17) $2(x + 1)(x + 4)$
18) $2(x - 1)(x + 3)$
19) $(2x + 1)(x + 4)$
20) $4(x - 2)(x + 3)$

Chapter 6: Polynomial Operations

Choosing a Factoring Method for Polynomials

1) $x(y-2)^2$
2) $x(y-4)^2$
3) $x(y+3)^2$
4) $x(y-4)^2$
5) $x(2y+9)^2$
6) $x(4y-5)^2$
7) $x(y+6)^2$
8) $x(2y+5)^2$
9) $x(3y-7)^2$
10) $x(4y-3)^2$
11) $4x(y+4)^2$
12) $2x(3y-5)^2$
13) $2x(y+5)^2$
14) $3x(y-6)^2$
15) $4x(y+3)^2$
16) $7x(y+4)^2$
17) $5x(y-9)^2$
18) $4x(y-7)^2$
19) $x(2y-5)^2$
20) $8x(y+3)^2$
21) $x(3y-4)^2$
22) $3x(3y+2)^2$
23) $2x(3y-2)^2$
24) $8x(2y-3)^2$
25) $5x(2y-7)^2$
26) $4x(4y+5)^2$

Factoring by GCF

1) $GCF = 5$
2) $GCF = 2$
3) $GCF = 2$
4) $GCF = 1$
5) $GCF = 6t$
6) $GCF = 9ab$
7) $GCF = 3x$
8) $GCF = 4a$
9) $GCF = 18x^2$
10) $GCF = 3x^2$
11) $GCF = 18x^3$
12) $GCF = 8x^2$
13) $GCF = 6x^4$
14) $GCF = 2x^3$
15) $GCF = 2x^4$
16) $GCF = 2x^3$
17) $GCF = 4x^3$
18) $GCF = 5m^2n$
19) $GCF = 3xy$
20) $GCF = 11m^2n^2$
21) $GCF = x^3yz^2$
22) $GCF = 20$
23) $GCF = 12a$
24) $GCF = 5x$

Operations with Polynomials

1) $6x + 4$
2) $-6x - 15$
3) $28x - 12$
4) $10x - 20$
5) $6x^2 - 21x$
6) $-6x^2 - 8x$
7) $16x^2 - 24x$
8) $3x^3 + 4x^2$
9) $x^4 + 5x^3$
10) $5x^5 - 3x^4$
11) $54x + 18$
12) $24x + 56$
13) $30x - 5$
14) $-24x + 9$
15) $18x^3 - 15x^2$
16) $35x^3 - 10x^2$
17) $-18x^4 + 24x^3$

Chapter 6: Polynomial Operations

18) $-14x^5 + 28x^4$

19) $8x^2 + 16x - 24$

20) $16x^2 - 8x + 4$

21) $6x^2 + 4x - 4$

22) $40x^3 + 24x^2 + 64x$

23) $27x^2 - 6x - 1$

24) $24x^2 + 10x - 25$

25) $35x^2 - 27x - 18$

26) $9x^2 + 12x - 32$

Even and Odd Functions

1) Even
2) Odd
3) Neither
4) Even
5) Odd
6) Even
7) Even
8) Neither
9) Even
10) Odd
11) Neither
12) Even
13) Odd
14) Odd
15) Even
16) Even
17) Odd
18) Even
19) Odd
20) Odd
21) Even
22) Odd
23) Odd

End Behavior of Polynomial Functions

1) $f(x) \to +\infty$, as $x \to -\infty$
   $f(x) \to +\infty$, as $x \to +\infty$

2) $f(x) \to -\infty$, as $x \to -\infty$
   $f(x) \to -\infty$, as $x \to +\infty$

3) $f(x) \to -\infty$, as $x \to -\infty$
   $f(x) \to +\infty$, as $x \to +\infty$

4) $f(x) \to +\infty$, as $x \to -\infty$
   $f(x) \to -\infty$, as $x \to +\infty$

5) $f(x) \to +\infty$, as $x \to -\infty$
   $f(x) \to +\infty$, as $x \to +\infty$

6) $f(x) \to -\infty$, as $x \to -\infty$
   $f(x) \to +\infty$, as $x \to +\infty$

7) $f(x) \to -\infty$, as $x \to -\infty$
   $f(x) \to +\infty$, as $x \to +\infty$

8) $f(x) \to -\infty$, as $x \to -\infty$
   $f(x) \to -\infty$, as $x \to +\infty$

9) $f(x) \to +\infty$, as $x \to -\infty$
   $f(x) \to -\infty$, as $x \to +\infty$

10) $f(x) \to +\infty$, as $x \to -\infty$
    $f(x) \to +\infty$, as $x \to +\infty$

11) $f(x) \to -\infty$, as $x \to -\infty$
    $f(x) \to -\infty$, as $x \to +\infty$

12) $f(x) \to -\infty$, as $x \to -\infty$
    $f(x) \to -\infty$, as $x \to +\infty$

13) $f(x) \to +\infty$, as $x \to -\infty$
    $f(x) \to -\infty$, as $x \to +\infty$

14) $f(x) \to -\infty$, as $x \to -\infty$
    $f(x) \to +\infty$, as $x \to +\infty$

Chapter 6: Polynomial Operations

Remainder and Factor Theorems

1) 7
2) 22
3) 32
4) 1
5) 4
6) 5
7) 120
8) −12
9) 34
10) 140
11) 296
12) 46

Polynomial Division (Long Division)

1) $x - 2 + \frac{2}{x-1}$
2) $x + 8 + \frac{24}{x-2}$
3) $x + 3 - \frac{14}{x+3}$
4) $x - 2 + \frac{8}{x-2}$
5) $x + 7 - \frac{1}{x-5}$
6) $x - 2 + \frac{36}{x+2}$
7) $2x + 5 + \frac{9}{x-3}$
8) $x - 8 - \frac{7}{x+9}$
9) $x + 5 + \frac{1}{x-6}$
10) $x + 4 + \frac{7}{x-7}$
11) $x + 5 - \frac{3}{x-5}$
12) $x - 9 - \frac{9}{2x+3}$
13) $x + 6 - \frac{10}{x+8}$
14) $x + 4 + \frac{7}{x-7}$
15) $x^2 - 3x + 4 - \frac{24}{x+3}$
16) $x^2 + 4x + 6$
17) $x^2 - 6x + 6$
18) $x^2 + 4x + 6$
19) $x^4 + 10x + 50 + \frac{208}{x-5}$
20) $x^2 - 5x + 1 - \frac{8}{x+3}$
21) $x^3 - 16x^2 - 64x - 92 - \frac{368}{x-4}$
22) $-x^3 - 12x^2 - 24x - 48 - \frac{82}{x-2}$

Polynomial Division (Synthetic Division)

1) $x - 2 + \frac{16}{x+2}$
2) $x + \frac{15}{x+5}$
3) $x^2 - 9 - \frac{27}{x-3}$
4) $3x - 1 + \frac{4}{x+2}$
5) $7x - 24 + \frac{78}{x+3}$
6) $4x^2 - 10x + 20 - \frac{40}{x+2}$
7) $4x + 5 + \frac{6}{x-1}$
8) $3x + 2 + \frac{6}{x-2}$

Chapter 6: Polynomial Operations

9) $x + 2 + \frac{8}{x+2}$

10) $x^2 + 3x + 9 + \frac{7}{x-3}$

11) $x + 3$

12) $x^2 - 9 - \frac{21}{x-3}$

13) $3x^2 - 2x + 2 - \frac{8}{x+2}$

14) $x^3 + 2x^2 - 6x + 12 - \frac{33}{x+3}$

15) $2x^2 + 13x + 84 + \frac{719}{x-9}$

16) $x^3 + 4x^2 - 9 - \frac{18}{x-2}$

17) $5x^3 - 10x^2 + 22x - 59 + \frac{130}{x+2}$

18) $4x^2 - 41x - 127 - \frac{290}{x-2}$

19) $x^2 - 8x - 117 - \frac{525}{x-5}$

20) $x^2 - 10x - 5 + \frac{35}{x-3}$

21) $x^2 - 6x - 4$

22) $x^2 + 12x + 11 - \frac{71}{x+3}$

23) $x^2 - x - 5 - \frac{12}{x-2}$

24) $x^3 + 4x^2 + 10x + 48 + \frac{150}{x-4}$

Finding Zeros of Polynomials

1) $\frac{1}{2}, -\frac{1}{2}$

2) $\frac{3}{5}, -\frac{3}{5}$

3) $\frac{-1+\sqrt{61}}{6}, \frac{-1-\sqrt{61}}{6}$

4) $1+\sqrt{7}, 1-\sqrt{7}$

5) $\frac{1}{3} + i\frac{\sqrt{11}}{3}, \frac{1}{3} - i\frac{\sqrt{11}}{3}$

6) $\frac{5}{6}, -3$

7) $-4, \frac{6}{5}$

8) $1+\sqrt{5}, 1-\sqrt{5}$

9) $0, -1, -4$

10) $0, 3, -1$

11) $0, -2, -3$

12) $0, -2, -6$

13) $0, 2, -2$

14) $2, \sqrt{3}, -\sqrt{3}$

15) $-3, 1, -1$

16) $-3, 1+\sqrt{3}, 1-\sqrt{3}$

17) $3, 2, -2$

18) $0, 2, -5$

19) $-3, -1, 2$

20) $5, -1, 0$

21) $0, -4, 5$

22) $0, -2+\sqrt{7}, -2-\sqrt{7}$

23) $\sqrt{5}, -\sqrt{5}, 3, -3$

24) $-5, 1+\sqrt{5}, 1-\sqrt{5}$

25) $\sqrt{3}, -\sqrt{3}, \sqrt{7}, -\sqrt{7}$

26) $2, -1.54$

Chapter 6: Polynomial Operations

Polynomial Identities

1) $(x + y)(x + 4y)$
2) $(x - 3y)(x + 2y)$
3) $2(4x - y)(x - y)$
4) $(3x + 2y)(x - 4y)$
5) $(5x + y)(2x - 3y)$
6) $2(3x + y)(3x - 2y)$
7) $(2x + 1)^3$
8) $(5x + 4y)(4x - 3y)$
9) $(2x - y)(x + 2y)$
10) $2(2x + y)(x - 3y)$
11) $(2x + 5)^3$
12) $(2x - 3)^3$
13) $(3x + 4)^3$
14) $(-3x + 2)^3$
15) $(3x + y + 1)^2$
16) $-8(2x - 1)^3$
17) $(3x + 1)^3$
18) $(2x + y + 3)^2$
19) $(5x + 2)^3$
20) $8(x + 4)^3$
21) $(4x + 3)^3$
22) $(3x + y + 1)^2$
23) $(2x + y)^3$
24) $(3x + 2y)^3$
25) $(4x - 3y)^3$
26) $(2x + 3y + 2)^2$

Chapter 7: Functions Operations

Math Topics that you'll learn in this Chapter:

- ✓ Function Notation
- ✓ Adding and Subtracting Functions
- ✓ Multiplying and Dividing Functions
- ✓ Composition of Functions
- ✓ Writing Functions
- ✓ Parent Functions
- ✓ Function Inverses
- ✓ Inverse Variation
- ✓ Graphing Functions
- ✓ Domain and Range of Function
- ✓ Piecewise Function
- ✓ Positive, Negative, Increasing, and Decreasing Functions on Intervals

Chapter 7: Functions Operations

Function Notation

✏️ **Evaluate each function.**

1) $f(x) = x - 3$, find $f(-2)$

2) $g(x) = x + 5$, find $g(6)$

3) $h(x) = x + 8$, find $h(2)$

4) $f(x) = -x - 7$, find $f(5)$

5) $f(x) = 2x - 7$, find $f(-1)$

6) $w(x) = -2 - 4x$, find $w(5)$

7) $g(n) = 6n - 3$, find $g(-2)$

8) $h(x) = -8x + 12$, find $h(3)$

9) $k(n) = 14 - 3n$, find $k(3)$

10) $g(x) = 4x - 4$, find $g(-2)$

11) $k(n) = 8n - 7$, find $k(4)$

12) $w(n) = -2n + 14$, find $w(5)$

13) $h(x) = 5x - 18$, find $h(8)$

14) $g(n) = 2n^2 + 2$, find $g(5)$

15) $f(x) = 3x^2 - 13$, find $f(2)$

16) $g(n) = 5n^2 + 7$, find $g(-3)$

17) $h(n) = 5n^2 - 10$, find $h(4)$

18) $g(x) = -3x^2 - 6x$, find $g(2)$

19) $k(n) = 4n^3 + n$, find $k(-5)$

20) $f(x) = -3x + 10$, find $f(3x)$

21) $k(a) = 4a + 9$, find $k(a - 1)$

22) $h(x) = 8x + 4$, find $h(5x)$

Chapter 7: Functions Operations

Adding and Subtracting Functions

✎ *Perform the indicated operation.*

1) $f(x) = x + 4$
   $g(x) = 2x + 5$
   Find $(f - g)(2)$
   _____

2) $g(x) = x - 2$
   $f(x) = -x - 6$
   Find $(g - f)(-2)$
   _____

3) $h(t) = 4t + 4$
   $g(t) = 3t + 2$
   Find $(h + g)(-1)$
   _____

4) $g(a) = 5a - 7$
   $f(a) = a^2 + 3$
   Find $(g + f)(2)$
   _____

5) $g(x) = 4x - 5$
   $f(x) = 6x^2 + 5$
   Find $(g - f)(-2)$
   _____

6) $h(x) = x^2 + 3$
   $g(x) = -4x + 1$
   Find $(h + g)(4)$
   _____

7) $f(x) = -3x - 9$
   $g(x) = x^2 + 5$
   Find $(f - g)(6)$
   _____

8) $h(n) = -4n^2 + 9$
   $g(n) = 5n + 6$
   Find $(h - g)(5)$
   _____

9) $g(x) = 4x^2 - 3x - 1$
   $f(x) = 6x + 10$
   Find $(g - f)(a)$
   _____

10) $g(t) = -6t - 7$
    $f(t) = -t^2 + 3t + 15$
    Find $(g + f)(t)$
    _____

Chapter 7: Functions Operations

Multiplying and Dividing Functions

✏ *Perform the indicated operation.*

1) $g(x) = x + 6$
   $f(x) = x + 4$
   Find $(g.f)(2)$

2) $f(x) = 3x$
   $h(x) = -x + 5$
   Find $(f.h)(-2)$

3) $g(a) = a + 5$
   $h(a) = 2a - 4$
   Find $(g.h)(4)$

4) $f(x) = 3x + 2$
   $h(x) = 2x - 3$
   Find $(\frac{f}{h})(2)$

5) $f(a) = a^2 - 2$
   $g(a) = -4 + 3a$
   Find $(\frac{f}{g})(2)$

6) $g(a) = 4a + 6$
   $f(a) = 2a - 8$
   Find $(\frac{g}{f})(3)$

7) $g(t) = t^2 + 6$
   $h(t) = 2t - 3$
   Find $(g.h)(-3)$

8) $g(x) = x^2 + 3x + 4$
   $h(x) = 2x + 6$
   Find $(g.h)(2)$

9) $g(a) = 2a^2 - 5a + 1$
   $f(a) = 2a^3 - 6$
   Find $(\frac{g}{f})(4)$

10) $g(x) = -3x^2 + 4 - 2x$
    $f(x) = x^2 - 5$
    Find $(g.f)(3)$

Composition of Functions

Using $f(x) = x + 6$ and $g(x) = 3x$, find:

1) $f(g(1)) = $ _____
2) $f(g(-1)) = $ _____
3) $g(f(-3)) = $ _____
4) $g(f(4)) = $ _____
5) $f(g(2)) = $ _____
6) $g(f(3)) = $ _____

Using $f(x) = 2x + 5$ and $g(x) = x - 2$, find:

7) $g(f(2)) = $ _____
8) $g(f(-2)) = $ _____
9) $f(g(5)) = $ _____
10) $f(f(4)) = $ _____
11) $g(f(3)) = $ _____
12) $g(f(-3)) = $ _____

Using $f(x) = 4x - 2$ and $g(x) = x - 5$, find:

13) $g(f(-2)) = $ _____
14) $f(f(4)) = $ _____
15) $f(g(5)) = $ _____
16) $f(f(3)) = $ _____
17) $g(f(-3)) = $ _____
18) $g(g(6)) = $ _____

Using $f(x) = 6x + 2$ and $g(x) = 2x - 3$, find:

19) $f(g(-3)) = $ _____
20) $g(f(5)) = $ _____
21) $f(g(4)) = $ _____
22) $f(f(3)) = $ _____

Chapter 7: Functions Operations

Writing Functions

✎ *According to the values of x and y in the following relationship, find the right equation.*

1) $\{(1,3),(2,6),(3,9),(4,12)\}$ $y =$ _____

2) $\{(1,2),(2,4),(3,6),(4,8)\}$ $y =$ _____

3) $\{(1,1),(2,4),(3,9),(4,16)\}$ $y =$ _____

4) $\{(1,4),(2,8),(3,12),(4,16)\}$ $y =$ _____

5) $\{(1,5),(2,7),(3,9),(4,11)\}$ $y =$ _____

6) $\{(1,4),(2,7),(3,10),(4,13)\}$ $y =$ _____

7) $\{(1,6),(2,10),(3,14),(4,18)\}$ $y =$ _____

8) $\{(1,-1),(2,-3),(3,-5),(4,-7)\}$ $y =$ _____

9) $\{(1,8),(2,13),(3,18),(4,23)\}$ $y =$ _____

10) $\{(1,9),(2,16),(3,23),(4,30)\}$ $y =$ _____

11) $\{(1,11),(2,16),(3,21),(4,26)\}$ $y =$ _____

12) $\{(1,10),(2,18),(3,26),(4,34)\}$ $y =$ _____

13) $\{(1,1),(2,7),(3,17),(4,31)\}$ $y =$ _____

14) $\{(1,1),(2,10),(3,25),(4,46)\}$ $y =$ _____

Chapter 7: Functions Operations

Parent Functions

✍ *Give the name of the parent function and describe the transformation represented.*

1) $y = x^2 - 3$ Name: _____

   Transformation: _____

2) $y = \sqrt{x-1}$ Name: _____

   Transformation: _____

3) $y = x^3 + 4$ Name: _____

   Transformation: _____

4) $y = \frac{1}{x+2}$ Name: _____

   Transformation: _____

5) $y = x^2 - 3$ Name: _____

   Transformation: _____

6) $y = x^3 + 4$ Name: _____

   Transformation: _____

7) $y = |x + 3|$ Name: _____

   Transformation: _____

8) $y = \frac{1}{x} - 4$ Name: _____

   Transformation: _____

9) $y = \sqrt{x+6}$ Name: _____

   Transformation: _____

10) $y = 2x^3 - 8$ Name: _____

    Transformation: _____

11) $y = \frac{1}{x-9}$ Name: _____

    Transformation: _____

12) $y = |x - 8|$ Name: _____

    Transformation: _____

Chapter 7: Functions Operations

Function Inverses

✎ *Find the inverse of each function.*

1) $g(x) = 6x \rightarrow g^{-1}(x) =$

2) $h(x) = \frac{1}{x-1} \rightarrow h^{-1}(x) =$

3) $g(x) = 12x \rightarrow g^{-1}(x) =$

4) $f(x) = \frac{1}{x} - 6 \rightarrow f^{-1}(x) =$

5) $h(x) = \frac{1}{x+4} \rightarrow h^{-1}(x) =$

6) $g(x) = \frac{7}{-x-3} \rightarrow g^{-1}(x) =$

7) $h(x) = \frac{x+9}{3} \rightarrow h^{-1}(x) =$

8) $h(x) = \frac{2x-10}{4} \rightarrow h^{-1}(x) =$

9) $f(x) = \frac{-15+x}{3} \rightarrow f^{-1}(x) =$

10) $s(x) = \sqrt{x} - 2 \rightarrow s^{-1}(x) =$

11) $h(x) = \frac{4}{x+2} \rightarrow h^{-1}(x) =$

12) $f(x) = (x-3)^3 \rightarrow f^{-1}(x) =$

13) $s(x) = -2x + 5 \rightarrow s^{-1}(x) =$

14) $k(x) = \frac{3}{-x-2} \rightarrow k^{-1}(x) =$

15) $f(x) = \sqrt[3]{x} - 3 \rightarrow f^{-1}(x) =$

16) $f(x) = \frac{1}{x} - 2 \rightarrow f^{-1}(x) =$

17) $s(x) = -3x + 1 \rightarrow s^{-1}(x) =$

18) $k(x) = x + 5 \rightarrow k^{-1}(x) =$

19) $h(x) = \frac{5x+16}{2} \rightarrow h^{-1}(x) =$

20) $g(x) = -x + 6 \rightarrow g^{-1}(x) =$

21) $h(x) = \frac{-x-5}{3} \rightarrow h^{-1}(x) =$

22) $w(x) = \frac{2}{7}x - \frac{10}{7} \rightarrow w^{-1}(x) =$

Chapter 7: Functions Operations

Inverse Variation

✎ *State whether each equation represents a direct or an inverse variation.*

1) $7x - y = 0$

2) $12xy - 10 = 20$

3) $-x - y = 0$

4) $x = \dfrac{2}{y}$

✎ *Solve.*

5) If y varies inversely as x and $y = 18$ when $x = 6$. What's the value of y when x is 4? _____

6) If y varies inversely as x and $y = 0.8$ when $x = 6$. What's the value of x when y is 3? _____

7) If y varies inversely as x and $y = 14$ when $x = 7$. What's the value of y when x is 8? _____

8) If y varies inversely as x and $y = 1.5$ when $x = 5$. What's the value of x when y is 2? _____

9) If y varies inversely as x and $y = 22$ when $x = 8$. What's the value of y when x is 5? _____

10) If y varies inversely as x and $y = 0.7$ when $x = 3$. What's the value of x when y is 4? _____

11) If y varies inversely as x and $y = 24$ when $x = 7$. What's the value of y when x is 6? _____

Chapter 7: Functions Operations

Graphing Functions

✎ *Graph the following functions.*

1) $y = 2x - 5$ 2) $y = 4x + 3$

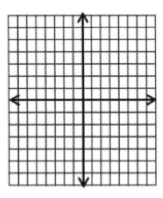

3) $y = 3x - 6$ 4) $y = 4x + 8$

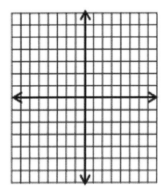
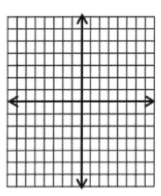

5) $y = 5x + 7$ 6) $y = -6x + 9$

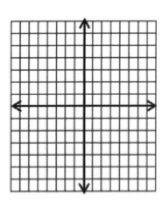
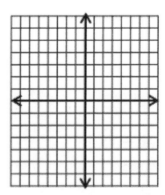

Chapter 7: Functions Operations

Domain and Range of Function

✎ **Find the domain and range of the functions.**

1) $x^3 - 4$
   Domain: _____
   Range: _____

2) $\sqrt{x-8} + 4$
   Domain: _____
   Range: _____

3) $\frac{2}{2x-1}$
   Domain: _____
   Range: _____

4) $-2x^3 + 6$
   Domain: _____
   Range: _____

5) $x^2 + 3x$
   Domain: _____
   Range: _____

6) $\frac{x}{x+2}$
   Domain: _____
   Range: _____

7) $-2(x+1)^2 + 5$
   Domain: _____
   Range: _____

8) $8x^3 + 2x$
   Domain: _____
   Range: _____

9) $\sqrt{x+2} - 6$
   Domain: _____
   Range: _____

10) $\frac{x^2}{3x+2}$
    Domain: _____
    Range: _____

11) $-2x^2 + 4x + 8$
    Domain: _____
    Range: _____

12) $\sqrt{3x^2 + 5} - 2$
    Domain: _____
    Range: _____

13) $-6x^3 + 5x^2 - 4$
    Domain: _____
    Range: _____

14) $\frac{3x^3}{2x-1}$
    Domain: _____
    Range: _____

Chapter 7: Functions Operations

Piecewise Function

✎ *Graph.*

1) $f(x) = \begin{cases} 2 + x, & x < -1 \\ x - 1, & x \geq 0 \end{cases}$

2) $f(x) = \begin{cases} 3 - x, & -2 < x < 2 \\ 2x, & -1 < x < 3 \end{cases}$

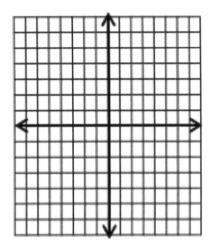 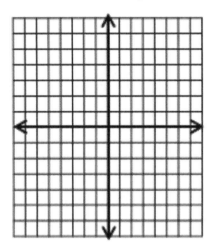

3) $f(x) = \begin{cases} x + 2, & 0 \leq x < 4 \\ -x - 1, & 1 < x < 4 \end{cases}$

4) $f(x) = \begin{cases} -2x, & -1 \leq x \leq 3 \\ 3x - 1, & -2 < x < 2 \end{cases}$

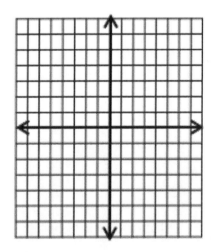 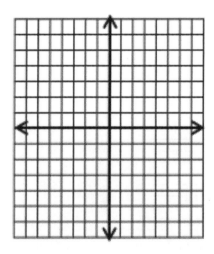

Chapter 7: Functions Operations

Positive, Negative, Increasing, and Decreasing Functions on Intervals

✍ *Determine the intervals where the function is increasing and decreasing.*

Submit your solution in interval notation.

1) $2x^2 + 1$

2) $-x^3 - 2$

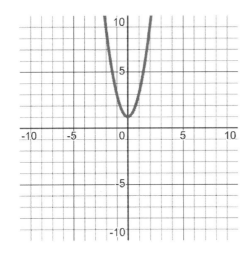
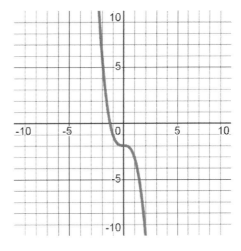

3) $(x-1)^2 + 2$

4) $x^3 - 2x^2 - 5$

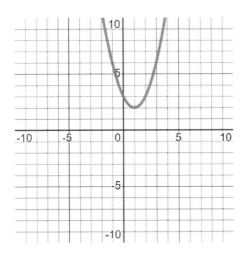
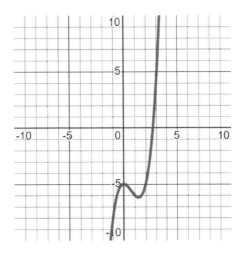

Chapter 7: Functions Operations

Answers – Chapter 7

Function Notation

1) -5
2) 11
3) 10
4) -12
5) -9
6) -22
7) -15
8) -12
9) 5
10) -12
11) 25
12) 4
13) 22
14) 52
15) -1
16) 52
17) 70
18) -24
19) -505
20) $-9x + 10$
21) $4a + 5$
22) $40x + 4$

Adding and Subtracting Functions

1) -3
2) 0
3) -1
4) 10
5) -42
6) 4
7) -68
8) -122
9) $4a^2 - 9a - 11$
10) $-t^2 - 3t + 8$

Multiplying and Dividing Functions

1) 48
2) -42
3) 36
4) 8
5) 1
6) -9
7) -135
8) 140
9) $\frac{13}{122}$
10) -116

Chapter 7: Functions Operations

Composition of Functions

1) $f(g(1)) = 9$
2) $f(g(-1)) = 3$
3) $g(f(-3)) = 9$
4) $g(f(4)) = 30$
5) $f(g(2)) = 12$
6) $g(f(3)) = 27$
7) $g(f(2)) = 7$
8) $g(f(-2)) = -1$
9) $f(g(5)) = 11$
10) $f(f(4)) = 31$
11) $g(f(3)) = 9$
12) $g(f(-3)) = -3$
13) $g(f(-2)) = -15$
14) $f(f(4)) = 54$
15) $f(g(5)) = -2$
16) $f(f(3)) = 38$
17) $g(f(-3)) = -19$
18) $g(g(6)) = -4$
19) $f(g(-3)) = -52$
20) $g(f(5)) = 61$
21) $f(g(4)) = 32$
22) $f(f(3)) = 122$

Writing Functions

1) $y = 3x$
2) $y = 2x$
3) $y = x^2$
4) $y = 4x$
5) $y = 2x + 3$
6) $y = 3x + 1$
7) $y = 4x + 2$
8) $y = -2x + 1$
9) $y = 5x + 3$
10) $y = 7x + 2$
11) $y = 5x + 6$
12) $y = 8x + 2$
13) $y = 2x^2 - 1$
14) $y = 3x^2 - 2$

Chapter 7: Functions Operations

Parent Functions

1) Name: Quadratic
   Transformation: shift 3 unit down
2) Name: square root
   Transformation: shift 1 unit right
3) Name: cubic
   Transformation: shift 4 units up
4) Name: rational
   Transformation: shift 2 units left
5) Name: quadratic
   Transformation: shift 3 unit down
6) Name: cubic
   Transformation: shift 4 units up
7) Name: absolute value
   Transformation: shift 3 units left
8) Name: rational
   Transformation: shift 4 units down
9) Name: square root
   Transformation: shift 6 unit left
10) Name: cubic
    Transformations: shift 8 unit down, stretch 2 times in $y-$direction,
11) Name: rational
    Transformation: shift 9 units right
12) Name: absolute value
    Transformation: shift 8 units right

Function Inverses

1) $g^{-1}(x) = \frac{x}{6}$
2) $h^{-1}(x) = \frac{1}{x} + 1$
3) $g^{-1}(x) = \frac{x}{12}$
4) $f^{-1}(x) = \frac{1}{x+6}$
5) $h^{-1}(x) = \frac{1}{x} - 4$
6) $g^{-1}(x) = -\frac{7+3x}{x}$
7) $h^{-1}(x) = 3x - 9$
8) $h^{-1}(x) = 2x + 5$
9) $f^{-1}(x) = 3x + 15$
10) $s^{-1}(x) = x^2 + 4x + 4$
11) $h^{-1}(x) = \frac{4-2x}{x}$
12) $f^{-1}(x) = \sqrt[3]{x} + 3$
13) $s^{-1}(x) = -\frac{1}{2}x + \frac{5}{2}$
14) $k^{-1}(x) = -\frac{3}{x} - 2$
15) $f^{-1}(x) = (x+3)^3$
16) $f^{-1}(x) = \frac{1}{x+2}$
17) $s^{-1}(x) = -\frac{1}{3}x + \frac{1}{3}$
18) $k^{-1}(x) = x - 5$
19) $h^{-1}(x) = \frac{2x-16}{5}$
20) $g^{-1}(x) = -x + 6$
21) $h^{-1}(x) = -3x - 5$
22) $w^{-1}(x) = 5 + \frac{7}{2}x$

Chapter 7: Functions Operations

Inverse Variation

1) Direct variation
2) Inverse variation
3) Direct variation
4) Inverse variation
5) $y = 27$
6) $x = 1.6$
7) $y = 12.25$
8) $x = 3.75$
9) $y = 35.2$
10) $x = 0.5$
11) $y = 28$

Graphing Functions

1) $y = 2x - 5$

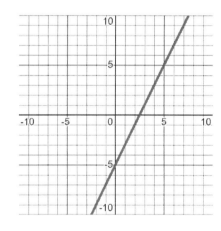

2) $y = 4x + 3$

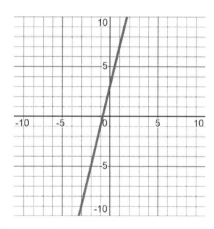

3) $y = 3x - 6$

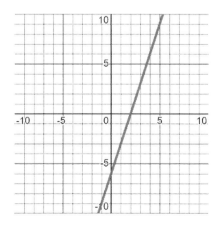

4) $y = 4x + 8$

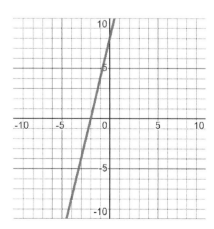

Chapter 7: Functions Operations

5) $y = 5x + 7$

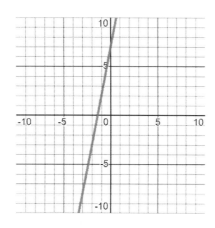

6) $y = -6x + 9$

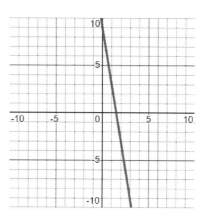

Domain and Range of Function

1) Domain: $-\infty < x < \infty$
   Range: $-\infty < f(x) < \infty$

2) Domain: $x \geq 8$
   Range: $f(x) \geq 4$

3) Domain: $x < \frac{1}{2}$ or $x > \frac{1}{2}$
   Range: $f(x) < 0$ or $f(x) > 0$

4) Domain: $-\infty < x < \infty$
   Range: $-\infty < f(x) < \infty$

5) Domain: $-\infty < x < \infty$
   Range: $f(x) \geq -\frac{9}{4}$

6) Domain: $x < -2$ or $x > -2$
   Range: $f(x) < 1$ or $f(x) > 1$

7) Domain: $-\infty < x < \infty$
   Range: $f(x) \leq 5$

8) Domain: $-\infty < x < \infty$
   Range: $-\infty < f(x) < \infty$

9) Domain: $x \geq -2$
   Range: $f(x) \geq -6$

10) Domain: $x < -\frac{2}{3}$ or $x > -\frac{2}{3}$
    Range: $f(x) \leq -\frac{8}{9}$ or $f(x) \geq 0$

11) Domain: $-\infty < x < \infty$
    Range: $f(x) \leq 10$

12) Domain: $-\infty < x < \infty$
    Range: $f(x) \geq \sqrt{5} - 2$

13) Domain: $-\infty < x < \infty$
    Range: $-\infty < f(x) < \infty$

14) Domain: $x < \frac{1}{2}$ or $x > \frac{1}{2}$
    Range: $-\infty < f(x) < \infty$

Chapter 7: Functions Operations

Piecewise Function

1) $f(x) = \begin{cases} 2 + x, & x < -1 \\ x - 1, & x \geq 0 \end{cases}$

2) $f(x) = \begin{cases} 3 - x, & -2 < x < 2 \\ 2x, & -1 < x < 3 \end{cases}$

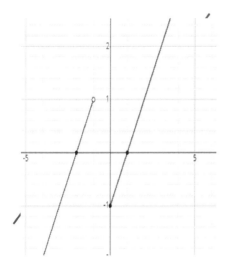

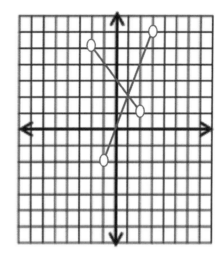

3) $f(x) = \begin{cases} x + 2, & 0 \leq x < 4 \\ -x - 1, & 1 < x < 4 \end{cases}$

4) $f(x) = \begin{cases} -2x, & -1 \leq x \leq 3 \\ 3x - 1, & -2 < x < 2 \end{cases}$

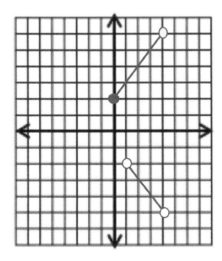

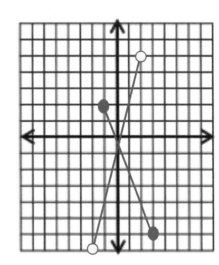

Chapter 7: Functions Operations

Positive, Negative, Increasing and Decreasing Functions on Intervals.

1) Increasing intervals: $(0, \infty)$

   Decreasing intervals: $(-\infty, 0)$

2) Decreasing intervals: $(0, \infty)$

   Decreasing intervals: $(-\infty, 0)$

3) Increasing intervals: $(1, \infty)$

   Decreasing intervals: $(-\infty, 1)$

4) Increasing intervals: $(\frac{4}{3}, \infty)$

   Decreasing intervals: $(0, \frac{4}{3})$

   Increasing intervals: $(-\infty, 0)$

Chapter 8: Exponential Functions

Math Topics that you'll learn in this Chapter:

- ✓ Exponential Function
- ✓ Linear, Quadratic and Exponential Models
- ✓ Linear vs Exponential Growth

Chapter 8: Exponential Functions

Exponential Function

✎ *Sketch the graph of each function.*

1) $2 \cdot \left(\dfrac{1}{3}\right)^x$

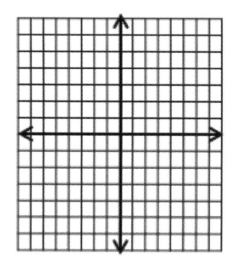

2) $5 \cdot (2)^x$

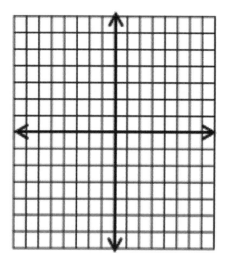

3) $\dfrac{1}{2} \cdot (4)^x$

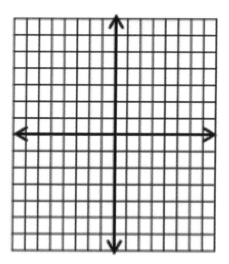

4) $-\dfrac{1}{3} \cdot \left(\dfrac{1}{2}\right)^x$

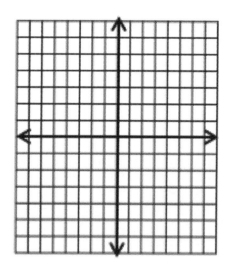

Chapter 8: Exponential Functions

Linear, Quadratic and Exponential Models

✎ *Identify the following equations as linear, quadratic, or exponential.*

1) $x^2 - 3x + 5$ _____

2) $2^x + 1$ _____

3) $2x - 9$ _____

4) $-6(2)^x$ _____

5) $(x-1)^2 - 3$ _____

6) $-5x + 1$ _____

7) $4 - \frac{2}{3}x$ _____

8) $8(\frac{1}{2})^x$ _____

✎ *Determine whether the following table of values represents a linear function, an exponential function, or a quadratic function.*

9) _____

x	-2	-1	0	1	2
y	$\frac{1}{2}$	1	2	4	8

10) _____

x	-2	-1	0	1	2
y	5	2	1	2	5

11) _____

x	-2	-1	0	1	2
y	-4	-1	2	5	8

Chapter 8: Exponential Functions

Linear vs Exponential Growth

✎ *Using the data in this table, determine whether this relationship is linear, exponential, or neither.*

1) _____

x	-2	-1	0	1	2
y	-6	-3	0	3	6

2) _____

x	-2	-1	0	1	2
y	$\frac{1}{9}$	$\frac{1}{3}$	1	3	9

3) _____

x	-2	-1	0	1	2
y	1	-2	-3	-2	1

4) _____

x	-2	-1	0	1	2
y	$-\frac{3}{4}$	$-\frac{1}{2}$	1	1	3

5) _____

x	-2	-1	0	1	2
y	-8	-6	-4	-2	0

Chapter 8: Exponential Functions

Answers – Chapter 8

Exponential Function

1) $2 \cdot \left(\frac{1}{3}\right)^x$

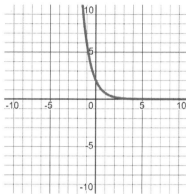

2) $5 \cdot (2)^x$

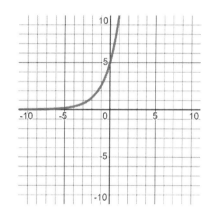

3) $\frac{1}{2} \cdot (4)^x$

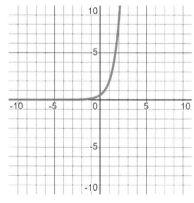

4) $-\frac{1}{3} \cdot \left(\frac{1}{2}\right)^x$

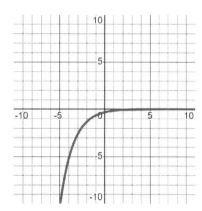

Linear, Quadratic and Exponential Models

1) Quadratic
2) Exponential
3) Linear
4) Exponential
5) Quadratic
6) Linear
7) Linear
8) Exponential
9) Exponential
10) Quadratic
11) Linear

Linear vs Exponential Growth

1) $y = 3x$, Linear

2) $(3)^x$, exponential

3) $y = x^2 - 3$, Quadratic

4) $2^x - 1$, exponential

5) $y = 2x - 4$, Linear

Chapter 9: Logarithms

Math Topics that you'll learn in this Chapter:

- ✓ Evaluating Logarithms
- ✓ Properties of Logarithms
- ✓ Natural Logarithms
- ✓ Solving Logarithmic Equations

Chapter 9: Logarithms

Evaluating Logarithms

✏️ *Evaluate each logarithm.*

1) $\log_2 4 =$

2) $\log_2 8 =$

3) $\log_3 27 =$

4) $\log_3 9 =$

5) $\log_4 16 =$

6) $\log_2 32 =$

7) $\log_8 64 =$

8) $\log_2 \frac{1}{2} =$

9) $\log_2 \frac{1}{8} =$

10) $\log_3 \frac{1}{3} =$

11) $\log_4 \frac{1}{16} =$

12) $\log_3 \frac{1}{9} =$

13) $\log_7 \frac{1}{49} =$

14) $\log_{64} \frac{1}{4} =$

15) $\log_{625} 5 =$

16) $\log_2 \frac{1}{64} =$

17) $\log_4 \frac{1}{64} =$

18) $\log_{36} \frac{1}{6} =$

✏️ *Circle the points which are on the graph of the given logarithmic functions.*

19) $y = 2 \log_3(x + 1) + 2$ (2, 4),   (8, 4),   (0, 3)

20) $y = 3 \log_3(3x) - 2$ (3, 6),   (3, 4), $(\frac{1}{3}, 2)$

21) $y = -2 \log_2 2(x + 1) + 1$ (3, -3),   (2, 1),   (5, 5)

22) $y = 4 \log_4(4x) + 7$ (1, 7),   (1, 11),   (4, 8)

23) $y = -\log_2 2(x + 3) + 1$ (-2, 0),   (1, 2),   (5, 3)

24) $y = -\log_5(x - 3) + 8$ (4, 8),   (8, 8),   (4, 4)

25) $y = 3 \log_4(x + 1) + 3$ (3, 3),   (3, 6),   (0, 4)

Chapter 9: Logarithms

Properties of Logarithms

✏️ **Expand each logarithm.**

1) $\log(8 \times 5) =$

2) $\log(9 \times 4) =$

3) $\log(3 \times 7) =$

4) $\log\left(\frac{3}{4}\right) =$

5) $\log\left(\frac{5}{7}\right) =$

6) $\log\left(\frac{2}{5}\right)^3 =$

7) $\log(2 \times 3^4) =$

8) $\log\left(\frac{5}{7}\right)^4 =$

9) $\log\left(\frac{2^3}{7}\right) \log\left(\frac{2^3}{7}\right) =$

10) $\log(x \times y)^5 =$

11) $\log(x^3 \times y \times z^4) =$

12) $\log\left(\frac{u^4}{v}\right) \log\left(\frac{u^4}{v}\right) =$

13) $\log\left(\frac{x}{y^6}\right) =$

✏️ **Condense each expression to a single logarithm.**

14) $\log 2 - \log 9 =$

15) $\log 5 + \log 3 =$

16) $5 \log 6 - 3 \log 4 =$

17) $4 \log 7 - 2 \log 9 =$

18) $3 \log 5 - \log 14 =$

19) $7 \log 3 - 4 \log 4 =$

20) $\log 7 - 2 \log 12 =$

21) $2 \log 5 + 3 \log 8 =$

22) $4 \log 3 + 5 \log 7 =$

23) $4 \log_5 a + 7 \log_5 b =$

24) $2 \log_3 x - 9 \log_3 y =$

25) $\log_4 u - 6 \log_4 v =$

26) $4 \log_6 u + 8 \log_6 v =$

27) $4 \log_3 u - 20 \log_3 v =$

Chapter 9: Logarithms

Natural Logarithms

✎ *Solve each equation for x.*

1) $e^x = 3$

2) $e^x = 4$

3) $e^x = 8$

4) $\ln x = 6$

5) $\ln(\ln x) = 5$

6) $e^x = 9$

7) $\ln(2x + 5) = 4$

8) $\ln(2x - 1) = 1$

9) $\ln(6x - 1) = 1$

10) $\ln x = \frac{1}{2}$

11) $\ln 2x = e^2$

12) $\ln x = \ln 4 + \ln 7$

13) $\ln x = 2 \ln 4 + \ln 5$

✎ *Evaluate each expression without using a calculator.*

14) $\ln 1 =$

15) $\ln e^3 =$

16) $2 \ln e =$

17) $\ln e^2 =$

18) $4 \ln e =$

19) $\ln(\frac{1}{e}) =$

20) $e^{\ln 10} =$

21) $e^{3 \ln 2} =$

22) $e^{5 \ln 2} =$

23) $\ln \sqrt{e} =$

✎ *Simplify the following expressions to simplest form.*

24) $e^{-2 \ln 5 + 2 \ln 3} =$

25) $e^{-\ln(\frac{1}{e})} =$

26) $2 \ln(e^3) =$

27) $\ln(\frac{1}{e})^2 =$

28) $e^{\ln 2 + 3 \ln 2} =$

29) $e^{\ln(\frac{2}{e})} =$

30) $5 \ln(1^{-e}) =$

31) $\ln(\frac{1}{e})^{-3} =$

32) $\ln(\frac{\sqrt{e}}{e}) =$

33) $e^{-2 \ln e + 2 \ln 2} =$

34) $e^{\ln \frac{1}{e}} =$

35) $3 \ln(e^e) =$

Chapter 9: Logarithms

Solving Logarithmic Equations

✍ **Find the value of the variables in each equation.**

1) $2\log_7 49 - 2x = 0$

2) $-\log_5 7x = 2$

3) $\log x + 5 = 2$

4) $\log x - \log 4 = 3$

5) $\log x + \log 2 = 4$

6) $\log 10 + \log x = 1$

7) $\log x + \log 8 = \log 48$

8) $3\log_3(x - 2) = -12$

9) $\log 6x = \log(x + 5)$

10) $\log(4p - 2) = \log(-5p + 5)$

11) $\log(4k - 5) = \log(2k - 1)$

12) $-10 + \log_3(n + 3) = -10$

13) $\log_9(x + 2) = \log_9(x^2 + 30)$

14) $\log_{12}(v^2 + 35) = \log_{12}(-2v - 1)$

15) $\log(16 + 2b) = \log(b^2 - 4b)$

16) $\log_9(x + 6) - \log_9(x) = \log_9 2$

17) $\log_5 6 + \log_5 2x^2 = \log_5 48$

18) $\log_6(x + 1) - \log_6 x = \log_6 29$

✍ **Find the value of x in each natural logarithm equation.**

19) $\ln 2 - \ln(3x + 2) = 1$

20) $\ln(x - 3) - \ln(x - 5) = \ln 5$

21) $\ln e^4 - \ln(x + 1) = 1$

22) $\ln(2x - 1) - \ln(x - 5) = \ln 5$

23) $\ln 2x + \ln(3x - 4) = \ln 4x$

24) $\ln(4x - 2) - 4\ln(x - 5) = \ln 10$

25) $\ln(4x + 2) - \ln 1 = 5$

26) $\ln(x - 3) + \ln() \ln(x - 5) = \ln 2$

27) $\ln 2 + \ln(3x + 2) = 4$

28) $2\ln 4x - \ln(x + 6) = 2\ln 3x$

29) $\ln x^2 + \ln x^3 = \ln 1$

30) $\ln x^4 - \ln(x + 4) = 4\ln x$

31) $2\ln(x - 3) = \ln(x^2 - 6x + 9)$

32) $\ln(x^2 + 12) = \ln(6x + 4)$

33) $2\ln x - 2\ln(x + 2) = 4\ln(x^2)$

34) $\ln(4x - 3) - \ln(2x - 4) = \ln 5$

35) $\ln 2 + 4\ln(x + 2) = \ln 2$

36) $2\ln e^2 + \ln(2x - 1) = \ln 5 + 4$

Chapter 9: Logarithms

Answers – Chapter 9

Evaluating Logarithms

1) 2
2) 3
3) 3
4) 2
5) 2
6) 5
7) 2
8) −1
9) −3
10) −1
11) −2
12) −2
13) −2
14) $-\frac{1}{3}$
15) $\frac{1}{4}$
16) −6
17) −3
18) $-\frac{1}{2}$
19) (2, 4)
20) (3, 4)
21) (3, −3)
22) (1, 11)
23) (−2, 1)
24) (4, 8)
25) (3, 6)

Properties of Logarithms

1) $\log 8 + \log 5$
2) $\log 9 + \log 4$
3) $\log 3 + \log 7$
4) $\log 3 - \log 4$
5) $\log 5 - \log 7$
6) $3 \log 2 - 3 \log 5$
7) $\log 2 + 4 \log 3$
8) $4 \log 5 - 4 \log 7$
9) $3 \log 2 - \log 7$
10) $5 \log x + 5 \log y$
11) $3 \log x + \log y + 4 \log z$
12) $4 \log u - \log v$
13) $\log x - 6 \log y$
14) $\log \frac{2}{9}$
15) $\log(5 \times 3)$
16) $\log \frac{6^5}{4^3}$
17) $\log \frac{7^4}{9^2}$
18) $\log \frac{5^3}{14}$
19) $\log \frac{3^7}{4^4}$
20) $\log \frac{7}{12^2}$
21) $\log (5^2 \times 8^3)$
22) $\log (3^4 \times 7^5)$
23) $\log_5 (a^4 \times b^7)$
24) $\log_3 \frac{x^2}{y^9}$
25) $\log_4 \frac{u}{v^6}$
26) $\log_6 (u^4 \times v^8)$
27) $\log_3 \frac{u^4}{v^{20}}$

Chapter 9: Logarithms

Natural Logarithms

1) $x = \ln 3$
2) $x = \ln 4, x = 2\ln(2)$
3) $x = \ln 8, x = 3\ln(2)$
4) $x = e^6$
5) $x = e^{e^5}$
6) $x = \ln 9, x = 2\ln(3)$
7) $x = \frac{e^4 - 5}{2}$
8) $x = \frac{e+1}{2}$
9) $x = \frac{e+1}{6}$
10) $x = \sqrt{e}$
11) $x = \frac{e^{e^2}}{2}$
12) $x = 28$
13) $x = 80$
14) 0
15) 3
16) 2
17) 2
18) 4
19) -1
20) 10
21) 8
22) 32
23) $\frac{1}{2}$
24) $\frac{9}{25} = 0.36$
25) e
26) 6
27) -2
28) 16
29) $\frac{2}{e}$
30) 0
31) 3
32) -0.5
33) $4e^{-2} = \frac{4}{e^2}$
34) $\frac{1}{e}$
35) $3e$

Solving Logarithmic Equations

1) $\{2\}$
2) $\{\frac{1}{175}\}$
3) $\{\frac{1}{1,000}\}$
4) $\{4,000\}$
5) $\{5,000\}$
6) $\{1\}$
7) $\{6\}$
8) $\{83\}$
9) $\{1\}$
10) $\{\frac{7}{9}\}$
11) $\{2\}$
12) $\{\frac{7}{9}\}\{-2\}$
13) No Solution
14) No Solution
15) $\{8, -2\}$
16) $\{6\}$
17) $\{\sqrt{3}, -\sqrt{3}\}$
18) $\{\frac{1}{28}\}$
19) $x = \frac{2-2e}{3e} = -0.42$
20) $\{\frac{11}{2}\}$
21) $e^3 - 1$
22) $\{8\}$
23) $\{2\}$
24) $\{6.23\}$
25) $x = \frac{e^5 - 2}{4}$
26) $x = 4 + \sqrt{3}$
27) $x = \frac{e^4 - 4}{6}$
28) No Solution
29) $\{1\}$
30) No Solution
31) $x > 3$
32) $\{2, 4\}$
33) $\{0.71667 \dots\}$
34) $\{\frac{17}{6}\}$
35) $\{-1\}$
36) $\{3\}$

Chapter 10: Radical Expressions

Math Topics that you'll learn in this Chapter:

- ✓ Simplifying Radical Expressions
- ✓ Multiplying Radical Expressions
- ✓ Simplifying Radical Expressions Involving Fractions
- ✓ Adding and Subtracting Radical Expressions
- ✓ Domain and Range of Radical Functions
- ✓ Solving Radical Equations

Chapter 10: Radical Expressions

Simplifying Radical Expressions

✏️ **Simplify.**

1) $\sqrt{35x^2} =$

2) $\sqrt{90x^2} =$

3) $\sqrt[3]{8a} =$

4) $\sqrt{100x^3} =$

5) $\sqrt{125a} =$

6) $\sqrt[3]{88w^3} =$

7) $\sqrt{80x} =$

8) $\sqrt{216v} =$

9) $\sqrt[3]{125x} =$

10) $\sqrt{64x^5} =$

11) $\sqrt{4x^2} =$

12) $\sqrt[3]{54a^2} =$

13) $\sqrt{405} =$

14) $\sqrt{512p^3} =$

15) $\sqrt{216m^4} =$

16) $\sqrt{264x^3y^3} =$

17) $\sqrt{49x^3y^3} =$

18) $\sqrt{16a^4b^3} =$

19) $\sqrt{20x^3y^3} =$

20) $\sqrt[3]{216yx^3} =$

21) $3\sqrt{75x^2} =$

22) $5\sqrt{80x^2} =$

23) $\sqrt[3]{256x^2y^3} =$

24) $\sqrt[3]{343x^4y^2} =$

25) $4\sqrt{125a} =$

26) $\sqrt[3]{625xy} =$

27) $2\sqrt{8x^2y^3r} =$

28) $4\sqrt{36x^2y^3z^4} =$

29) $2\sqrt[3]{512x^3y^4} =$

30) $5\sqrt{64a^2b^3c^5} =$

Chapter 10: Radical Expressions

Multiplying Radical Expressions

✎ Simplify.

1) $\sqrt{5} \times \sqrt{5} =$

2) $\sqrt{5} \times \sqrt{10} =$

3) $\sqrt{2} \times \sqrt{18} =$

4) $\sqrt{14} \times \sqrt{21} =$

5) $\sqrt{5} \times -4\sqrt{20} =$

6) $3\sqrt{12} \times \sqrt{6} =$

7) $5\sqrt{42} \times \sqrt{3} =$

8) $\sqrt{3} \times -\sqrt{25} =$

9) $\sqrt{99} \times \sqrt{48} =$

10) $5\sqrt{45} \times 3\sqrt{176} =$

11) $\sqrt{12}(3 + \sqrt{3}) =$

12) $\sqrt{23x^2} \times \sqrt{23x} =$

13) $-5\sqrt{12} \times -\sqrt{3} =$

14) $2\sqrt{20x^2} \times \sqrt{5x^2} =$

15) $\sqrt{12x^2} \times \sqrt{2x^3} =$

16) $-12\sqrt{7x} \times \sqrt{5x^3} =$

17) $-5\sqrt{9x^3} \times 6\sqrt{3x^2} =$

18) $-2\sqrt{12}(3 + \sqrt{12}) =$

19) $\sqrt{18x}(4 - \sqrt{6x}) =$

20) $\sqrt{3x}(6\sqrt{x^3} + \sqrt{27}) =$

21) $\sqrt{15r}(5 + \sqrt{5}) =$

22) $-5\sqrt{3x} \times 4\sqrt{6x^3} =$

23) $-2\sqrt{18x} \times 4\sqrt{2x}$

24) $-3\sqrt{5v^2}(-3\sqrt{15v}) =$

25) $(\sqrt{5} - \sqrt{3})(\sqrt{5} + \sqrt{3}) =$

26) $(-4\sqrt{6} + 2)(\sqrt{6} - 5) =$

27) $(2 - 2\sqrt{3})(-2 + \sqrt{3}) =$

28) $(11 - 4\sqrt{5})(6 - \sqrt{5}) =$

29) $(-2 - \sqrt{3x})(3 + \sqrt{3x}) =$

30) $(-2 + 3\sqrt{2r})(-2 + \sqrt{2r}) =$

31) $(-4\sqrt{2n} + 2)(-2\sqrt{2} - 4) =$

32) $(-1 + 2\sqrt{3})(2 - 3\sqrt{3x}) =$

Chapter 10: Radical Expressions

Simplifying Radical Expressions Involving Fractions

✎ *Simplify.*

1) $\dfrac{\sqrt{5}}{\sqrt{3}} =$

2) $\dfrac{\sqrt{8}}{\sqrt{100}} =$

3) $\dfrac{\sqrt{2}}{2\sqrt{3}} =$

4) $\dfrac{4}{\sqrt{5}} =$

5) $\dfrac{2\sqrt{5r}}{\sqrt{m^3}} =$

6) $\dfrac{8\sqrt{3}}{\sqrt{k}} =$

7) $\dfrac{6\sqrt{14x^2}}{2\sqrt{18x}} =$

8) $\dfrac{\sqrt{7x^2y^2}}{\sqrt{5x^3v^2}} =$

9) $\dfrac{1}{1+\sqrt{2}} =$

10) $\dfrac{1-5\sqrt{a}}{\sqrt{11a}} =$

11) $\dfrac{\sqrt{a}}{\sqrt{a}+\sqrt{b}} =$

12) $\dfrac{1+\sqrt{2}}{3+\sqrt{5}} =$

13) $\dfrac{2+\sqrt{5}}{6-\sqrt{3}} =$

14) $\dfrac{5}{-3-3\sqrt{3}} =$

15) $\dfrac{2}{3+\sqrt{5}} =$

16) $\dfrac{\sqrt{7}-\sqrt{3}}{\sqrt{3}-\sqrt{7}} =$

17) $\dfrac{\sqrt{7}+\sqrt{5}}{\sqrt{5}+\sqrt{2}} =$

18) $\dfrac{3\sqrt{2}-\sqrt{7}}{4\sqrt{2}+\sqrt{5}} =$

19) $\dfrac{\sqrt{5}+2\sqrt{2}}{4-\sqrt{5}} =$

20) $\dfrac{5\sqrt{3}-3\sqrt{2}}{3\sqrt{2}-2\sqrt{3}} =$

21) $\dfrac{\sqrt{8a^5b^3}}{\sqrt{2ab^2}} =$

22) $\dfrac{6\sqrt{45x^3}}{3\sqrt{5x}} =$

Chapter 10: Radical Expressions

Adding and Subtracting Radical Expressions

✏️ **Simplify.**

1) $\sqrt{3} + \sqrt{27} =$

2) $3\sqrt{8} + 3\sqrt{2} =$

3) $4\sqrt{3} - 2\sqrt{12} =$

4) $3\sqrt{18} - 2\sqrt{2} =$

5) $2\sqrt{45} - 2\sqrt{5} =$

6) $-\sqrt{12} - 5\sqrt{3} =$

7) $-4\sqrt{2} - 5\sqrt{32} =$

8) $5\sqrt{10} + 2\sqrt{40} =$

9) $4\sqrt{12} - 3\sqrt{27} =$

10) $-3\sqrt{2} + 4\sqrt{18} =$

11) $-10\sqrt{7} + 6\sqrt{28} =$

12) $5\sqrt{3} - \sqrt{27} =$

13) $-\sqrt{12} + 3\sqrt{3} =$

14) $-3\sqrt{6} - \sqrt{54} =$

15) $3\sqrt{8} + 3\sqrt{2} =$

16) $2\sqrt{12} - 3\sqrt{27} =$

17) $\sqrt{50} - \sqrt{32} =$

18) $4\sqrt{8} - 6\sqrt{2} =$

19) $-4\sqrt{12} + 12\sqrt{108} =$

20) $2\sqrt{45} - 2\sqrt{5} =$

21) $7\sqrt{18} - 3\sqrt{2} =$

22) $-12\sqrt{35} + 7\sqrt{140} =$

23) $-6\sqrt{19} - 3\sqrt{76} =$

24) $-\sqrt{54x} - 3\sqrt{6x} =$

25) $\sqrt{5y^2} + y\sqrt{45} =$

26) $\sqrt{8mn^2} + 2n\sqrt{18m} =$

27) $-8\sqrt{27a} - 5\sqrt{3a} =$

28) $-4\sqrt{7ab} - \sqrt{28ab} =$

29) $\sqrt{27a^2b} + a\sqrt{12b} =$

30) $3\sqrt{6a^3} - 2\sqrt{24a^3} + 2a\sqrt{54a} =$

Chapter 10: Radical Expressions

Domain and Range of Radical Functions

✍ *Identify the domain and range of each function.*

1) $y = \sqrt{x+2} - 3$

2) $y = \sqrt[3]{x-1} - 1$

3) $y = \sqrt{x-2} + 5$

4) $y = \sqrt[3]{(x+1)} - 4$

5) $y = 3\sqrt{3x+6} + 5$

6) $y = \sqrt[3]{(2x-1)} - 4$

7) $y = 6\sqrt{3x^2+6} + 5$

8) $y = \sqrt[3]{(2x^2-2)} - 4$

9) $y = 4\sqrt{4x^3+32} - 1$

10) $y = \sqrt[3]{(4x+8)} - 2x$

11) $y = 7\sqrt{-2(2x+4)} + 1$

12) $y = \sqrt[5]{(4x^2-5)} - 2$

13) $y = 2x\sqrt{5x^4+6} - 2x$

14) $y = 6\sqrt[3]{(8x^6+2x+8)} - 2$

✍ *Sketch the graph of each function.*

15) $y = \sqrt{x} + 8$

16) $y = 2\sqrt{x} - 4$

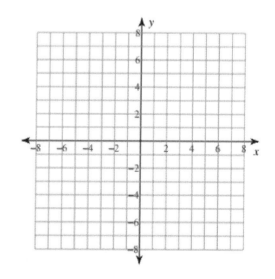
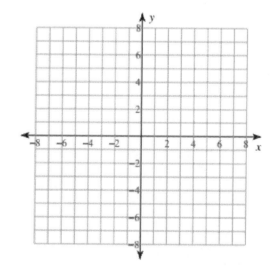

Chapter 10: Radical Expressions

Solving Radical Equations

✎ Solve each equation. Remember to check for extraneous solutions.

1) $\sqrt{a} = 5$

2) $\sqrt{v} = 3$

3) $\sqrt{r} = 4$

4) $2 = 4\sqrt{x}$

5) $\sqrt{x+1} = 9$

6) $1 = \sqrt{x-5}$

7) $6 = \sqrt{r-2}$

8) $\sqrt{x-6} = 8$

9) $5 = \sqrt{x-3}$

10) $\sqrt{m+8} = 8$

11) $10\sqrt{9a} = 60$

12) $5\sqrt{3x} = 15$

13) $1 = \sqrt{3x-5}$

14) $\sqrt{12-x} = x$

15) $\sqrt{r+3} - 1 = 7$

16) $-12 = -6\sqrt{r+4}$

17) $20 = 2\sqrt{36v}$

18) $x = \sqrt{42-x}$

19) $\sqrt{110-a} = a$

20) $\sqrt{2n-12} = 2$

21) $\sqrt{3r-5} = r-3$

22) $\sqrt{-16+10x} = x$

23) $\sqrt{3x+12} = \sqrt{x+8}$

24) $\sqrt{v} = \sqrt{2v-6}$

25) $\sqrt{11-x} = \sqrt{x-7}$

26) $\sqrt{m+8} = \sqrt{3m+8}$

27) $\sqrt{2r+40} = \sqrt{-16-2r}$

28) $\sqrt{k+3} = \sqrt{1-k}$

29) $-10\sqrt{x-10} = -60$

30) $\sqrt{72-x} = \sqrt{\dfrac{x}{5}}$

Chapter 10: Radical Expressions

Answers – Chapter 10

Simplifying Radical Expressions

1) $x\sqrt{35}$
2) $3x\sqrt{10}$
3) $2\sqrt[3]{a}$
4) $10x\sqrt{x}$
5) $5\sqrt{5a}$
6) $2w\sqrt[3]{11}$
7) $4\sqrt{5x}$
8) $6\sqrt{6v}$
9) $5\sqrt[3]{x}$
10) $8x^2\sqrt{x}$
11) $2x$
12) $3\sqrt[3]{2a^2}$
13) $9\sqrt{5}$
14) $16p\sqrt{2p}$
15) $6m^2\sqrt{6}$
16) $2x.y\sqrt{66xy}$
17) $7xy\sqrt{xy}$
18) $4a^2b\sqrt{b}$
19) $2xy\sqrt{5xy}$
20) $6x\sqrt[3]{y}$
21) $15x\sqrt{3}$
22) $20x\sqrt{5}$
23) $4y\sqrt[3]{4x^2}$
24) $7x\sqrt[3]{xy^2}$
25) $20\sqrt{5a}$
26) $5\sqrt[3]{5xy}$
27) $4xy\sqrt{2yr}$
28) $24xyz^2\sqrt{y}$
29) $16xy\sqrt[3]{y}$
30) $40abc^2\sqrt{bc}$

Multiplying Radical Expressions

1) 5
2) $5\sqrt{2}$
3) 6
4) $7\sqrt{6}$
5) -40
6) $18\sqrt{2}$
7) $15\sqrt{14}$
8) $-5\sqrt{3}$
9) $12\sqrt{33}$
10) $180\sqrt{55}$
11) $6\sqrt{3}+6$
12) $23x\sqrt{x}$
13) 30
14) $20x^2$
15) $2x^2\sqrt{6x}$
16) $-12x^2\sqrt{35}$
17) $-90x^2\sqrt{3x}$
18) $-12\sqrt{3}-24$
19) $12\sqrt{2x}-6x\sqrt{3}$
20) $6x^2\sqrt{3}+9\sqrt{x}$
21) $5\sqrt{15r}+5\sqrt{3r}$
22) $-60x^2\sqrt{2}$
23) $-48x$
24) $45v\sqrt{3v}$
25) 2
26) $22\sqrt{6}-34$
27) $6\sqrt{3}-10$
28) $86-35\sqrt{5}$
29) $-3x-5\sqrt{3x}-6$
30) $6r-8\sqrt{2r}+4$
31) $16\sqrt{n}+16\sqrt{2n}-4\sqrt{2}-8$
32) $-2+3\sqrt{3x}+4\sqrt{3}-18\sqrt{x}$

Effortless Math Education

Chapter 10: Radical Expressions

Simplifying Radical Expressions Involving Fractions

1) $\frac{\sqrt{15}}{3}$

2) $\frac{\sqrt{2}}{5}$

3) $\frac{\sqrt{6}}{6}$

4) $\frac{4\sqrt{5}}{5}$

5) $\frac{2\sqrt{5mr}}{m^2}$

6) $\frac{8\sqrt{3k}}{k}$

7) $\sqrt{7x}$

8) $\frac{y\sqrt{35x}}{5xv}$

9) $-1 + \sqrt{2}$

10) $\frac{\sqrt{11}a - 5a\sqrt{11}}{11a}$

11) $\frac{a - \sqrt{ab}}{a - b}$

12) $\frac{3 - \sqrt{5} + 3\sqrt{2} - \sqrt{10}}{4}$

13) $\frac{12 + 2\sqrt{3} + 6\sqrt{5} + \sqrt{15}}{33}$

14) $-\frac{5(-1+\sqrt{3})}{6}$

15) $\frac{3-\sqrt{5}}{2}$

16) -1

17) $\frac{\sqrt{35} - \sqrt{14} + 5 - \sqrt{10}}{3}$

18) $\frac{24 - 3\sqrt{10} - 4\sqrt{14} + \sqrt{35}}{27}$

19) $\frac{4\sqrt{5} + 5 + 8\sqrt{2} + 2\sqrt{10}}{11}$

20) $\frac{3\sqrt{6}+4}{2}$

21) $2a^2\sqrt{b}$

22) $6x$

Adding and Subtracting Radical Expressions

1) $4\sqrt{3}$

2) $9\sqrt{2}$

3) 0

4) $7\sqrt{2}$

5) $4\sqrt{5}$

6) $-7\sqrt{3}$

7) $-24\sqrt{2}$

8) $9\sqrt{10}$

9) $-\sqrt{3}$

10) $9\sqrt{2}$

11) $2\sqrt{7}$

12) $2\sqrt{3}$

13) $\sqrt{3}$

14) $-6\sqrt{6}$

15) $9\sqrt{2}$

16) $-5\sqrt{3}$

17) $\sqrt{2}$

18) $2\sqrt{2}$

19) $64\sqrt{3}$

20) $4\sqrt{5}$

21) $18\sqrt{2}$

22) $2\sqrt{35}$

23) $-12\sqrt{19}$

24) $-6\sqrt{6x}$

25) $4y\sqrt{5}$

26) $8n\sqrt{2m}$

27) $-29\sqrt{3a}$

28) $-6\sqrt{7ab}$

29) $5a\sqrt{3b}$

30) $5a\sqrt{6a}$

Chapter 10: Radical Expressions

Domain and Range of Radical Functions

1) domain: $x \geq -2$
   range: $y \geq -3$

2) domain: {all real numbers}
   range: {all real numbers}

3) domain: $x \geq 2$
   range: $y \geq 5$

4) domain: {all real numbers}
   range: {all real numbers}

5) domain: $x \geq -2$
   range: $y \geq 5$

6) domain: {all real numbers}
   range: {all real numbers}

7) domain: {all real numbers}
   range: $y \geq 6\sqrt{6} + 5$

8) domain: {all real numbers}
   range: {all real numbers}

9) domain: $x \geq -2$
   range: $y \geq -1$

10) domain: {all real numbers}
    range: {all real numbers}

11) domain: $x \leq -2$
    range: $y \geq 1$

12) domain: {all real numbers}
    range: {all real numbers}

13) domain: {all real numbers}
    range: {all real numbers}

14) domain: {all real numbers}
    range: {all real numbers}

15)

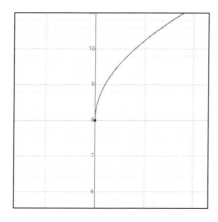

16)

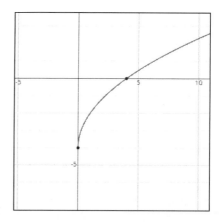

Chapter 10: Radical Expressions

Solving Radical Equations

1) {25}
2) {9}
3) {16}
4) {$\frac{1}{4}$}
5) {80}
6) {6}
7) {38}
8) {70}
9) {28}
10) {56}
11) {4}
12) {3}
13) {2}
14) {3}
15) {61}
16) {0}
17) {$\frac{25}{9}$}
18) {6}
19) {10}
20) {8}
21) {7}
22) {2, 8}
23) {−2}
24) {6}
25) {9}
26) {0}
27) {−14}
28) {−1}
29) {46}
30) {60}

Chapter 11: Rational and Irrational Expressions

Math Topics that you'll learn in this Chapter:

- ✓ Rational and Irrational Numbers
- ✓ Simplifying Rational Expressions
- ✓ Graphing Rational Expressions
- ✓ Multiplying Rational Expressions
- ✓ Dividing Rational Expressions
- ✓ Adding and Subtracting Rational Expressions
- ✓ Rational Equations
- ✓ Simplify Complex Fractions
- ✓ Maximum and Minimum Points
- ✓ Solving Rational Inequalities
- ✓ Irrational Functions
- ✓ Direct, Inverse, Joint, and Combined Variation

Chapter 11: Rational and Irrational Expressions

Rational and Irrational Numbers

✎ *Determine if the number is rational or irrational number.*

1) $\sqrt{25}$ _____ 13) $\sqrt{49}$ _____

2) $\sqrt{7}$ _____ 14) $\frac{17}{54}$ _____

3) 4.8 _____ 15) $\sqrt{103}$ _____

4) 24 _____ 16) $3.62\overline{23}$ _____

5) $90.790180\ldots/$ _____ 17) 0.25 _____

6) $\frac{22}{38}$ _____ 18) $23.4\overline{279}$ _____

7) $\sqrt{3}$ _____ 19) 17 _____

8) $2.514796\ldots/$ _____ 20) $\sqrt{29}$ _____

9) 22 _____ 21) $\frac{14}{8}$ _____

10) 0.15 _____ 22) $65.714813\ldots/$ _____

11) $\frac{11}{3}$ _____ 23) $13.5\overline{186}$ _____

12) 16 _____ 24) $\sqrt{13}$ _____

Chapter 11: Rational and Irrational Expressions

Simplifying Rational Expressions

✎ **Simplify.**

1) $\dfrac{6x^2}{4x} =$

2) $\dfrac{18x^4}{8x^2} =$

3) $\dfrac{16x^3}{20x^3} =$

4) $\dfrac{64x^3}{24x} =$

5) $\dfrac{25x^5}{15x^3} =$

6) $\dfrac{4}{2x-2} =$

7) $\dfrac{21}{3x-6} =$

8) $\dfrac{16}{2x-2} =$

9) $\dfrac{15x-3}{24} =$

10) $\dfrac{40}{10x-5} =$

11) $\dfrac{4x+16}{28} =$

12) $\dfrac{x^2-10x+25}{x-5} =$

13) $\dfrac{x^2-49}{x^2+3x-28} =$

14) $\dfrac{x^2+4x+4}{x^2-5x-14} =$

15) $\dfrac{x+3}{3x+9} =$

16) $\dfrac{2x^2-2x-12}{x-3} =$

17) $\dfrac{16}{4x-4} =$

18) $\dfrac{36x^3}{42x^3} =$

19) $\dfrac{x^2-3x-4}{x^2+2x-24} =$

20) $\dfrac{81x^3}{18x} =$

21) $\dfrac{x-3}{x^2-x-6} =$

22) $\dfrac{x^2-3x-28}{x-7} =$

23) $\dfrac{6x+18}{30} =$

24) $\dfrac{16}{4x-4} =$

141

Chapter 11: Rational and Irrational Expressions

Graphing Rational Expressions

✏️ *Graph rational expressions.*

1) $f(x) = \frac{x^2+x-2}{x-2}$

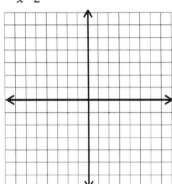

2) $f(x) = \frac{x^2-6x+8}{2x-4}$

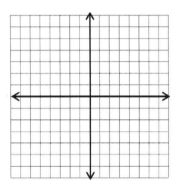

3) $f(x) = \frac{x^2+2x-9}{x-3}$

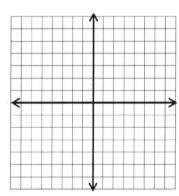

4) $f(x) = \frac{2x^3-15x+45}{x^2-2x-4}$

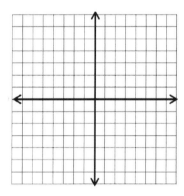

5) $f(x) = \frac{x^3-8x}{2x-3}$

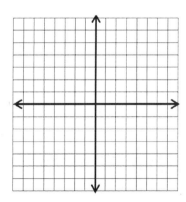

6) $f(x) = \frac{x^4+x^2+2x}{x^2+4x}$

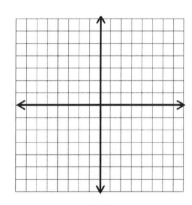

Chapter 11: Rational and Irrational Expressions

Multiplying Rational Expressions

✎ Simplify each expression.

1) $\dfrac{84}{3} \times \dfrac{48x}{95} =$

2) $\dfrac{53}{43} \times \dfrac{46x^2}{31} =$

3) $\dfrac{79x}{25} \times \dfrac{85}{27x^2} =$

4) $\dfrac{96x^3}{7x} \times \dfrac{119}{68x} =$

5) $\dfrac{96}{38x} \times \dfrac{25}{45} =$

6) $\dfrac{93}{21x} \times \dfrac{34x}{51x} =$

7) $\dfrac{85}{16x} \times \dfrac{48x}{95} =$

8) $\dfrac{2}{43x} \times \dfrac{46x^5}{38x} =$

9) $\dfrac{27x}{81} \times \dfrac{14x}{51x^2} =$

10) $\dfrac{5x+50}{x+10} \times \dfrac{x-2}{5} =$

11) $\dfrac{x-7}{x+6} \times \dfrac{10x+60}{x-7} =$

12) $\dfrac{1}{x+10} \times \dfrac{10x+30}{x+3} =$

13) $\dfrac{12x}{14} \times \dfrac{14}{16x} =$

14) $\dfrac{79x}{25} \times \dfrac{85}{27x^2} =$

15) $\dfrac{8(x+1)}{7x} \times \dfrac{9}{8(x+1)} =$

16) $\dfrac{2(x+6)}{4} \times \dfrac{x-3}{2(x-1)} =$

17) $\dfrac{9(x+4)}{x+4} \times \dfrac{9x}{9(x-5)} =$

18) $\dfrac{4x+20}{x+5} \times \dfrac{x-2}{4} =$

19) $\dfrac{x-3}{x+4} \times \dfrac{5x+30}{x-5} =$

20) $\dfrac{1}{x+4} \times \dfrac{4x+20}{x+5} =$

21) $\dfrac{3x^2+18x}{x+6} \times \dfrac{1}{x+8} =$

22) $\dfrac{21x^2-21x}{18x^2-18x} \times \dfrac{6x}{6x^2} =$

23) $\dfrac{1}{x-9} \times \dfrac{x^2+6x-27}{x+9} =$

24) $\dfrac{x^2-10x+25}{10x-100} \times \dfrac{x-10}{45-9x} =$

www.EffortlessMath.com

Chapter 11: Rational and Irrational Expressions

Dividing Rational Expressions

✍ **Divide.**

1) $\dfrac{12x}{3} \div \dfrac{5}{8} =$

2) $\dfrac{10x^2}{7} \div \dfrac{3x}{12} =$

3) $\dfrac{12x}{3} \div \dfrac{5}{8} =$

4) $\dfrac{9x}{x+5} \div \dfrac{9x}{2x+10} =$

5) $\dfrac{x^2}{9} \div \dfrac{3}{18x} =$

6) $\dfrac{11x}{x-7} \div \dfrac{11x}{12x-84} =$

7) $\dfrac{x+5}{5x^2-10x} \div \dfrac{1}{5x} =$

8) $\dfrac{x-2}{7x-12} \div \dfrac{x}{x+3} =$

9) $\dfrac{5x}{x-10} \div \dfrac{5x}{x-5} =$

10) $\dfrac{1}{2x} \div \dfrac{8x}{2x^2+16x} =$

11) $\dfrac{x^2+10x+16}{x^2+6x+8} \div \dfrac{1}{x+4} =$

12) $\dfrac{x^2-2x-15}{8x+20} \div \dfrac{2}{4x+10} =$

13) $\dfrac{x-4}{x^2-2x-8} \div \dfrac{1}{x-5} =$

14) $\dfrac{8+2x-x^2}{x^2-2x-8} \div \dfrac{4x}{x+6} =$

15) $\dfrac{x+10}{9x^2-90x} \div \dfrac{1}{9x} =$

16) $\dfrac{x-2}{x+6x-16} \div \dfrac{11x}{x+9} =$

17) $\dfrac{x^2-x-12}{8x+2} \div \dfrac{4}{4x+1} =$

18) $\dfrac{x-7}{-x^2+10x-21} \div \dfrac{1}{x-3} =$

19) $\dfrac{3x}{x-5} \div \dfrac{3x}{10x-50} =$

20) $\dfrac{x+5}{x+13x+40} \div \dfrac{4x}{x+9} =$

21) $\dfrac{x+4}{x+14x+40} \div \dfrac{6x}{x+9} =$

22) $\dfrac{14x+12}{3} \div \dfrac{63x+54}{3x} =$

23) $\dfrac{7x^3+49x^2}{x^2+12x+35} \div \dfrac{2}{2x^3-12x^2} =$

24) $\dfrac{x^2+10x+16}{x^2+6x+8} \div \dfrac{1}{x+8} =$

www.EffortlessMath.com

Chapter 11: Rational and Irrational Expressions

Adding and Subtracting Rational Expressions

✎ *Simplify each expression.*

1) $\dfrac{2}{x+3} + \dfrac{3}{x-2} =$

2) $\dfrac{3}{x+7} - \dfrac{4}{x-8} =$

3) $\dfrac{4}{x+1} - \dfrac{2}{x+2} =$

4) $\dfrac{2x}{5x+4} + \dfrac{6x}{2x+3} =$

5) $\dfrac{4x}{x+2} + \dfrac{x-3}{x+1} =$

6) $\dfrac{x}{x+1} + \dfrac{x+1}{x+2} =$

7) $\dfrac{x}{3x+2} + \dfrac{3x}{2x+3} =$

8) $\dfrac{4}{x+1} - \dfrac{2}{x+2} =$

9) $\dfrac{2}{3x^2+12x} + \dfrac{8}{2x} =$

10) $\dfrac{x}{10x+5} + \dfrac{5x}{2x+1} =$

11) $\dfrac{2}{6x+10} + \dfrac{x-6}{6x+10} =$

12) $\dfrac{x+5}{4x^2+20x} - \dfrac{x-5}{4x^2+20x} =$

13) $\dfrac{2}{x^2-5x+4} + \dfrac{2}{x^2-4} =$

14) $\dfrac{x-5}{x^2-6} - \dfrac{x-1}{6-x^2} =$

15) $\dfrac{4}{6x+8} + \dfrac{x-8}{6x+8} =$

16) $\dfrac{x+2}{x-4} + \dfrac{x-2}{x+3} =$

17) $\dfrac{x-7}{x^2-16} - \dfrac{x-1}{16-x^2} =$

18) $\dfrac{5}{x+5} + \dfrac{4x}{2x+6} =$

19) $2 + \dfrac{x-3}{x+1} =$

20) $\dfrac{3x-1}{5x+4} + \dfrac{x+3}{2x+6} =$

21) $\dfrac{5xy}{x^2-y^2} - \dfrac{x-y}{x+y} =$

22) $\dfrac{5x+5}{5x^2+35x-40} + \dfrac{7x}{3x} =$

23) $3 + \dfrac{x}{x+2} - \dfrac{2}{x^2-4} =$

24) $\dfrac{x+2}{3x^2+10x} + \dfrac{x-2}{3x^2+10x} =$

Chapter 11: Rational and Irrational Expressions

Rational Equations

✎ *Solve each equation. Remember to check for extraneous solutions.*

1) $\dfrac{x-1}{x+3} = \dfrac{4}{x-3}$

2) $\dfrac{3}{x-2} = \dfrac{2x}{x-2}$

3) $\dfrac{4}{b-7} = \dfrac{-2b}{b+3}$

4) $\dfrac{9}{n+1} = \dfrac{n}{n-1}$

5) $\dfrac{x}{4} = \dfrac{x+2}{6}$

6) $\dfrac{2-x}{1-x} = \dfrac{12}{4-x}$

7) $\dfrac{2}{x^2-x} = \dfrac{1}{x-1}$

8) $\dfrac{5x}{2x^2-4} = \dfrac{10}{x-5}$

9) $\dfrac{2x-3}{x+1} = \dfrac{x+6}{x-2}$

10) $\dfrac{1}{x} = \dfrac{6}{5x} + 1$

11) $\dfrac{x+6}{x+3} = \dfrac{x+6}{x+1}$

12) $\dfrac{1}{6b^2} + \dfrac{1}{6b} = \dfrac{1}{b^2}$

13) $\dfrac{3x-2}{9x+1} = \dfrac{2x-5}{6x-5}$

14) $\dfrac{1}{n^2} + \dfrac{1}{n} = \dfrac{1}{2n^2}$

15) $\dfrac{1}{8b^2} = \dfrac{1}{4b^2} - \dfrac{1}{b}$

16) $\dfrac{1}{n-8} - 1 = \dfrac{7}{n-8}$

17) $\dfrac{5}{r-2} = -\dfrac{10}{r+2} + 7$

18) $1 = \dfrac{1}{x^2+2x} + \dfrac{x-1}{x}$

19) $\dfrac{1}{x} = 8 + \dfrac{6}{9x}$

20) $\dfrac{x+5}{x^2-2x} - 1 = \dfrac{1}{x^2-2x}$

21) $\dfrac{x-2}{x+3} - 1 = \dfrac{1}{x+2}$

22) $\dfrac{1}{6x^2} = \dfrac{1}{3x^2} - \dfrac{1}{x}$

23) $\dfrac{x+5}{x^2-x} = \dfrac{1}{x^2+x} - \dfrac{x-6}{x+1}$

24) $1 = \dfrac{1}{x^2-2x} + \dfrac{x-1}{x}$

Chapter 11: Rational and Irrational Expressions
Simplify Complex Fractions

✎ *Simplify each expression.*

1) $\dfrac{\frac{12}{3}}{\frac{2}{15}} =$

2) $\dfrac{\frac{14}{3}}{-6\frac{2}{11}} =$

3) $\dfrac{-1\frac{11}{12}}{-3} =$

4) $\dfrac{\frac{4}{5}}{\frac{2}{25}-\frac{5}{16}} =$

5) $\dfrac{8}{\frac{8}{x}+\frac{2}{3x}} =$

6) $\dfrac{x}{\frac{2}{5}-\frac{2}{x}} =$

7) $\dfrac{\frac{2}{x+2}}{\frac{8}{x^2+6x+8}} =$

8) $\dfrac{\frac{12}{x-1}}{\frac{12}{5}-\frac{12}{25}} =$

9) $\dfrac{1+\frac{2}{x-4}}{1-\frac{6}{x-4}} =$

10) $\dfrac{\frac{x+6}{4}}{\frac{x^2}{2}-\frac{5}{2}} =$

11) $\dfrac{\frac{x-2}{x-6}}{\frac{8}{x-2}+\frac{2}{9}} =$

12) $\dfrac{9}{\frac{9}{x}+\frac{2}{3x}} =$

13) $\dfrac{x^2}{\frac{4}{5}-\frac{4}{x}} =$

14) $\dfrac{\frac{4}{x-3}-\frac{2}{x+2}}{\frac{8}{x^2+6x+8}} =$

15) $\dfrac{\frac{16}{x-1}}{\frac{16}{5}-\frac{16}{25}} =$

16) $\dfrac{2+\frac{6}{x-4}}{2-\frac{4}{x-4}} =$

17) $\dfrac{\frac{1}{2}-\frac{x+5}{4}}{\frac{x^2}{2}-\frac{5}{2}} =$

18) $\dfrac{\frac{x-6}{2}-\frac{x-2}{x-6}}{\frac{36}{x-2}+\frac{4}{9}} =$

147

Chapter 11: Rational and Irrational Expressions

Maximum and Minimum Points

✏️ **Find the maximum and minimum points of the function.**

1) $f(x) = 2x^2 - 4x + 6$

   Maximum: _____
   Minimum: _____

2) $f(x) = x^3 + 4x + 1$

   Maximum: _____
   Minimum: _____

3) $f(x) = x^3 - 3x + 2$

   Maximum: _____
   Minimum: _____

4) $f(x) = 3x^2 + 4x + 3$

   Maximum: _____
   Minimum: _____

5) $f(x) = 4x^2 - 3$

   Maximum: _____
   Minimum: _____

6) $f(x) = x^3 + x^2 - 8x - 6$

   Maximum: _____
   Minimum: _____

7) $f(x) = \frac{4}{x^2 + 2}$

   Maximum: _____
   Minimum: _____

8) $f(x) = x^3 + 2x$

   Maximum: _____
   Minimum: _____

9) $f(x) = -x^3 - 6x^2 - 9x + 2$

   Maximum: _____
   Minimum: _____

10) $f(x) = 4x^2 - 16x + 3$

    Maximum: _____
    Minimum: _____

11) $f(x) = 9x + \frac{1}{x}$

    Maximum: _____
    Minimum: _____

12) $f(x) = \frac{x}{(1+x)^2}$

    Maximum: _____
    Minimum: _____

13) $f(x) = 3x^4 - 8x^3 + 6$

    Maximum: _____
    Minimum: _____

14) $f(x) = -2x^3 - 4x^2 + 2$

    Maximum: _____
    Minimum: _____

Chapter 11: Rational and Irrational Expressions
Solving Rational Inequalities

Solve.

1) $\dfrac{x-4}{x-1} \geq 0$

2) $\dfrac{x+6}{x-5} \geq 0$

3) $\dfrac{x-8}{x-2} \leq 0$

4) $\dfrac{3x-1}{x-1} \geq 0$

5) $\dfrac{4x}{2x+2} < 0$

6) $\dfrac{5x-2}{x+3} \geq 0$

7) $\dfrac{x^2-9}{x+3} < 0$

8) $\dfrac{x^2}{2x-1} > 0$

9) $\dfrac{(x+3)(x+5)}{x+2} \geq 0$

10) $\dfrac{x+5}{x-4} \geq 0$

11) $\dfrac{(x-4)(x+6)}{x-3} < 0$

12) $\dfrac{x^2-2x}{x-2} \leq 4$

13) $\dfrac{x^2+5x}{x-3} < 0$

14) $\dfrac{2x-5}{x-3} \geq 0$

15) $\dfrac{3x+8}{x-2} \geq -2$

16) $\dfrac{x+49}{x-7} \geq 5$

17) $\dfrac{x+32}{x+4} \leq 3$

18) $\dfrac{3}{x+6} \leq -\dfrac{4}{x+7}$

19) $\dfrac{9}{x-3} \leq -\dfrac{12}{x-5}$

20) $\dfrac{7}{x+5} \geq -\dfrac{6}{x+4}$

21) $\dfrac{-x+5}{x+6} > -2$

22) $-\dfrac{5}{x+2} \leq -\dfrac{4}{x+6}$

23) $-\dfrac{15}{x-5} \leq -\dfrac{11}{x-6}$

24) $\dfrac{2}{2x-4} > \dfrac{6}{x-2}$

149

Chapter 11: Rational and Irrational Expressions

Irrational Functions

✎ *What is the domain of the functions?*

1) $y = \sqrt{x-4} + 6$

   Domain: _____

2) $y = \dfrac{x-2}{\sqrt{x-1}}$

   Domain: _____

3) $y = \dfrac{3x}{\sqrt{x-2}}$

   Domain: _____

4) $y = \dfrac{x-4}{2\sqrt{x+6}}$

   Domain: _____

5) $y = \dfrac{x+2}{\sqrt{x^2-2}}$

   Domain: _____

6) $y = \dfrac{2x-8}{\sqrt{x+4}}$

   Domain: _____

7) $y = \dfrac{\sqrt{x-1}}{\sqrt{x^2+1}}$

   Domain: _____

8) $y = \dfrac{x^2 - \sqrt{x}}{\sqrt{x}-1}$

   Domain: _____

9) $y = \dfrac{x-1}{\sqrt{x^2+2}-1}$

   Domain: _____

10) $y = \dfrac{\sqrt{x-2}}{\sqrt{2x^2+4}}$

    Domain: _____

11) $y = \dfrac{1}{2}\sqrt{x-1}$

    Domain: _____

12) $y = \dfrac{2\sqrt{x}-1}{\sqrt{x^2-2}}$

    Domain: _____

13) $y = -\dfrac{4}{5}\sqrt{3x+4}$

    Domain: _____

14) $y = -\dfrac{3}{4}\sqrt{x-1} + 5$

    Domain: _____

Chapter 11: Rational and Irrational Expressions

Direct, Inverse, Joint, and Combined Variation

Solve.

1) When x is 7 and y is 4, find the constant of variation and an equation that inversely relates y and x.

2) Refer to the figure on the right. Write an equation to represent the area of S, Identify the type of variation and the constant of variation.

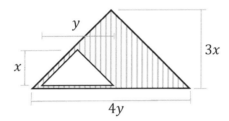

3) y varies jointly as x and z. If $y = 12$ when $x = 9$ and $z = 8$, find y when $x = 16$ and $z = 9$.

4) y varies jointly as x and z. If $y = 18$ when $x = 2$ and $z = 3$, find y when $x = 7$ and $z = 8$.

5) We know that y varies directly with x and inversely with z. Given that $y = 20$ when $x = 10$ and $z = 6$, find y when $x = 20$ and $z = 5$.

6) For the combined variation equation of $y = 4\frac{x}{z}$, find x when $y = 3$ and $z = 8$.

Chapter 11: Rational and Irrational Expressions

Answers – Chapter 11

Rational and Irrational Numbers

1) Rational
2) Irrational
3) Rational
4) Rational
5) Irrational
6) Rational
7) Irrational
8) Irrational
9) Rational
10) Rational
11) Rational
12) Rational
13) Rational
14) Rational
15) Irrational
16) Rational
17) Rational
18) Rational
19) Rational
20) Irrational
21) Rational
22) Irrational
23) Rational
24) Irrational

Simplifying Rational Expressions

1) $\frac{3x}{2}$
2) $\frac{9x^2}{4}$
3) $\frac{4}{5}$
4) $\frac{8x^2}{3}$
5) $\frac{5x^2}{3}$
6) $\frac{2}{x-1}$
7) $\frac{7}{x-2}$
8) $\frac{8}{x-1}$
9) $\frac{5x-1}{8}$
10) $\frac{8}{2x-1}$
11) $\frac{x+4}{7}$
12) $x - 5$
13) $\frac{x-7}{x-4}$
14) $\frac{x+2}{x-7}$
15) $\frac{1}{3}$
16) $2x + 4$
17) $\frac{4}{x-1}$
18) $\frac{6}{7}$
19) $\frac{x+1}{x+6}$
20) $\frac{9x^2}{2}$
21) $\frac{1}{x+2}$
22) $x + 4$
23) $\frac{x+3}{5}$
24) $\frac{4}{x-1}$

Chapter 11: Rational and Irrational Expressions

Graphing Rational Expressions

1) $f(x) = \dfrac{x^2+x-2}{x-2}$

2) $f(x) = \dfrac{x^2-6x+8}{2x-4}$

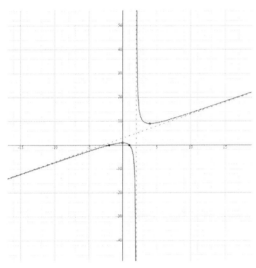
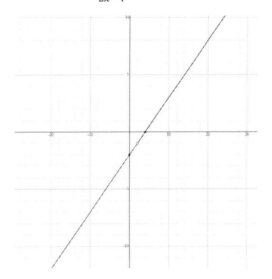

3) $f(x) = \dfrac{x^2+2x-9}{x-3}$

4) $f(x) = \dfrac{2x^3-15x+45}{x^2-2x-4}$

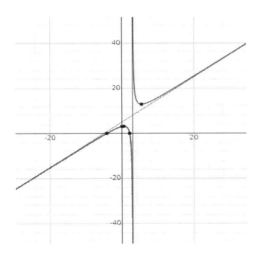
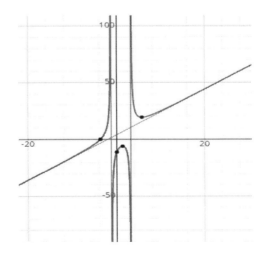

Chapter 11: Rational and Irrational Expressions

5) $f(x) = \frac{x^3 - 8x}{2x - 3}$

6) $f(x) = \frac{x^4 + x^2 + 2x}{x^2 + 4x}$

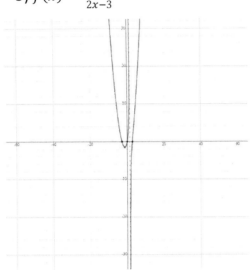
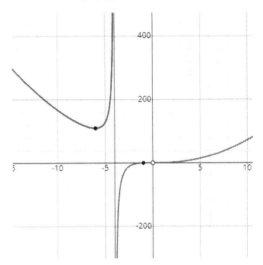

Multiplying Rational Expressions

1) $\frac{1,344x}{95}$

2) $\frac{2,438x^2}{1,333}$

3) $\frac{1,343}{135x}$

4) $24x$

5) $\frac{80}{57x}$

6) $\frac{62}{21x}$

7) $\frac{51}{19}$

8) $\frac{46x^3}{817}$

9) $\frac{14}{153}$

10) $x - 2$

11) 10

12) $\frac{10}{x+10}$

13) $\frac{3}{4}$

14) $\frac{1,343}{135x}$

15) $\frac{9}{7x}$

16) $\frac{(x+6)(x-3)}{4(x-1)}$

17) $\frac{9x}{x-5}$

18) $x - 2$

19) $\frac{(x-3)(5x+30)}{(x+4)(x-5)}$

20) $\frac{4}{x+4}$

21) $\frac{3x}{x+8}$

22) $\frac{7}{6x}$

23) $\frac{x-3}{x-9}$

24) $-\frac{(x-5)}{90}$

Chapter 11: Rational and Irrational Expressions

Dividing Rational Expressions

1) $\frac{32}{5}x$

2) $\frac{40x}{7}$

3) $\frac{32}{5}x$

4) 2

5) $\frac{2x^3}{3}$

6) 12

7) $\frac{x+5}{x-2}$

8) $\frac{(x-2)(x+3)}{x(7x-12)}$

9) $\frac{(x-5)}{(x-10)}$

10) $\frac{x+8}{8x}$

11) $x+8$

12) $\frac{(x+3)(x-5)}{4}$

13) $\frac{x-5}{x+2}$

14) $-\frac{x+6}{4x}$

15) $\frac{x+10}{x-10}$

16) $\frac{(x+9)(x-2)}{11x(7x-16)}$

17) $\frac{(x+3)(x-4)}{8}$

18) -1

19) 10

20) $\frac{(x+5)(x+9)}{4x(14x+40)}$

21) $\frac{(x+9)(x+4)}{6x(15x+40)}$

22) $\frac{2x}{9}$

23) $\frac{7x^4(x-6)}{x+5}$

24) $\frac{(x+8)^2}{x+4}$

Adding and Subtracting Rational Expressions

1) $\frac{5x+5}{(x+3)(x-2)}$

2) $\frac{-x-52}{(x+7)(x-8)}$

3) $\frac{2x+6}{(x+1)(x+2)}$

4) $\frac{34x^2+30x}{(5x+4)(2x+3)}$

5) $\frac{5x^2+3x-6}{(x+2)(x+1)}$

6) $\frac{2x^2+4x+1}{(x+1)(x+2)}$

7) $\frac{11x^2+9x}{(3x+2)(2x+3)}$

8) $\frac{2x+6}{(x+1)(x+2)}$

9) $\frac{50+12x}{3x(x+4)}$

10) $\frac{26x}{5(2x+1)}$

11) $\frac{-4+x}{6x+10}$

12) $\frac{5}{2x(x+5)}$

13) $\frac{4x^2-10x}{(x-1)(x-4)(x+2)(x-2)}$

14) $\frac{2x-6}{x^2-6}$

15) $\frac{-4+x}{6x+8}$

16) $\frac{2x^2-x+14}{(x-4)(x+3)}$

17) $\frac{2}{x+4}$

18) $\frac{2x^2+15x+15}{(x+5)(x+3)}$

19) $\frac{3x-1}{x+1}$

20) $\frac{11x+2}{2(5x+4)}$

21) $\frac{-x^3+6xy^2-y^3+6x^2y}{(x^2-y^2)(x+y)}$

22) $\frac{52x-53+7x^2}{3(x+8)(x-1)}$

23) $\frac{4x^2-2x-14}{(x+2)(x-2)}$

24) $\frac{2}{3x+10}$

Chapter 11: Rational and Irrational Expressions

Rational Equations

1) $\{9, -1\}$
2) $\{\frac{3}{2}\}$
3) $\{2, 3\}$
4) $\{4 + \sqrt{7}, 4 - \sqrt{7}\}$
5) $\{4\}$
6) $\{-3 + \sqrt{13}, -3 - \sqrt{13}\}$
7) $\{2\}$
8) $\{-\frac{8}{3}, 1\}$
9) $\{14, 0\}$
10) $\{-\frac{1}{5}\}$
11) $\{-6\}$
12) $\{5\}$
13) $\{-\frac{15}{16}\}$
14) $\{-\frac{1}{2}\}$
15) $\{\frac{1}{8}\}$
16) $\{2\}$
17) $\{-\frac{6}{7}, 3\}$
18) $\{-1\}$
19) $\{\frac{1}{24}\}$
20) $\{4, -1\}$
21) $\{-\frac{13}{6}\}$
22) $\{\frac{1}{6}\}$
23) $\{-0.43484\}$
24) $\{3\}$

Simplify Complex Fractions

1) 30
2) $-\frac{77}{102}$
3) $\frac{23}{36}$
4) $-\frac{320}{93}$
5) $\frac{12x}{13}$
6) $\frac{5x^2}{2x-10}$
7) $\frac{(x+4)}{4}$
8) $\frac{25}{4(x-1)}$
9) $\frac{x-2}{x-10}$
10) $\frac{x+6}{2x^2-10}$
11) $\frac{9(x-2)^2}{(2x+68)(x-6)}$
12) $\frac{27x}{29}$
13) $\frac{5x^3}{4x-20}$
14) $\frac{(x+7)(x+4)}{4(x-3)}$
15) $\frac{25}{4x-4}$
16) $\frac{x-1}{x-6}$
17) $\frac{-3-x}{2x^2-10}$
18) $\frac{9x^3-144x^2+612x-720}{584x+8x^2-3,792}$

Chapter 11: Rational and Irrational Expressions

Maximum and Minimum Points

1) Minimum: $(1,4)$
2) Maximum: *none*
   Minimum: *none*
3) Maximum: $(-1,4)$
   Minimum: $(1,0)$
4) Minimum: $(-\frac{2}{3}, \frac{5}{3})$
5) Minimum: $(0,-3)$
6) Maximum: $(-2, 6)$
   Minimum: $(\frac{4}{3}, -\frac{338}{27})$
7) Maximum: $(0,2)$
8) Maximum: *none*
   Minimum: *none*
9) Maximum: $(-1, 6)$
   Minimum: $(-3, 2)$
10) Minimum: $(2, -13)$
11) Maximum: $(-\frac{1}{3}, -6)$
    Minimum: $(\frac{1}{3}, 6)$
12) Maximum: $(1, \frac{1}{4})$
13) Minimum: $(2, -10)$
14) Maximum: $(0, 2)$
    Minimum: $(-\frac{4}{3}, -\frac{10}{27})$

Solving Rational Inequalities

1) $(-\infty, 1) \cup [4, \infty)$
2) $(-\infty, -6] \cup (5, \infty)$
3) $(2, 8]$
4) $(-\infty, \frac{1}{3}] \cup (1, \infty)$
5) $(-1, 0)$
6) $(-\infty, -3) \cup [\frac{2}{5}, \infty)$
7) $(-\infty, -3) \cup (-3, 3)$
8) $(\frac{1}{2}, \infty)$
9) $[-5, -3] \cup (-2, \infty)$
10) $(-\infty, -5] \cup (4, \infty)$
11) $(-\infty, -6) \cup (3, 4)$
12) $(-\infty, 2) \cup (2, 4]$
13) $(-\infty, -5) \cup (0, 3)$
14) $(-\infty, \frac{5}{2}] \cup (3, \infty)$
15) $(-\infty, -\frac{4}{5}] \cup (2, \infty)$
16) $(7, 21]$
17) $(-\infty, -4) \cup [10, \infty)$
18) $(-\infty, -7) \cup [-\frac{45}{7}, -6)$
19) $(-\infty, 3) \cup [\frac{27}{7}, 5)$
20) $(-5, -\frac{58}{13}] \cup (-4, \infty)$
21) $(-\infty, -17) \cup (-6, \infty)$
22) $[-22, -6) \cup (-2, \infty)$
23) $(5, 6) \cup [\frac{35}{4}, \infty)$
24) $(-\infty, 2)$

Chapter 11: Rational and Irrational Expressions

Irrational Functions

1) Domain: $[4, +\infty)$
2) Domain: $[0,1) \cup (1, +\infty)$
3) Domain: $(2, +\infty)$
4) Domain: $(-6, +\infty)$
5) Domain: $(-\infty, -\sqrt{2}) \cup (\sqrt{2}, +\infty)$
6) Domain: $[0, \infty)$
7) Domain: $[0, \infty)$
8) Domain: $[0,1) \cup (1, +\infty)$
9) Domain: $(-\infty, +\infty)$
10) Domain: $[2, \infty)$
11) Domain: $[1, +\infty)$
12) Domain: $(\sqrt{2}, +\infty)$
13) Domain: $[-\frac{4}{3}, +\infty)$
14) Domain: $[1, +\infty)$

Direct, Inverse, Joint, and Combined Variation

1) $y = \frac{28}{x}$
2) The area varies jointly as x and y. The constant of variation is $\frac{11}{2}$.
3) $y = 24$
4) $y = 168$
5) $y = 48$
6) $x = 6$

Chapter 12: Conics

Math Topics that you'll learn in this Chapter:

- ✓ Equation of a Parabola
- ✓ Finding the Focus, Vertex, and Directrix of a Parabola
- ✓ Standard From of a Circle
- ✓ Finding the Center and the Radius of Circles
- ✓ Equation of Ellipse
- ✓ Hyperbola in Standard Form
- ✓ Classifying a Conic Section (in Standard Form)

Chapter 12: Conics

Equation of a Parabola

✎ *Write the equation of the following parabolas.*

1) Vertex $(0, 0)$ and Focus $(0, 2)$ _____

2) Vertex $(1, 0)$ and Focus $(2, -2)$ _____

3) Vertex $(0, 1)$ and Focus $(0, -8)$ _____

4) Vertex $(3, 2)$ and Focus $(3, 4)$ _____

5) Vertex $(1, 1)$ and Focus $(1, 6)$ _____

6) Vertex $(-1, 2)$ and Focus $(-1, 5)$ _____

7) Vertex $(2, 2)$ and Focus $(2, 4)$ _____

8) Vertex $(0, 1)$ and Focus $(0, 3)$ _____

9) Vertex $(2, 1)$ and Focus $(4, 1)$ _____

10) Vertex $(5, 0)$ and Focus $(9, 0)$ _____

11) Vertex $(-2, 4)$ and Focus $(2, 4)$ _____

12) Vertex $(0, -4)$ and Focus $(4, -4)$ _____

Chapter 12: Conics

Finding the Focus, Vertex, and Directrix of a Parabola

✎ *Identify the Focus, Vertex, and Directrix of each. Then sketch the graph.*

1) $x^2 + 8y = 0$

Focus:
Vertex:
Directrix:

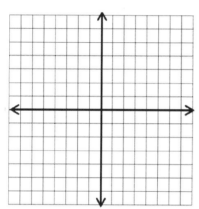

2) $x^2 = 16y$

Focus:
Vertex:
Directrix:

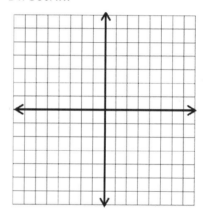

3) $y = (x + 3)^2 - 2$

Focus:
Vertex:
Directrix:

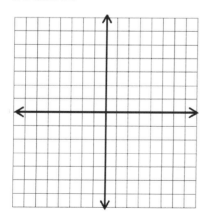

4) $(x + 2)^2 = -4(y + 2)$

Focus:
Vertex:
Directrix:

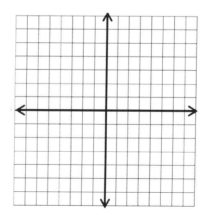

161

Chapter 12: Conics

Standard From of a Circle

✏️ **Write the standard form equation of each circle.**

1) $x^2 + y^2 - 2y - 15 = 0$

2) $8x + x^2 - 2y = 64 - y^2$

3) $x^2 + y^2 - 6x - 4y + 12 = 0$

4) $x^2 + y^2 + 4x + 6y + 12 = 0$

5) $x^2 + y^2 - 18x - 24y + 161 = 0$

6) $x^2 + y^2 + 16x - 28y + 224 = 0$

7) $x^2 + y^2 + 26x + 18y + 106 = 0$

8) $x^2 + y^2 + 4x + 28y + 175 = 0$

9) $x^2 + y^2 - 8x - 6y + 21 = 0$

10) $y^2 + 2x + x^2 = 24y - 120$

✏️ **Use the information provided to write the standard form equation of each circle.**

11) Center: $(-5, -6)$, Radius: 9 _____

12) Center: $(-12, -5)$, Area: 4π _____

13) Center: $(-11, -14)$, Area: 16π _____

14) Center: $(-3, 2)$, Area: 2π _____

15) Center: $(15, 14)$, Area: $2\pi\sqrt{15}$ _____

16) Center: $(-4, -8)$, Radius: 4 _____

17) Center: $(-6, -15)$, Radius: $\sqrt{5}$ _____

18) Center: $(-10, -15)$, Radius: 3 _____

Chapter 12: Conics

Finding the Center and the Radius of Circles

✎ *Identify the center and radius of each.*

1) $(x + 6)^2 + (y + 12)^2 = 18$ Center: _____, Radius: _____
2) $(x + 1)^2 + (y + 3)^2 = 4$ Center: _____, Radius: _____
3) $(x - 4)^2 + (y - 9)^2 = 16$ Center: _____, Radius: _____
4) $(x - 8)^2 + (y + 11)^2 = 24$ Center: _____, Radius: _____
5) $(x + 12)^2 + (y - 18)^2 = 81$ Center: _____, Radius: _____
6) $(x - 9)^2 + (y + 14)^2 = 144$ Center: _____, Radius: _____
7) $(x - 2)^2 + (y + 5)^2 = 10$ Center: _____, Radius: _____
8) $x^2 + (y - 1)^2 = 4$ Center: _____, Radius: _____
9) $(x - 2)^2 + (y + 6)^2 = 9$ Center: _____, Radius: _____
10) $(x + 14)^2 + (y - 5)^2 = 16$ Center: _____, Radius: _____
11) $x^2 + (y - 6)^2 = 22$ Center: _____, Radius: _____
12) $(y - 11)^2 + (x - 6)^2 = 9$ Center: _____, Radius: _____

✎ *State the center and radius of each equation and graph.*

13) $(x - 2)^2 + (y - 6)^2 = 4$

Center: _____, Radius: _____

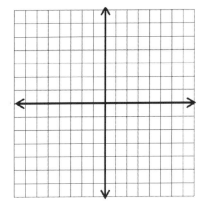

14) $(x + 3)^2 + (y - 7)^2 = 9$

Center: _____, Radius: _____

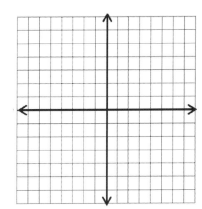

Chapter 12: Conics

Equation of Ellipse

✎ *Identify the vertices, co-vertices, foci.*

1) $\dfrac{x^2}{81} + \dfrac{y^2}{49} = 1$

   Vertices: _____

   Co–vertices: _____

   Foci: _____

2) $\dfrac{x^2}{121} + \dfrac{y^2}{169} = 1$

   Vertices: _____

   Co–vertices: _____

   Foci: _____

3) $\dfrac{x^2}{169} + \dfrac{y^2}{64} = 1$

   Vertices: _____

   Co–vertices: _____

   Foci: _____

4) $\dfrac{x^2}{95} + \dfrac{y^2}{30} = 1$

   Vertices: _____

   Co–vertices: _____

   Foci: _____

5) $\dfrac{x^2}{36} + \dfrac{y^2}{16} = 1$

   Vertices: _____

   Co–vertices: _____

   Foci: _____

6) $\dfrac{x^2}{49} + \dfrac{y^2}{169} = 1$

   Vertices: _____

   Co–vertices: _____

   Foci: _____

7) $\dfrac{(x+5)^2}{81} + \dfrac{(y-1)^2}{144} = 1$

   Vertices: _____

   Co–vertices: _____

   Foci: _____

8) $\dfrac{(x-3)^2}{49} + \dfrac{(y-9)^2}{4} = 1$

   Vertices: _____

   Co–vertices: _____

   Foci: _____

9) $\dfrac{x^2}{64} + \dfrac{(y-8)^2}{9} = 1$

   Vertices: _____

   Co–vertices: _____

   Foci: _____

10) $\dfrac{x^2}{64} + \dfrac{(y-6)^2}{121} = 1$

    Vertices: _____

    Co–vertices: _____

    Foci: _____

Chapter 12: Conics

Hyperbola in Standard Form

✎ *Identify the vertices, foci, and direction of opening of each.*

1) $\dfrac{y^2}{25} - \dfrac{x^2}{16} = 1$
   Vertices: _____
   Foci: _____
   Direction: _____

2) $\dfrac{x^2}{121} - \dfrac{y^2}{36} = 1$
   Vertices: _____
   Foci: _____
   Direction: _____

3) $\dfrac{x^2}{121} - \dfrac{y^2}{81} = 1$
   Vertices: _____
   Foci: _____
   Direction: _____

4) $\dfrac{x^2}{81} - \dfrac{y^2}{4} = 1$
   Vertices: _____
   Foci: _____
   Direction: _____

5) $\dfrac{(x+2)^2}{169} - \dfrac{(y+8)^2}{4} = 1$
   Vertices: _____
   Foci: _____
   Direction: _____

6) $\dfrac{(y+8)^2}{36} - \dfrac{(x+2)^2}{25} = 1$
   Vertices: _____
   Foci: _____
   Direction: _____

7) $\dfrac{(y-7)^2}{100} - \dfrac{(x+9)^2}{100} = 1$
   Vertices: _____
   Foci: _____
   Direction: _____

8) $\dfrac{(x-5)^2}{36} - \dfrac{(y-4)^2}{81} = 1$
   Vertices: _____
   Foci: _____
   Direction: _____

9) $\dfrac{(y-10)^2}{144} - \dfrac{(x+10)^2}{16} = 1$
   Vertices: _____
   Foci: _____
   Direction: _____

10) $\dfrac{(y+5)^2}{4} - \dfrac{(x-8)^2}{49} = 1$
    Vertices: _____
    Foci: _____
    Direction: _____

11) $\dfrac{(y-9)^2}{169} - \dfrac{(x+5)^2}{49} = 1$
    Vertices: _____
    Foci: _____
    Direction: _____

12) $\dfrac{(x-7)^2}{25} - \dfrac{(y-1)^2}{195} = 1$
    Vertices: _____
    Foci: _____
    Direction: _____

13) $\dfrac{(x)^2}{4} - \dfrac{(y-1)^2}{16} = 1$
    Vertices: _____
    Foci: _____
    Direction: _____

14) $\dfrac{(y-2)^2}{10} - \dfrac{(x)^2}{15} = 1$
    Vertices: _____
    Foci: _____
    Direction: _____

Chapter 12: Conics

Classifying a Conic Section (in Standard Form)

✏️ **Classify each conic section and write its equation in standard form.**

1) $x^2 + y^2 - 8x + 8y - 4 = 0$

2) $y = 6x^2 - 60x + 149$

3) $x^2 - 4x + 4y^2 - 32y + 32 = 0$

4) $x^2 - 2x - 36y^2 - 360y - 935 = 0$

5) $y = -3x^2 - 36x - 108$

6) $x^2 + y^2 - 8x + 8y - 4 = 0$

7) $x^2 + y^2 + 6x + 10y + 33 = 0$

8) $x^2 - 4x - 36y^2 + 288y - 608 = 0$

9) $9x^2 + 4y^2 + 16y - 128 = 0$

10) $x^2 + 8x - 25y^2 + 50y - 34 = 0$

11) $y = 5x^2 + 40x - 155$

12) $4x^2 + 9y^2 - 54y + 45 = 0$

13) $-9x^2 - 54x + 4y^2 - 40y - 125 = 0$

14) $x^2 - 4x + 4y^2 - 32y + 32 = 0$

✏️ **Classify each conic section.**

15) $x^2 - 4y^2 + 6x - 8y + 1 = 0$

16) $3x^2 + 3x + y + 79 = 0$

17) $x^2 + y^2 + 4x - 2y - 18 = 0$

18) $-y^2 + x + 8y - 17 = 0$

19) $49x^2 + 9y^2 + 392x + 343 = 0$

20) $-9x^2 + y^2 - 72x - 153 = 0$

21) $-2y^2 + x - 20y - 49 = 0$

22) $-x^2 + 10x + y - 21 = 0$

Chapter 12: Conics

Answers – Chapter 12

Equation of a Parabola

1) Vertex $(0,0)$ and Focus $(0,2)$: $x^2 = 8y$

2) Vertex $(1,0)$ and Focus $(1,-2)$: $(x-1)^2 = -8y$

3) Vertex $(0,1)$ and Focus $(0,-8)$: $(x+0)^2 = -36(y-1)$

4) Vertex $(3,2)$ and Focus $(3,4)$: $(x-3)^2 = 8(y-2)$

5) Vertex $(1,1)$ and Focus $(1,6)$: $(x-1)^2 = 20(y-1)$

6) Vertex $(-1,2)$ and Focus $(-1,5)$: $(x+1)^2 = 12(y-2)$

7) Vertex $(2,2)$ and Focus $(2,4)$: $(x-2)^2 = 8(y-2)$

8) Vertex $(0,1)$ and Focus $(0,3)$: $x^2 = 8(y-1)$

9) Vertex $(2,1)$ and Focus $(4,1)$: $(y-1)^2 = 8(x-2)$

10) Vertex $(5,0)$ and Focus $(9,0)$: $y^2 = 16(x-5)$

11) Vertex $(-2,4)$ and Focus $(2,4)$: $(y-4)^2 = 16(x+2)$

12) Vertex $(0,-4)$ and Focus $(4,-4)$: $(y+4)^2 = 16x$

Finding the Focus, Vertex, and Directrix of a Parabola

1) $x^2 + 8y = 0$

Focus: $(0,-2)$
Vertex: $(0,0)$
Directrix: $y = 2$

2) $x^2 = 16y$

Focus: $(0,4)$
Vertex: $(0,0)$
Directrix: $\boldsymbol{y = -4}$

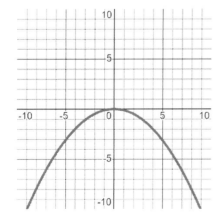
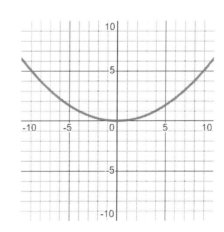

3) $y = (x+3)^2 - 2$

Focus: $(-3, -\frac{7}{4})$

Vertex: $(-3, -2)$

Directrix: $\boldsymbol{y = -\frac{9}{4}}$

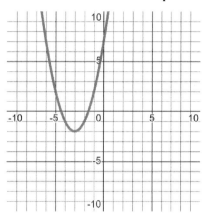

4) $(x+2)^2 = -4(y+2)$

Focus: $(-2, -3)$

Vertex: $(-2, -2)$

Directrix: $\boldsymbol{y = -1}$

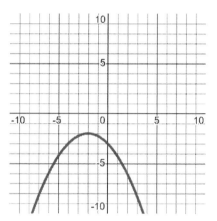

Standard From of a Circle

1) $(x-0)^2 + (y-1)^2 = 4^2$

2) $(x+4)^2 + (y-1)^2 = 9^2$

3) $(x-3)^2 + (y-2)^2 = 1^2$

4) $(x+2)^2 + (y+3)^2 = 1^2$

5) $(x-9)^2 + (y-12)^2 = 8^2$

6) $(x+8)^2 + (y-14)^2 = 6^2$

7) $(x+13)^2 + (y+9)^2 = 12^2$

8) $(x+2)^2 + (y+14)^2 = 5^2$

9) $(x-4)^2 + (y-3)^2 = 2^2$

10) $(x+1)^2 + (y-12)^2 = 5^2$

11) $(x+5)^2 + (y+6)^2 = 81$

12) $(x+12)^2 + (y+5)^2 = 4$

13) $(x+11)^2 + (y+14)^2 = 16$

14) $(x+3)^2 + (y-2)^2 = 2$

15) $(x-15)^2 + (y-14)^2 = 2\sqrt{15}$

16) $(x+4)^2 + (y+8)^2 = 16$

17) $(x+6)^2 + (y+15)^2 = 5$

18) $(x+10)^2 + (y+15)^2 = 9$

Chapter 12: Conics

Finding the Center and the Radius of Circles

1) Center: $(-6, -12)$, Radius: $\sqrt{18}$

2) Center: $(-1, -3)$, Radius: 2

3) Center: $(4, 9)$, Radius: 4

4) Center: $(8, -11)$, Radius: $\sqrt{24}$

5) Center: $(-12, 18)$, Radius: 9

6) Center: $(9, -14)$, Radius: 12

7) Center: $(2, -5)$, Radius: $\sqrt{10}$

8) Center: $(0, 1)$, Radius: 2

9) Center: $(2, -6)$, Radius: 3

10) Center: $(-14, 5)$, Radius: 4

11) Center: $(0, 6)$, Radius: $\sqrt{22}$

12) Center: $(6, 11)$, Radius: 3

13) $(x-2)^2 + (y-6)^2 = 4$

Center: $(\mathbf{2, 6})$, Radius: $\mathbf{2}$

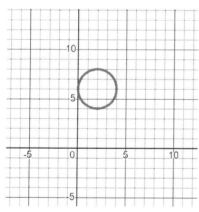

14) $(x+3)^2 + (y-7)^2 = 9$

Center: $(-3, \ 7)$, Radius: 3

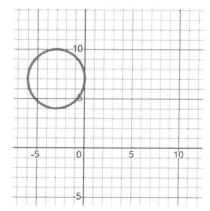

Chapter 12: Conics

Equation of Ellipse

1) Vertices: $(9, 0), (-9, 0)$
   Co–vertices: $(0, 7), (0, -7)$
   Foci: $(4\sqrt{2}, 0), (-4\sqrt{2}, 0)$

2) Vertices: $(0, -13), (0, 13)$
   Co–vertices: $(-11, 0), (11, 0)$
   Foci: $(0, -4\sqrt{3}), (0, 4\sqrt{3})$

3) Vertices: $(13, 0), (-13, 0)$
   Co–vertices: $(0, -8), (0, 8)$
   Foci: $(\sqrt{105}, 0), (-\sqrt{105}, 0)$

4) Vertices: $(-\sqrt{95}, 0), (\sqrt{95}, 0)$
   Co–vertices: $(0, -\sqrt{30}), (0, \sqrt{30})$
   Foci: $(-\sqrt{65}, 0), (\sqrt{65}, 0)$

5) Vertices: $(-6, 0), (6, 0)$
   Co–vertices: $(0, -4), (0, 4)$
   Foci: $(-2\sqrt{5}, 0), (2\sqrt{5}, 0)$

6) Vertices: $(0, -13), (0, 13)$
   Co–vertices: $(-7, 0), (7, 0)$
   Foci: $(0, -2\sqrt{30}), (0, 2\sqrt{30})$

7) Vertices: $(-5, -11), (-5, 13)$
   Co–vertices: $(-14, 1), (4, 1)$
   Foci: $(-5, 1 - 3\sqrt{7}), (-5, 1 + 3\sqrt{7})$

8) Vertices: $(-4, 9), (10, 9)$
   Co–vertices: $(3, 7), (3, 11)$
   Foci: $(3 - 3\sqrt{5}, 9), (3 + 3\sqrt{5}, 9)$

9) Vertices: $(-8, 8), (8, 8)$
   Co–vertices: $(0, 5), (0, 11)$
   Foci: $(-\sqrt{55}, 8), (\sqrt{55}, 8)$

10) Vertices: $(0, -5), (0, 17)$
    Co–vertices: $(-8, 6), (8, 6)$
    Foci: $(0, 6 - \sqrt{57}), (0, 6 + \sqrt{57})$

Hyperbola in Standard Form

1) Vertices: $(0, 5), (0, -5)$
   Foci: $(0, \sqrt{41}), (0, -\sqrt{41})$
   Opens up/down

2) Vertices: $(11, 0), (-11, 0)$
   Foci: $(\sqrt{157}, 0), (-\sqrt{157}, 0)$
   Opens left/right

3) Vertices: $(11, 0), (-11, 0)$
   Foci: $(\sqrt{202}, 0), (-\sqrt{202}, 0)$
   Opens left/right

4) Vertices: $(9, 0), (-9, 0)$
   Foci: $(\sqrt{85}, 0), (-\sqrt{85}, 0)$
   Opens left/right

5) Vertices: $(11, -8), (-15, -8)$
   Foci: $(-2 \pm \sqrt{173}, -8)$
   Opens left/right

6) Vertices: $(-2, -2), (-2, -14)$
   Foci: $(-2, -8 \pm \sqrt{61})$
   Opens up/down

Chapter 12: Conics

7) Vertices: $(-9, 17), (-9, -3)$
   Foci: $(-9, 7 \pm 10\sqrt{2})$
   Opens up/down

8) Vertices: $(11, 4), (-1, 4)$
   Foci: $(5 \pm 3\sqrt{13}, 4)$
   Opens left/right

9) Vertices: $(-10, 22), (-10, -2)$
   Foci: $(-10, 10 \pm 4\sqrt{10})$
   Opens up/down

10) Vertices: $(8, -3), (8, -7)$
    Foci: $(8, -5 \pm \sqrt{53})$
    Opens up/down

11) Vertices: $(-5, 22), (-5, -4)$
    Foci: $(-5, 9 \pm \sqrt{218})$
    Opens up/down

12) Vertices: $(12, 1), (2, 1)$
    Foci: $(7 \pm 2\sqrt{55}, 1)$
    Opens left/right

13) Vertices: $(2, 1), (-2, 1)$
    Foci: $(2\sqrt{5}, 1), (-2\sqrt{5}, 1)$
    Opens left/right

14) Vertices: $(0, 2 + \sqrt{10}), (0, 2 - \sqrt{10})$
    Foci: $(0, 7), (0, -3)$
    Opens up/down

Classifying a Conic Section (in Standard Form)

1) Circle, $(x - 4)^2 + (y + 4)^2 = 6^2$
2) Parabola, $y = 6(x - 5)^2 - 1$
3) Ellipse, $\frac{(x-2)^2}{6^2} + \frac{(y-4)^2}{3^2} = 1$
4) Hyperbola, $\frac{(x-1)^2}{6^2} - \frac{(y+5)^2}{1^2} = 1$
5) Parabola, $y = -3(x + 6)^2$
6) Circle, $(x - 4)^2 + (y + 4)^2 = 6^2$
7) Circle, $(x + 3)^2 + (y + 5)^2 = 1^2$
8) Hyperbola, $\frac{(x-2)^2}{6^2} - \frac{(y-4)^2}{1^2} = 1$
9) Ellipse, $\frac{(x-0)^2}{4^2} + \frac{(y+2)^2}{6^2} = 1$
10) Hyperbola, $\frac{(x+4)^2}{5^2} - \frac{(y-1)^2}{1^2} = 1$
11) Parabola, $y = 5(x + 4)^2 - 235$
12) Ellipse, $\frac{(x-0)^2}{3^2} + \frac{(y-3)^2}{2^2} = 1$
13) Hyperbola, $\frac{(y-5)^2}{6^2} - \frac{(x+3)^2}{4^2} = 1$
14) Ellipse, $\frac{(x-2)^2}{6^2} + \frac{(y-4)^2}{3^2} = 1$
15) Hyperbola
16) Parabola
17) Circle
18) Parabola
19) Ellipse
20) Hyperbola
21) Parabola
22) Parabola

Chapter 13: Sequences and Series

Math Topics that you'll learn in this Chapter:

- ✓ Arithmetic Sequences
- ✓ Geometric Sequences
- ✓ Arithmetic Series
- ✓ Finite Geometric Series
- ✓ Infinite Geometric Series
- ✓ Pascal's Triangle
- ✓ Binomial Theorem
- ✓ Sigma Notation (Summation Notation)
- ✓ Alternating Series

Chapter 13: Sequences and Series

Arithmetic Sequences

✎ **Find the next three terms of each arithmetic sequence.**

1) $15, 11, 7, 3, -1, \ldots$

2) $-21, -14, -7, 0, \ldots$

3) $3, 6, 9, 12, 15, \ldots$

4) $4, 8, 12, 16, 20, \ldots$

✎ **Given the first term and the common difference of an arithmetic sequence find the first five terms and the explicit formula.**

5) $a_1 = 24, d = 2$

6) $a_1 = -15, d = -5$

7) $a_1 = 18, d = 10$

8) $a_1 = -38, d = -100$

✎ **Given a term in an arithmetic sequence and the common difference find the first five terms and the explicit formula.**

9) $a_{36} = -276, d = -7$

10) $a_{37} = 249, d = 8$

11) $a_{38} = -53.2, d = -1.1$

12) $a_{40} = -1{,}191, d = -30$

✎ **Given a term in an arithmetic sequence and the common difference find the recursive formula and the three terms in the sequence after the last one given.**

13) $a_{22} = -44, d = -2$

14) $a_{12} = 28.6, d = 1.8$

15) $a_{18} = 27.4, d = 1.1$

16) $a_{21} = -1.4, d = 0.6$

Chapter 13: Sequences and Series

Geometric Sequences

✍ *Determine if the sequence is geometric. If it is, find the common ratio.*

1) $1, -5, 25, -125, \ldots$

2) $-2, -4, -8, -16, \ldots$

3) $4, 16, 36, 64, \ldots$

4) $-3, -15, -75, -375, \ldots$

✍ *Given the first term and the common ratio of a geometric sequence find the first five terms and the explicit formula.*

5) $a_1 = 0.8, r = -5$

6) $a_1 = 1, r = 2$

✍ *Given the recursive formula for a geometric sequence find the common ratio, the first five terms, and the explicit formula.*

7) $a_n = a_{n-1} \cdot 2, a_1 = 2$

8) $a_n = a_{n-1} \cdot -3, a_1 = -3$

9) $a_n = a_{n-1} \cdot 5, a_1 = 2$

10) $a_n = a_{n-1} \cdot 3, a_1 = -3$

✍ *Given two terms in a geometric sequence find the 8th term and the recursive formula.*

11) $a_4 = 12$ and $a_5 = -6$

12) $a_5 = 768$ and $a_2 = 12$

Chapter 13: Sequences and Series

Arithmetic Series

✍ **Find the first five terms of the sequence.**

1) $a_1 = 4, d = 5$ ___, ___, ___, ___, ___ .

2) $a_1 = -2, d = -3$ ___, ___, ___, ___, ___ .

3) $a_1 = 12, d = 7$ ___, ___, ___, ___, ___ .

4) $a_1 = 28, d = 12$ ___, ___, ___, ___, ___ .

5) $a_1 = 67, d = 13$ ___, ___, ___, ___, ___ .

6) $a_1 = 118, d = 85$ ___, ___, ___, ___, ___ .

7) $a_1 = -9, d = -16$ ___, ___, ___, ___, ___ .

8) $a_1 = -120, d = -100$ ___, ___, ___, ___, ___ .

9) $a_1 = 55, d = 23$ ___, ___, ___, ___, ___ .

10) $a_1 = 12.5, d = 4.2$ ___, ___, ___, ___, ___ .

✍ **Find the sum of the first four terms of the sequence.**

11) $a_3 = 12, d = 3$

12) $a_5 = 46, d = 5$

13) $a_{10} = 66, d = 4$

14) $a_8 = 38, d = 6$

15) $a_{12} = 88, d = 7$

16) $a_{22} = 226, d = 9$

Chapter 13: Sequences and Series

Finite Geometric Series

✎ *Evaluate the related series of each sequence.*

1) $-1, 5, -25, 125$

2) $-2, 6, -18, 54, -162$

3) $-1, 4, -16, 64$

4) $2, 12, 72, 432$

5) $-4, -8, -16, -32, -64$

6) $1, 5, 25, 125, 625$

✎ *Evaluate each geometric series described.*

7) $1 + 2 + 4 + 8 \ldots, n = 6$ _____

8) $1 - 4 + 16 - 64 \ldots, n = 9$ _____

9) $-2 - 6 - 18 - 54 \ldots, n = 9$ _____

10) $2 - 10 + 50 - 250 \ldots, n = 8$ _____

11) $1 - 5 + 25 - 125 \ldots, n = 7$ _____

12) $-3 - 6 - 12 - 24 \ldots, n = 9$ _____

13) $a_1 = -1, r = 4, n = 8$ _____

14) $a_1 = -2, r = -3, n = 9$ _____

15) $\sum_{n=1}^{8} 2 \cdot (-2)^{n-1}$ _____

16) $\sum_{n=1}^{9} 4 \cdot 3^{n-1}$ _____

17) $\sum_{n=1}^{10} 4 \cdot (-3)^{n-1}$ _____

18) $\sum_{m=1}^{9} -2^{m-1}$ _____

19) $\sum_{m=1}^{8} 3 \cdot 5^{m-1}$ _____

20) $\sum_{k=1}^{7} 2 \cdot 5^{k-1}$ _____

Chapter 13: Sequences and Series

Infinite Geometric Series

✎ *Determine if each geometric series converges or diverges.*

1) $a_1 = -3, r = 4$

2) $a_1 = 5.5, r = 0.5$

3) $a_1 = -1, r = 3$

4) $a_1 = 3.2, r = 0.2$

5) $a_1 = 5, r = 2$

6) $-1, 3, -9, 27, \ldots$

7) $2, -1, \frac{1}{2}, -\frac{1}{4}, \frac{1}{8}, \ldots$

8) $81 + 27 + 9 + 3 \ldots$

9) $-3 + \frac{12}{5} - \frac{48}{25} + \frac{192}{125} \ldots$

10) $\frac{128}{3,125} - \frac{64}{625} + \frac{32}{125} - \frac{16}{25} \ldots$

✎ *Evaluate each infinite geometric series described.*

11) $a_1 = 3, r = -\frac{1}{5}$

12) $a_1 = 1, r = -3$

13) $a_1 = 1, r = -4$

14) $a_1 = 3, r = \frac{1}{2}$

15) $1 + 0.5 + 0.25 + 0.125 + \cdots$

16) $81 - 27 + 9 - 3 \ldots,$

17) $1 - 0.6 + 0.36 - 0.216 \ldots,$

18) $3 + \frac{9}{4} + \frac{27}{16} + \frac{81}{64} \ldots,$

19) $\sum_{k=1}^{\infty} 4^{k-1}$

20) $\sum_{i=1}^{\infty} (\frac{1}{3})^{i-1}$

21) $\sum_{k=1}^{\infty} (-\frac{1}{3})^{k-1}$

22) $\sum_{n=1}^{\infty} 16(\frac{1}{4})^{n-1}$

Chapter 13: Sequences and Series

Pascal's Triangle

Use Pascal's triangle to expand the following binomial expressions.

1) $(x+6)^3$

2) $(1+3x)^2$

3) $(\sqrt{x}-\sqrt{3})^4$

4) $(1-5x)^5$

5) $(2x-1)^3$

6) $(x+4)^6$

7) $(y-3x)^5$

8) $(y+2)^7$

9) $(y-x)^9$

10) $(2x+y)^4$

Solve.

11) Determine the third element in the fourth row of Pascal's triangle.

12) Find the coefficients of expansions of $(x+y)^3$ using Pascal's triangle.

13) Find the sum of the elements in the 12th row of the Pascal's triangle.

14) Determine the elements in row 10 of Pascal's triangle.

15) Find the coefficients of expansions of $(x+y)^5$ using Pascal's triangle.

Chapter 13: Sequences and Series

Binomial Theorem

Expand completely.

1) $(2x - 1)^4 =$

2) $(x - y)^3 =$

3) $(x^4 - y)^5 =$

4) $(2x^3 + 1)^5 =$

5) $(y - x^2)^3 =$

6) $(y^3 - 4x)^3 =$

7) $(3x + 1)^4 =$

8) $(y - 3x)^3 =$

9) $(4x - 1)^4 =$

10) $(4x^3 + 4x)^4 =$

11) $(2x^2 - 1)^6 =$

12) $(1 + 3x^2)^4 =$

Solve.

13) Write the 5th term of the expansion of $(1 - 4b^2)^4$. _____

14) Write the 2nd term of the expansion of $(1 - 3n^4)^4$. _____

15) Write the 5th term of the expansion of $(2 - 4y)^4$. _____

16) Write the 2nd term of the expansion of $(2x + y)^3$. _____

17) Write the 4th term of the expansion of $(4y + x)^4$. _____

18) Write the 4th term of the expansion of $(2x - 3)^5$. _____

Chapter 13: Sequences and Series

Sigma Notation (Summation Notation)

✎ Solve.

1) $\sum_{n=1}^{7} 2a$

2) $\sum_{x=1}^{4}(50 - x)$

3) $\sum_{x=2}^{6}(100 - x)$

4) $\sum_{k=1}^{4} k(k + 3)$

5) $\sum_{n=1}^{5}(n^2 - 2)$

6) $\sum_{n=1}^{4} n^3$

7) $\sum_{k=1}^{3} \frac{k}{k+2}$

8) $\sum_{n=3}^{5} -\frac{2}{n}$

9) $\sum_{x=1}^{3} \frac{x^2}{x+2}$

10) $\sum_{n=2}^{6}(n^2 + n)$

11) $\sum_{i=3}^{7} \frac{i+2}{i-2}$

12) $\sum_{k=-3}^{3}(k^2 - k)$

13) $\sum_{k=1}^{4} k(k + 2)$

14) $\sum_{m=1}^{5} m$

15) $\sum_{n=1}^{7}(30 - n)$

16) $\sum_{a=4}^{9}(20 - a^2)$

17) $\sum_{n=1}^{4}(5n^2 + 4)$

18) $\sum_{k=0}^{4}(100 - k)$

19) $\sum_{m=1}^{6} \frac{m^2+1}{m}$

20) $\sum_{k=1}^{7} k^2$

Chapter 13: Sequences and Series

Alternating Series

✏️ **Determine whether the following series converge or diverge.**

1) $\sum_{n=1}^{\infty}(-1)^{n-1}\frac{2}{n+1}$

2) $\sum_{n=2}^{\infty}\frac{(-1)^n}{\sqrt{n+4}}$

3) $\sum_{n=4}^{\infty}(-1)^{n-1}\frac{n}{n+2}$

4) $\sum_{n=1}^{\infty}(-1)^{n-1}\frac{1}{n^2}$

5) $\sum_{n=1}^{\infty}\frac{(-1)^{n-1}n}{n}$

6) $\sum_{n=1}^{\infty}(-1)^{n-1}\frac{1}{n}$

7) $\sum_{n=1}^{\infty}\frac{(-1)^{n-1}}{2n+5}$

8) $\sum_{n=1}^{\infty}(-1)^{n-1}\frac{n}{3n-2}$

9) $\sum_{n=1}^{\infty}(-1)^{n-1}\frac{1}{n^3}$

10) $\sum_{n=1}^{\infty}(-1)^{n-1}\frac{n}{n^2}$

11) $\sum_{n=1}^{\infty}(-1)^{n-1}\frac{\cos n}{n^2}$

12) $\sum_{n=1}^{\infty}(-1)^{n+1}\frac{\sin n}{n^2}$

13) $\sum_{n=1}^{\infty}(-1)^n\frac{n+3}{n^2+2n+5}$

14) $\sum_{n=1}^{\infty}\frac{(-1)^n}{\sqrt{n}}$

15) $\sum_{n=3}^{\infty}(-1)^n\frac{3n-3}{5n-10}$

16) $\sum_{n=3}^{\infty}(-1)^n\frac{n}{8^n}$

17) $\sum_{n=1}^{\infty}(1)^{n-1}\frac{5}{n+1}$

18) $\sum_{n=1}^{\infty}(-1)^{n-1}\frac{n}{n^2+6n+8}$

Chapter 13: Sequences and Series

Answers – Chapter 13

Arithmetic Sequences

1) $-5, -9, -13$
2) $7, 14, 21$
3) $18, 21, 24$
4) $24, 28, 32$
5) First Five Terms: $24, 26, 28, 30, 32$, Explicit: $a_n = 2n + 22$
6) First Five Terms: $-15, -20, -25, -30, -35$, Explicit: $a_n = -5n - 10$
7) First Five Terms: $18, 28, 38, 48, 58$, Explicit: $a_n = 10n + 8$
8) First Five Terms: $-38, -138, -238, -338, -438$, Explicit: $a_n = -100n + 62$
9) First Five Terms: $-31, -38, -45, -52, -59$, Explicit: $a_n = -7n - 24$
10) First Five Terms: $-39, -31, -23, -15, -7$, Explicit: $a_n = 8n - 47$
11) First Five Terms: $-12.5, -13.6, -14.7, -15.8, -16.9$, Explicit: $a_n = -1.1n - 11.4$
12) First Five Terms: $-21, -51, -81, -111, -141$, Explicit: $a_n = -30n + 9$
13) Next 3 terms: $-46, -48, -50$, Recursive: $a_n = a_{n-1} - 2, a_1 = -2$
14) Next 3 terms: $30.4, 32.2, 34$, Recursive: $a_n = a_{n-1} + 1.8, a_1 = 8.8$
15) Next 3 terms: $28.5, 29.6, 30.7$, Recursive: $a_n = a_{n-1} + 1.1, a_1 = 8.7$
16) Next 3 terms: $-0.8, -0.2, 0.4$, Recursive: $a_n = a_{n-1} + 0.6, a_1 = -13.4$

Geometric Sequences

1) $r = -5$
2) $r = 2$
3) not geometric
4) $r = 5$
5) First Five Terms: $0.8, -4, 20, -100, 500$
   Explicit: $a_n = 0.8 \cdot (-5)^{n-1}$
6) First Five Terms: $1, 2, 4, 8, 16$
   Explicit: $a_n = 2^{n-1}$
7) Common Ratio: $r = 2$
   First Five Terms: $2, 4, 8, 16, 32$
   Explicit: $a_n = 2 \cdot 2^{n-1}$
8) Common Ratio: $r = -3$
   First Five Terms: $-3, 9, -27, 81, -243$
   Explicit: $a_n = -3 \cdot (-3)^{n-1}$
9) Common Ratio: $r = 5$
   First Five Terms: $10, 50, 250, 1,250$
   Explicit: $a_n = 2 \cdot 5^{n-1}$
10) Common Ratio: $r = 3$
    First Five Terms: $-3, -9, -27, -81, -243$
    Explicit: $a_n = -3 \cdot 3^{n-1}$
11) $a_8 = \frac{3}{4}$,
    Recursive: $a_n = a_{n-1} \cdot \frac{-1}{2}, a_1 = -96$
12) $a_8 = 49,152$,
    Recursive: $a_n = a_{n-1} \cdot 4, a_1 = 3$

Chapter 13: Sequences and Series

Arithmetic Series

1) 4, 9, 14, 19, 24
2) −2, −5, −8, −11, −14
3) 12, 19, 26, 33, 40
4) 28, 40, 52, 64, 76
5) 67, 80, 93, 106, 119
6) 118, 203, 288, 373, 458
7) −9, −25, −41, −57, −73
8) −120, −220, −320, −420, −520
9) 55, 78, 101, 124, 147
10) 12.5, 16.7, 20.9, 25.1, 29.3
11) 42
12) 134
13) 144
14) 20
15) 86
16) 202

Finite Geometric Series

1) 104
2) −122
3) 51
4) 518
5) −124
6) 781
7) 63
8) 52,429
9) −19,682
10) −130,208
11) 13,021
12) −1513
13) −21,845
14) −9,842
15) −170
16) 39,364
17) −59048
18) −511
19) 292,968
20) 39,062

Infinite Geometric Series

1) Diverges
2) Converges
3) Diverges
4) Converges
5) Diverges
6) Diverges
7) Converges
8) Converges
9) Converges
10) Diverges
11) $\frac{5}{2}$
12) Infinite
13) Infinite
14) 6
15) 2
16) $\frac{243}{4}$
17) 0.625
18) 12
19) Infinite
20) $\frac{3}{2}$
21) $\frac{3}{4}$
22) $\frac{4}{3}$

| Effortless Math Education | Chapter 13: Sequences and Series |

Pascal's Triangle

1) $x^3 + 18x^2 + 108x + 216$
2) $1 + 6x + 9x^2$
3) $x^2 - 4\sqrt{3}x\sqrt{x} + 18x - 12\sqrt{3}\sqrt{x} + 9$
4) $1 - 25x + 250x^2 - 1250x^3 + 3125x^4 - 3125x^5$
5) $8x^3 - 12x^2 + 6x - 1$
6) $x^6 + 24x^5 + 240x^4 + 1,280x^3 + 3,840x^2 + 6,144x + 4,096$
7) $y^5 - 15y^4x + 90y^3x^2 - 270y^2x^3 + 405yx^4 - 243x^5$
8) $y^7 + 14y^6 + 84y^5 + 280y^4 + 560y^3 + 672y^2 + 448y + 128$
9) $y^9 - 9y^8x + 36y^7x^2 - 84y^6x^3 + 126y^5x^4 - 126y^4x^5 + 84y^3x^6 - 36y^2x^7 + 9yx^8 - x^9$
10) $16x^4 + 32x^3y + 24x^2y^2 + 8xy^3 + y^4$
11) 3
12) 1,3,3,1
13) 4,096
14) 1,9,36,84,126,126,84,36,9,1
15) 1,5,10,10,5,1

Binomial Theorem

1) $16x^4 - 32x^3 + 24x^2 - 8x + 1$
2) $x^3 - 3x^2y + 3xy^2 - y^3$
3) $x^{20} - 5x^{16}y + 10x^{12}y^{12} - 10x^8y^3 + 5x^4y^4 - y^5$
4) $32x^{15} + 80x^{12} + 80x^9 + 40x^6 + 10x^3 + 1$
5) $y^3 - 3y^2x^2 + 3yx^4 - x^6$
6) $y^9 - 12y^6x + 48y^3x^2 - 64x^3$
7) $81x^4 + 108x^3 + 54x^2 + 12x + 1$
8) $y^3 - 9y^2x + 27yx^2 - 27x^3$

Chapter 13: Sequences and Series

9) $256x^4 - 256x^3 + 96x^2 - 16x + 1$

10) $256x^{12} + 1024x^{10} + 1536x^8 + 1024x^6 + 256x^4$

11) $64x^{12} - 192x^{10} + 240x^8 - 160x^6 + 60x^4 - 12x^2 + 1$

12) $1 + 12x^2 + 54x^4 + 108x^6 + 81x^8$

13) $256b^8$

14) $-12n^4$

15) $256y^4$

16) $12x^2y$

17) $16yx^3$

18) $-1,080x^2$

Sigma Notation (Summation Notation)

1) 56
2) 190
3) 480
4) 60
5) 45
6) 100
7) $1\frac{13}{30}$
8) $-\frac{47}{30}$
9) $\frac{47}{15}$
10) 110
11) $\frac{212}{15}$
12) 28
13) 50
14) 15
15) 182
16) -151
17) 166
18) 490
19) $\frac{469}{20}$
20) 140

Alternate Series

1) Converges
2) Converges
3) Diverges
4) Converges
5) Diverges
6) Converges
7) Converges
8) Diverges
9) Converges
10) Converges
11) Converges
12) Converges
13) Converges
14) Converges
15) Diverges
16) Converges
17) Diverges
18) Converges

Chapter 14: Trigonometric Functions

Math Topics that you'll learn in this Chapter:

- ✓ Trig Ratios of General Angles
- ✓ Trigonometric Ratios
- ✓ Right-Triangle Trigonometry
- ✓ Angles of Rotation
- ✓ The Unit Circle, Sine, and Cosine
- ✓ The Reciprocal Trigonometric Functions
- ✓ Function Values of Special Angles
- ✓ Function Values from the Calculator
- ✓ Reference Angles and the Calculator
- ✓ Coterminal Angles and Reference Angles
- ✓ Angles and Angle Measure
- ✓ Evaluating Trigonometric Function
- ✓ Missing Sides and Angles of a Right Triangle
- ✓ Arc length and Sector Area
- ✓ The Inverse of Trigonometric Functions
- ✓ Solving Trigonometric Equations

Chapter 14: Trigonometric Functions

Trig Ratios of General Angles

✏️ *Evaluate.*

1) $\sin -60° =$ _____

2) $\sin 150° =$ _____

3) $\cos 315° =$ _____

4) $\cos 180° =$ _____

5) $\sin 120° =$ _____

6) $\sin -330° =$ _____

7) $\tan -90° =$ _____

8) $\cot 90° =$ _____

9) $\tan 270° =$ _____

10) $\cot 150° =$ _____

11) $\sec 120° =$ _____

12) $\csc -360° =$ _____

13) $\cot -270° =$ _____

14) $\sec 90° =$ _____

15) $\cos -90° =$ _____

16) $\sec 60° =$ _____

17) $\csc 480° =$ _____

18) $\cot -135° =$ _____

✏️ *Find the exact value of each trigonometric function. Some may be undefined.*

19) $\sec \pi =$ _____

20) $\tan -\frac{3\pi}{2} =$ _____

21) $\cos \frac{11\pi}{6} =$ _____

22) $\cot \frac{5\pi}{3} =$ _____

23) $\sec -\frac{3\pi}{4} =$ _____

24) $\sec \frac{\pi}{3} =$ _____

25) $\csc \frac{5\pi}{6} =$ _____

26) $\cot \frac{4\pi}{3} =$ _____

27) $\csc -\frac{3\pi}{4} =$ _____

28) $\cot \frac{2\pi}{3} =$ _____

Chapter 14: Trigonometric Functions

Trigonometric Ratios

✏️ *Find the given trigonometric ratio.*

1) $\tan X = $ _____

2) $\sin X = $ _____

3) $\cos X = $ _____

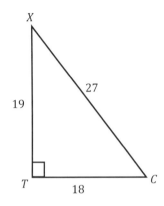
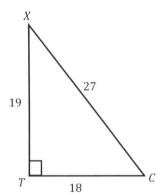
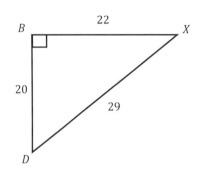

4) $\cos C = $ _____

5) $\tan A = $ _____

6) $\sin A = $ _____

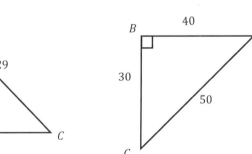
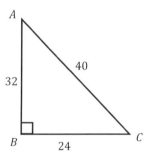

✏️ *Find the value of each trigonometric ratio using a calculator.*

7) $\cos 60°$

10) $\cos 24°$

8) $\sec 45°$

11) $\sin 39°$

9) $\cos 52°$

12) $\sec 75°$

Chapter 14: Trigonometric Functions

Right-Triangle Trigonometry

✏️ *Find the measure of each side indicated. Round to the nearest tenth.*

1) _____   3) _____   5) _____

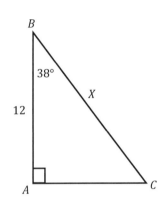 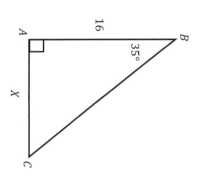 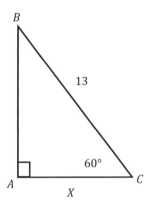

2) _____   4) _____   6) _____

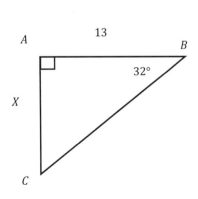 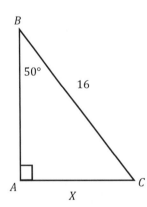 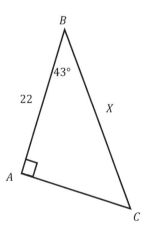

190

www.EffortlessMath.com

Chapter 14: Trigonometric Functions

Angles of Rotation

✏ Find.

1) Find the reference angle of 130°. _____

2) Find the reference angle of 150°. _____

3) Find the reference angle of 115°. _____

✏ Find a coterminal angle between 0° and 360°.

4) −320°

5) 425°

6) −630°

7) 440°

8) −390°

9) 378°

10) −115°

11) 765°

12) −215°

13) 410°

14) −205°

15) 390°

✏ Find a coterminal angle between 0° and 2π°.

16) $\frac{15\pi}{4}$

17) $-\frac{11\pi}{3}$

18) $\frac{19\pi}{8}$

19) $-\frac{13\pi}{4}$

20) $\frac{12\pi}{5}$

21) $-\frac{5\pi}{2}$

22) $\frac{14\pi}{3}$

23) $-\frac{5\pi}{6}$

Chapter 14: Trigonometric Functions

The Unit Circle, Sine, and Cosine

✎ Solve.

1) $P\left(-\frac{\sqrt{3}}{2},\frac{1}{2}\right)$ is a point on the unit circle, and the terminal side of an angle in standard position has a measure of θ. Find $\sin\theta$ and $\cos\theta$. _____

2) $P\left(\frac{\sqrt{2}}{2},-\frac{\sqrt{2}}{2}\right)$ is a point on the unit circle, and the terminal side of an angle in standard position has a measure of θ. Find $\sin\theta$ and $\cos\theta$. _____

3) Use the unit circle to find the sine, cosine, and tangent ratios of an angle with a measure of 135°.

$\sin 315° =$ _____, $\cos 315° =$ _____, $\tan 315° =$ _____

4) Use the unit circle to find the sine, cosine, and tangent ratios of an angle with a measure of 420°.

$\sin 420° =$ _____, $\cos 420° =$ _____, $\tan 420° =$ _____

5) Use the unit circle to find the sine, cosine, and tangent ratios of an angle with a measure of $\frac{7\pi}{3}$.

$\sin\frac{7\pi}{3} =$ _____, $\cos\frac{7\pi}{3} =$ _____, $\tan\frac{7\pi}{3} =$ _____

6) Use the unit circle to find the sine, cosine, and tangent ratios of an angle with a measure of $\frac{3\pi}{4}$.

$\sin\frac{3\pi}{4} =$ _____, $\cos\frac{3\pi}{4} =$ _____, $\tan\frac{3\pi}{4} =$ _____

Chapter 14: Trigonometric Functions

The Reciprocal Trigonometric Functions

✎ *Find the value of the trig function indicated.*

1) Find $\cot \theta$ if $\csc \theta = \frac{25}{7}$

   $\cot \theta =$ ___

2) Find $\csc \theta$ if $\cot \theta = \frac{7}{23}$

   $\csc \theta =$ ___

3) Find $\csc \theta$ if $\cot \theta = \frac{2\sqrt{5}}{15}$

   $\csc \theta =$ ___

4) Find $\operatorname{cosec} \theta$ if $\sec \theta = \frac{17}{8}$

   $\operatorname{cosec} \theta =$ ___

5) Find $\sec \theta$ if $\cot \theta = \frac{5}{2}$

   $\sec \theta =$ ___

6) Find $\cot \theta$ if $\csc \theta = \frac{41}{9}$

   $\cot \theta =$ ___

7) Find $\sec \theta$ if $\cot \theta = \frac{1}{2}$

   $\sec \theta =$ ___

8) Find $\cot \theta$ if $\csc \theta = \frac{5}{3}$

   $\cot \theta =$ ___

9) Find $\csc \theta$ if $\sin \theta = \frac{3}{5}$

   $\csc \theta =$ ___

10) Find $\csc \theta$ if $\sin \theta = \frac{5}{7}$

    $\csc \theta =$ ___

11) Find $\sin \theta$ if $\cot \theta = \frac{3\sqrt{2}}{\sqrt{3}}$

    $\sin \theta =$ ___

12) Find $\cos \theta$ if $\csc \theta = \frac{85}{13}$

    $\cos \theta =$ ___

13) Find $\csc \theta$ if $\sec \theta = \frac{\sqrt{5}}{2}$

    $\csc \theta =$ ___

14) Find $\cot \theta$ if $\sec \theta = \frac{5}{3}$

    $\cot \theta =$ ___

15) Find $\csc \theta$ if $\sec \theta = \frac{5}{4}$

    $\csc \theta =$ ___

16) Find $\csc \theta$ if $\sec \theta = \frac{13}{12}$

    $\csc \theta =$ ___

Chapter 14: Trigonometric Functions
Function Values of Special Angles

✏️ **Find the exact value of the following.**

1) $\sin 45° \cos 30°$

2) $\sin 60° + \cos 60°$

3) $\tan 45° \cos 60°$

4) $\sin 60° + \tan 30°$

5) $\sin 60° \tan 30°$

6) $\cos 30° + \sin 60°$

7) $\sin 45° \cos 45°$

8) $\sin^2 30° + \cos^2 60°$

9) $\tan^2 60° \, 2\tan^2 45°$

10) $\sin^4 30° - \cos^4 60°$

11) $\cot^2 30° \sin^2 30°$

12) $4\cos^2 45° + 2\cot^2 45°$

13) $\sin 30° \sin 45° \sin 60°$

14) $\sin 60° \cos 60° \tan 60°$

15) $4 \sec 30° \tan 60°$

16) $2\cos^2 60° + 3\sec^2 30°$

17) $4\sin^2 60° + 2\cot^2 30°$

18) $\sin 30° + \cos 60° + \tan 45°$

19) $\cos 60° + \tan 30° + \sin 30°$

20) $2\sin 30° + \cos 60° + \sec 60°$

21) $2\sin 60° \cos 30° + \sin 30° \cos 60°$

22) $\tan^2 60° - 2\tan^2 30° - \cot^2 30° + 2\sin^2 45°$

23) $2\cot^2 45° + \cos^2 60° - \sec^2 60° - \sin^2 60°$

24) $3\cos^2 90° + 2\sin^2 90° + 2\tan^2 45°$

Chapter 14: Trigonometric Functions

Function Values from the Calculator

✎ **Find angles to four decimal places.**

1) $\csc 66° =$

2) $\sec 56° =$

3) $\cos 120° =$

4) $\tan 44° =$

5) $\sin 46° =$

6) $\cot 110° =$

7) $\cos 66° =$

8) $\csc 132° =$

9) $\sin 34° =$

10) $\tan 32° =$

11) $\sec 70° =$

12) $\sin 145° =$

13) $\cos 175° =$

14) $\sec 95° =$

15) $\tan 80° =$

16) $\sin 215° =$

17) $\csc 65° =$

18) $\cot 44° =$

19) $\cos 245° =$

20) $\sec 110° =$

21) $\tan 115° =$

22) $\sin 320° =$

Chapter 14: Trigonometric Functions

Reference Angles and the Calculator

✎ **Find the reference angle.**

1) $135° =$

2) $-210° =$

3) $160° =$

4) $-330° =$

5) $280° =$

6) $-120° =$

7) $320° =$

8) $-250° =$

9) $145° =$

10) $-375° =$

11) $390° =$

12) $-255° =$

13) $420° =$

14) $-130° =$

15) $290° =$

16) $-450° =$

17) $\frac{2\pi}{3} =$

18) $\frac{15\pi}{8} =$

19) $\frac{7\pi}{4} =$

20) $-\frac{7\pi}{10} =$

21) $\frac{14\pi}{9} =$

22) $-\frac{16\pi}{9} =$

23) $\frac{5\pi}{6} =$

24) $-\frac{16\pi}{3} =$

Chapter 14: Trigonometric Functions

Coterminal Angles and Reference Angles

✎ **Find a positive and a negative coterminal angle for each given angle.**

1) $75°=$

2) $115°=$

3) $85°=$

4) $170°=$

5) $220°=$

6) $95°=$

7) $120°=$

8) $55°=$

9) $135°=$

10) $140°=$

11) $185°=$

12) $235°=$

13) $95°=$

14) $165°=$

15) $\frac{\pi}{3}=$

16) $\frac{\pi}{4}=$

17) $\frac{5\pi}{4}=$

18) $\frac{2\pi}{5}=$

19) $-\frac{5\pi}{6}=$

20) $-\frac{\pi}{12}=$

21) $\frac{7\pi}{9}=$

22) $\frac{3\pi}{4}=$

Chapter 14: Trigonometric Functions

Angles and Angle Measure

✎ **Convert each degree measure to a radian measure.**

1) $45° =$

2) $90° =$

3) $30° =$

4) $70° =$

5) $50° =$

6) $85° =$

7) $120° =$

8) $110° =$

9) $130° =$

10) $250° =$

11) $210° =$

12) $600° =$

✎ **Convert each radian measure to a degree measure.**

13) $\frac{\pi}{4} =$

14) $\frac{\pi}{5} =$

15) $\frac{\pi}{6} =$

16) $\frac{\pi}{3} =$

17) $\frac{3\pi}{4} =$

18) $\frac{5\pi}{6} =$

19) $-\frac{3\pi}{2} =$

20) $-\frac{7\pi}{3} =$

21) $\frac{11\pi}{5} =$

22) $\frac{15\pi}{12} =$

23) $-\frac{14\pi}{5} =$

24) $\frac{25\pi}{12} =$

Chapter 14: Trigonometric Functions

Evaluating Trigonometric Function

✏ *Find the exact value of each trigonometric function.*

1) $\cos 120° =$

2) $\sin -\frac{\pi}{4} =$

3) $\cos 135° =$

4) $\sec 150° =$

5) $\sin 225° =$

6) $\cot -45° =$

7) $\csc 60° =$

8) $\tan -\frac{\pi}{3} =$

9) $\cos \frac{5\pi}{3} =$

10) $\sec 120° =$

11) $\cos 240° =$

12) $\sin -\frac{11\pi}{6} =$

13) $\cos 255° =$

14) $\sec -\frac{7\pi}{6} =$

15) $\cos \frac{13\pi}{5} =$

16) $\cot 120° =$

17) $\csc -\frac{\pi}{6} =$

18) $\tan 225° =$

19) $\cos -\frac{3\pi}{2} =$

20) $\sec 345° =$

21) $\tan -\frac{13\pi}{8} =$

22) $\cot 240° =$

Chapter 14: Trigonometric Functions

Missing Sides and Angles of a Right Triangle

✎ **Find the missing sides. Round answers to the nearest tenth.**

1) _____

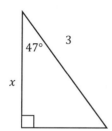

2) _____

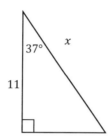

3) _____

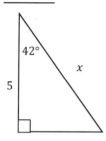

4) _____

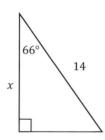

5) _____

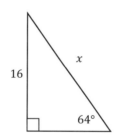

6) _____

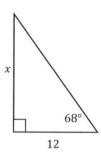

7) _____

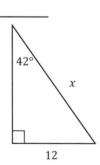

8) _____

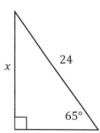

9) _____

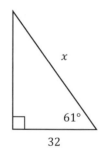

200

www.EffortlessMath.com

Chapter 14: Trigonometric Functions

Arc Length and Sector Area

✍ **Find the length of each arc. Round your answers to the nearest tenth.**
(π = 3.14)

1) $r = 28\ cm,\ \theta = 45°$

2) $r = 15\ ft,\ \theta = 95°$

3) $r = 22\ ft,\ \theta = 60°$

4) $r = 12\ m,\ \theta = 85°$

✍ **Find the area of each sector. Round your answers to the nearest tenth.**
(π = 3.14)

5) _____

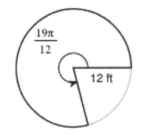

6) _____

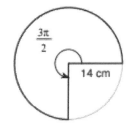

7) _____

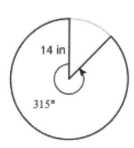

8) _____

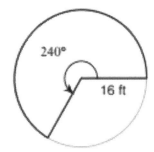

201

Chapter 14: Trigonometric Functions

The Inverse of Trigonometric Functions

✏️ **Find the exact value of each inverse trigonometric ratio in radians.**

1) $\cos^{-1}\left(-\frac{\sqrt{3}}{2}\right) =$

2) $\sin^{-1}\left(-\frac{\sqrt{2}}{2}\right) =$

3) $\cos^{-1}\left(\frac{1}{2}\right) =$

4) $\tan^{-1}\left(\frac{\sqrt{3}}{3}\right) =$

5) $\tan^{-1}(-\sqrt{3}) =$

6) $\sin^{-1}\left(-\frac{\sqrt{3}}{2}\right) =$

7) $\csc^{-1}\left(\frac{2\sqrt{3}}{3}\right) =$

8) $\tan^{-1}(1) =$

9) $\cos^{-1}\left(\frac{\sqrt{2}}{2}\right) =$

10) $\sec^{-1}(1) =$

✏️ **Find the value of each expression.**

11) $\cos^{-1}\left(\cos\frac{2\pi}{3}\right) =$

12) $\tan^{-1}\left(\tan\frac{3\pi}{4}\right) =$

13) $\tan^{-1}(\sec\pi) =$

14) $\sin^{-1}\left(\cos\frac{\pi}{3}\right) =$

15) $\cos^{-1}\left(\cos\frac{13\pi}{6}\right) =$

16) $\tan^{-1}(\sin 90) =$

17) $\cos^{-1}\left(\sin\frac{\pi}{6}\right) =$

18) $\sin^{-1}\left(\sin\frac{11\pi}{6}\right) =$

Chapter 14: Trigonometric Functions

Solving Trigonometric Equations

✏️ **Find the value of each expression.**

1) $\cos x - 2 = -1$

2) $2\sec x + 4 = 0$

3) $\cot x - \sqrt{3} = 0$

4) $\sin x + 2 = 1$

5) $4\cos x + 2\sqrt{2} = 0$

6) $\sin x + \cos x = \sqrt{2}$

7) $4\cos^2 x - 3 = 0$

8) $2\sin^2 x - 1 = 0$

9) $4\sin^2 x + 4 = 5$

10) $4 + \cos x = 4$

11) $\tan^2 x - 3 = 0$

12) $3\sin x + 2\sin^2 x = -1$

13) $-\cos x + \sin x = 1$

14) $\cos^2 x = 2 + 2\sin x$

15) $\tan x \sin x - 4\tan x = -3\tan x$

16) $3\csc x = -2 + 2\csc x$

17) $3 + \csc x = 1$

18) $\frac{\sqrt{3}}{3} = \cot\left(x + \frac{\pi}{6}\right)$

19) $2 = \csc\left(x + \frac{2\pi}{3}\right)$

20) $\cos^2 x = 1 - 2\sin$

Chapter 14: Trigonometric Functions

Answers – Chapter 14

Trig Ratios of General Angles

1) $-\frac{\sqrt{3}}{2}$
2) $\frac{1}{2}$
3) $\frac{\sqrt{2}}{2}$
4) -1
5) $\frac{\sqrt{3}}{2}$
6) $\frac{1}{2}$
7) Undefined
8) 0
9) Undefined
10) $-\sqrt{3}$
11) -2
12) Undefined
13) 0
14) Undefined
15) 0
16) 2
17) $\frac{2\sqrt{3}}{3}$
18) 1
19) -1
20) Undefined
21) $\frac{\sqrt{3}}{2}$
22) $-\frac{\sqrt{3}}{3}$
23) $-\sqrt{2}$
24) 2
25) 2
26) $\frac{\sqrt{3}}{3}$
27) $-\sqrt{2}$
28) $-\frac{\sqrt{3}}{3}$

Trigonometric Ratios

1) $\frac{18}{19}$
2) $\frac{18}{27}$
3) $\frac{22}{29}$
4) $\frac{20}{29}$
5) $\frac{3}{4}$
6) $\frac{3}{5}$
7) $\frac{1}{2}$
8) $\sqrt{2}$
9) 0.6157
10) 0.9135
11) 0.6293
12) 3.8637

Right-Triangle Trigonometry

1) 15.2
2) 8.1
3) 11.2
4) 12.3
5) 6.5
6) 30.1

Effortless Math Education

Chapter 14: Trigonometric Functions

Angles of Rotation

1) 50°
2) 30°
3) 65°
4) 40°
5) 65°
6) 90°
7) 80°
8) 330°
9) 18°
10) 245°
11) 45°
12) 145°
13) 50°
14) 155°
15) 30°
16) $\frac{7\pi}{4}$
17) $\frac{\pi}{3}$
18) $\frac{3\pi}{8}$
19) $\frac{3\pi}{4}$
20) $\frac{2\pi}{5}$
21) $\frac{3\pi}{2}$
22) $\frac{2\pi}{3}$
23) $\frac{7\pi}{6}$

The Unit Circle, Sine, and Cosine

1) $\sin\theta = y$ −coordinate of $P = \frac{1}{2}$

   $\cos\theta = x$ −coordinate of $P = -\frac{\sqrt{3}}{2}$

2) $\sin\theta = y$-coordinate of $P = -\frac{\sqrt{2}}{2}$

   $\cos\theta = x$ −coordinate of $P = \frac{\sqrt{2}}{2}$

3) $\sin 315° = -\frac{\sqrt{2}}{2}, \cos 315° = \frac{\sqrt{2}}{2}, \tan 315° = -1$

4) $\sin 420° = \frac{\sqrt{3}}{2}, \cos 420° = \frac{1}{2}, \tan 420° = \sqrt{3}$

5) $\sin\frac{7\pi}{3} = \frac{\sqrt{3}}{2}, \cos\frac{7\pi}{3} = \frac{1}{2}, \tan\frac{7\pi}{3} = \sqrt{3}$

6) $\sin\frac{3\pi}{4} = \frac{\sqrt{2}}{2}, \cos\frac{3\pi}{4} = -\frac{\sqrt{2}}{2}, \tan\frac{3\pi}{4} = -1$

Chapter 14: Trigonometric Functions

The Reciprocal Trigonometric Functions

1) $\frac{24}{7}$

2) $\frac{17\sqrt{2}}{23}$

3) $\frac{7\sqrt{5}}{15}$

4) $\frac{17}{15}$

5) $\frac{\sqrt{29}}{5}$

6) $\frac{40}{9}$

7) $\sqrt{5}$

8) $\frac{4}{3}$

9) $\frac{5}{3}$

10) $\frac{7}{5}$

11) $\frac{\sqrt{7}}{7}$

12) $\frac{84}{85}$

13) $\sqrt{5}$

14) $\frac{3}{4}$

15) $\frac{5}{3}$

16) $\frac{13}{5}$

Function Values of Special Angles

1) $\frac{\sqrt{6}}{4}$

2) $\frac{\sqrt{3}+1}{2}$

3) $\frac{1}{2}$

4) $\frac{5\sqrt{3}}{6}$

5) $\frac{1}{2}$

6) $\sqrt{3}$

7) $\frac{1}{2}$

8) $\frac{1}{2}$

9) 6

10) 0

11) $\frac{3}{4}$

12) 4

13) $\frac{\sqrt{6}}{8}$

14) $\frac{3}{4}$

15) 8

16) $\frac{9}{2}$

17) 9

18) 2

19) $1 + \frac{\sqrt{3}}{3}$

20) $\frac{7}{2}$

21) $\frac{7}{4}$

22) $\frac{1}{3}$

23) $-\frac{5}{2}$

24) 4

Chapter 14: Trigonometric Functions

Function Values from the Calculator

1) 1.0946
2) 1.7882
3) −0.5
4) 0.9656
5) 0.7193
6) −0.3639
7) 0.4067
8) 1.3456
9) 0.5591
10) 0.6248
11) 2.9238
12) 0.5735
13) −0.9961
14) −11.4737
15) 5.6712
16) −0.5735
17) 1.1033
18) 1.0355
19) −0.4226
20) −2.9238
21) −2.1445
22) −0.6427

Reference Angles and the Calculator

1) 45°
2) 30°
3) 20°
4) 30°
5) 80°
6) 60°
7) 40°
8) 70°
9) 35°
10) 15°
11) 30°
12) 75°
13) 60°
14) 50°
15) 70°
16) 90°
17) $\frac{\pi}{3}$
18) $\frac{\pi}{8}$
19) $\frac{\pi}{4}$
20) $\frac{3\pi}{10}$
21) $\frac{4\pi}{9}$
22) $\frac{2\pi}{9}$
23) $\frac{\pi}{6}$
24) $\frac{\pi}{3}$

Chapter 14: Trigonometric Functions

Coterminal Angles and Reference Angles

1) −285° and a 435°
2) −245° and a 475°
3) −275° and a 445°
4) −190° and a 530°
5) −140° and a 580°
6) −265° and a 455°
7) −240° and a 480°
8) −305° and a 415°
9) −225° and a 495°
10) −220° and a 500°
11) −175° and a 545°
12) −125° and a 595°
13) −265° and a 455°
14) −195° and a 525°
15) $-\frac{5\pi}{3}$ and a $\frac{7\pi}{3}$
16) $-\frac{7\pi}{4}$ and a $\frac{9\pi}{4}$
17) $-\frac{3\pi}{4}$ and a $\frac{13\pi}{4}$
18) $-\frac{8\pi}{5}$ and a $\frac{12\pi}{5}$
19) $-\frac{17\pi}{6}$ and a $\frac{7\pi}{6}$
20) $-\frac{25\pi}{12}$ and a $\frac{23\pi}{12}$
21) $-\frac{11\pi}{9}$ and a $\frac{25\pi}{9}$
22) $-\frac{5\pi}{4}$ and a $\frac{11\pi}{4}$

Angles and Angle Measure

1) $\frac{\pi}{4}$
2) $\frac{\pi}{2}$
3) $\frac{\pi}{6}$
4) $\frac{7\pi}{18}$
5) $\frac{5\pi}{18}$
6) $\frac{17\pi}{36}$
7) $\frac{2\pi}{3}$
8) $\frac{11\pi}{18}$
9) $\frac{13\pi}{18}$
10) $\frac{25\pi}{18}$
11) $\frac{7\pi}{6}$
12) $\frac{10\pi}{3}$
13) 45°
14) 36°
15) 30°
16) 60°
17) 135°
18) 150°
19) −270°
20) −420°
21) 396°
22) 225°
23) −504°
24) 375°

Effortless Math Education

Chapter 14: Trigonometric Functions

Evaluating Trigonometric Function

1) $-\frac{1}{2}$

2) $-\frac{\sqrt{2}}{2}$

3) $-\frac{\sqrt{2}}{2}$

4) $-\frac{2\sqrt{3}}{3}$

5) $-\frac{\sqrt{2}}{2}$

6) -1

7) $\frac{2\sqrt{3}}{3}$

8) $-\sqrt{3}$

9) $\frac{1}{2}$

10) -2

11) $-\frac{1}{2}$

12) $\frac{1}{2}$

13) $\frac{\sqrt{2}-\sqrt{6}}{4}$

14) $-\frac{2\sqrt{3}}{3}$

15) $-\frac{\sqrt{2}\sqrt{3-\sqrt{5}}}{4}$

16) $-\frac{\sqrt{3}}{3}$

17) -2

18) 1

19) 0

20) $-\sqrt{2}+\sqrt{6}$

21) $\sqrt{2}+1$

22) $\frac{\sqrt{3}}{3}$

Missing Sides and Angles of a Right Triangle

1) 2

2) 13.8

3) 6.7

4) 5.7

5) 17.8

6) 29.7

7) 17.9

8) 21.8

9) 66

Arc Length and Sector Area

1) 22 cm

2) 24.9 ft

3) 23 ft

4) 17.8 m

5) 358 ft^2

6) 461.6 cm^2

7) 538.5 in^2

8) 535.9 ft^2

Chapter 14: Trigonometric Functions

The Inverse of Trigonometric Functions

1) $\dfrac{5\pi}{6}$

2) $-\dfrac{\pi}{4}$

3) $\dfrac{\pi}{3}$

4) $\dfrac{\pi}{6}$

5) $-\dfrac{\pi}{3}$

6) $-\dfrac{\pi}{3}$

7) $\dfrac{\pi}{3}$

8) $\dfrac{\pi}{4}$

9) $\dfrac{\pi}{4}$

10) 0

11) $\dfrac{2\pi}{3}$

12) $-\dfrac{\pi}{4}$

13) $-\dfrac{\pi}{4}$

14) $\dfrac{\pi}{6}$

15) $\dfrac{\pi}{6}$

16) $\dfrac{\pi}{4}$

17) $\dfrac{\pi}{3}$

18) $-\dfrac{\pi}{6}$

Solving Trigonometric Equations

1) 2π

2) $\dfrac{2\pi}{3}, \dfrac{4\pi}{3}$

3) $\dfrac{\pi}{6}$

4) $\dfrac{3\pi}{2}$

5) $\dfrac{3\pi}{4}, \dfrac{5\pi}{4}$

6) $\dfrac{\pi}{4}$

7) $\dfrac{\pi}{6}, \dfrac{11\pi}{6}, \dfrac{5\pi}{6}, \dfrac{7\pi}{6}$

8) $\dfrac{\pi}{4}, \dfrac{3\pi}{4}, \dfrac{5\pi}{4}, \dfrac{7\pi}{4}$

9) $\dfrac{\pi}{6}, \dfrac{5\pi}{6}, \dfrac{7\pi}{6}, \dfrac{11\pi}{6}$

10) $\dfrac{\pi}{2}, \dfrac{3\pi}{2}$

11) $\dfrac{\pi}{3}, \dfrac{2\pi}{3}$

12) $\dfrac{7\pi}{6}, \dfrac{11\pi}{6}, \dfrac{3\pi}{2}$

13) $\dfrac{\pi}{2}, \pi$

14) $\dfrac{3\pi}{2}$

15) $0, \pi$

16) $\dfrac{7\pi}{6}, \dfrac{11\pi}{6}$

17) $\dfrac{7\pi}{6}, \dfrac{11\pi}{6}$

18) $\dfrac{\pi}{6}$

19) $\dfrac{\pi}{6}, -\dfrac{\pi}{2}$

20) $2\pi, \pi$

Chapter 15: More Topics Trigonometric Functions

Math Topics that you'll learn in this Chapter:

- ✓ Pythagorean Identities
- ✓ Domain and Range of Trigonometric Functions
- ✓ Cofunctions
- ✓ Law of Sines
- ✓ Law of Cosines
- ✓ Sum and Difference Identities
- ✓ Double-Angle and Half-Angle Identities
- ✓ Using the Law of Cosines to Find Angle Measure

Chapter 15: More Topics Trigonometric Functions

Pythagorean Identities

✎ *Simplify each trigonometric expression using Pythagorean identities.*

1) $\sin x \tan x + \cos x =$

2) $(\sin x + \cos x)^2 =$

3) $(1 + \cot^2 x) \sin^2 x =$

4) $\csc^2 x - \cot^2 x =$

5) $2 \sin^2 x + \cos^2 x =$

6) $\sin^2 x - \sin^2 x \cos^2 x =$

7) $\tan x (\csc x - \sin x) =$

8) $\cot x \sec x \sin x =$

9) $\cos x (\csc x - \sec x) - \cot x =$

10) $\dfrac{\sin^2 x}{1 - \cos x} =$

11) $\sin^2 x + 2 \cos^2 x - 1 =$

12) $\dfrac{-1 + \sec^2 x}{\sec^2 x} =$

13) $2 \sec^2 x \sin^2 x =$

14) $\cos x (\sec x - \cos x) =$

15) $\dfrac{\sec^2 x - 1}{\tan x} =$

16) $\sec x \cot x - \cot x \cos x =$

17) $\dfrac{\sin^3 x + \cos^3 x}{1 - \sin x \cos x} =$

18) $\dfrac{\cot x \sec^2 x - \cot x}{\sin x \tan x + \cos x} =$

19) $\csc^2 x - \cot^2 x + \tan^2 x =$

20) $\dfrac{(\sin^2 x + \cos^2 x)(\sec^2 x - \tan^2 x)}{\cot x} =$

Chapter 15: More Topics Trigonometric Functions

Domain and Range of Trigonometric Functions

✏️ *Find the domain and range of Functions.*

1) $y = \cos x - 4$

   Domain: _____

   Range: _____

2) $y = \sin x - 3$

   Domain: _____

   Range: _____

3) $y = \dfrac{1}{2 - \sin 2x}$

   Domain: _____

   Range: _____

4) $y = 7\sin x + 4$

   Domain: _____

   Range: _____

5) $y = 3 \tan x$

   Domain: _____

   Range: _____

6) $y = \sec^{-1} x$

   Domain: _____

   Range: _____

7) $y = \tan^{-1} x$

   Domain: _____

   Range: _____

8) $y = \csc^{-1} x$

   Domain: _____

   Range: _____

9) $y = \dfrac{1}{\cos x - 4}$

   Domain: _____

   Range: _____

10) $y = \cot^{-1} x$

    Domain: _____

    Range: _____

11) $y = 3\cos x + 6$

    Domain: _____

    Range: _____

12) $y = -6 \sin x - 8$

    Domain: _____

    Range: _____

Chapter 15: More Topics Trigonometric Functions

Cofunctions

✎ **Solve using cofunction identities.**

1) $\sin x = \cos 35°$

   $x = $ _____

2) $\cot x = \tan 80°$

   $x = $ _____

3) $\csc 68° = \sec x$

   $x = $ _____

4) $\sec(3x) = \csc(x + 22°)$

   $x = $ _____

5) $\sin 42° = \cos x$

   $x = $ _____

6) $\sec x = \csc 55°$

   $x = $ _____

7) $\tan x = \cot 25°$

   $x = $ _____

8) $\csc x = \sec 33°$

   $x = $ _____

9) $\tan 4x = \cot 26°$

   $x = $ _____

10) $\csc(x + 22°) = \sec(25°)$

    $x = $ _____

11) $\cot\left(\frac{\pi}{8}\right) = \tan(x)$

    $x = $ _____

12) $\csc\left(\frac{\pi}{2}\right) = \sec(x)$

    $x = $ _____

13) $\sin\left(\frac{9\pi}{20}\right) = \cos(x)$

    $x = $ _____

14) $\cot\left(\frac{3\pi}{20}\right) = \tan(x)$

    $x = $ _____

15) $\cos\left(\frac{\pi}{3}\right) = \sin(x)$

    $x = $ _____

Chapter 15: More Topics Trigonometric Functions
Law of Sines

✎ *Find each measurement indicated. Round your answers to the nearest tenth.*

1) _____

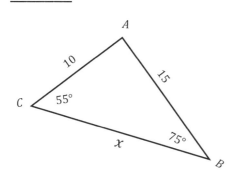

2) _____

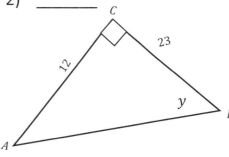

3) _____

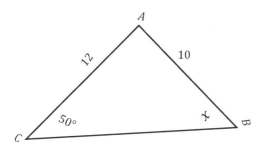

4) _____

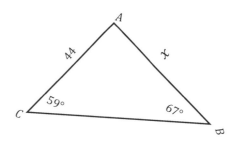

5) In $\triangle ABC$, $m\angle C = 14°$, $m\angle A = 24°$, $c = 9\ cm$ _____

6) In $\triangle ABC$, $m\angle B = 56.3°$, $m\angle C = 37.6°$, $b = 15\ cm$ _____

7) In $\triangle ABC$, $m\angle C = 75°$ $a = 14\ cm$, $c = 19\ cm$ _____

8) In $\triangle ABC$, $m\angle A = 22°$, $m\angle C = 13°$, $a = 9\ cm$ _____

Chapter 15: More Topics Trigonometric Functions
Law of Cosines

✎ *Find each measurement indicated. Round your answers to the nearest tenth.*

1) _____

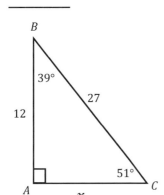

2) _____

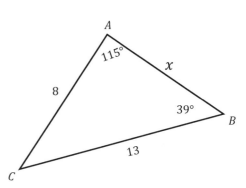

3) _____

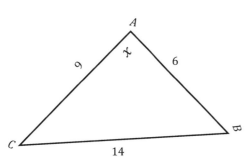

4) _____

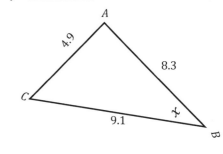

5) In $\triangle ABC, a = 15\ cm, b = 10\ cm, c = 7\ cm$ _____

6) In $\triangle ABC, m\angle C = 125°, b = 8, a = 24$ _____

7) In $\triangle ABC, a = 6, b = 14, c = 12$ _____

8) In $\triangle ABC, m\angle A = 107°, b = 14, c = 23$ _____

9) In $\triangle ABC, a = 28, b = 17, c = 15$ _____

Chapter 15: More Topics Trigonometric Functions

Sum and Difference Identities

✍ *Find the value of angles.*

1) $\cos 75° =$

2) $\sin 30° =$

3) $\sin (30° + 45°) =$

4) $\cos (-15°) =$

5) $\tan (75°) =$

6) $\sin (-75°) =$

7) $\sin (-165°) =$

8) $\csc(120°) =$

9) $\tan(345°) =$

10) $\cos (375°) =$

11) $\tan(105°) =$

12) $\sin (-15°) =$

13) $\tan(15°) =$

14) $\sin (-105°) =$

15) $\csc(915°) =$

16) $\tan(-15°) =$

17) $\cos(195°) =$

18) $\cot \left(\frac{2\pi}{4} + \frac{5\pi}{4} \right) =$

19) $\tan \left(-\frac{7\pi}{12} \right) =$

20) $\cos \left(\frac{17\pi}{6} \right) =$

21) $\sin \left(\frac{11\pi}{12} \right) =$

22) $\sec \left(\frac{\pi}{12} \right) =$

23) $\sin \left(\frac{15\pi}{4} \right) =$

24) $\tan \left(\frac{13\pi}{12} \right) =$

Chapter 15: More Topics Trigonometric Functions

Double-Angle and Half-Angle Identities

✏️ **Solve.**

1) If $sin(\theta) = \frac{2}{5}$ and θ is in the second quadrant, find exact values for $cos(2\theta)$.

2) If $cos(\theta) = -\frac{4}{5}$ and θ is in the second quadrant, find exact values for $sin(2\theta)$.

3) If $cot(\theta) = -\frac{4}{3}$ and θ is in the second quadrant, find exact values for $sin(2\theta)$.

4) If $sin(\theta) = \frac{9}{22}$ and θ is in the second quadrant, find exact values for $cos(2\theta)$.

5) If $cos(\theta) = -\frac{3}{4}$ and θ is in the second quadrant, find exact values for $sin(2\theta)$.

6) If $sin(\theta) = \frac{7}{25}$ and θ is in the second quadrant, find exact values for $cos(\frac{\theta}{2})$.

✏️ **Use a half-angle identity to find the exact value of each expression.**

7) $cos\ 30° =$

8) $cos\ 105° =$

9) $tan\left(\frac{7\pi}{8}\right) =$

10) $sin\ 165° =$

11) $cos\left(\frac{3\pi}{8}\right) =$

12) $sin\left(-\frac{5\pi}{12}\right) =$

13) $sin\ 15° =$

14) $sec\left(\frac{9\pi}{8}\right) =$

Chapter 15: More Topics Trigonometric Functions

Using the Law of Cosines to Find Angle Measure

✎ *Calculate the angles labeled θ in each triangle.*

1) _____

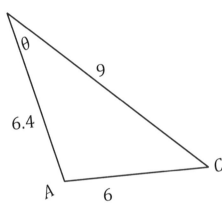

2) _____

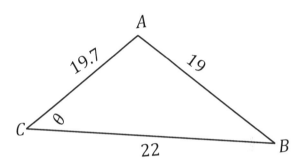

3) _____

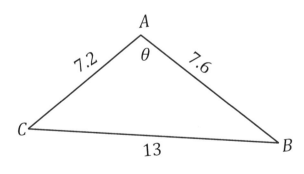

4) _____

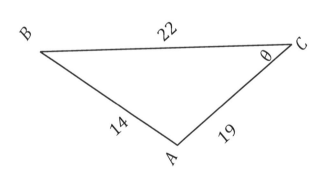

Chapter 15: More Topics Trigonometric Functions

Answers – Chapter 15

Pythagorean Identities

1) $\sec x$
2) $1 + \sin(2x)$
3) 1
4) 1
5) $1 + \sin^2 x$
6) $\sin^4 x$
7) $\cos x$
8) 1
9) -1
10) $1 + \cos x$
11) $\cos^2 x$
12) $\sin^2 x$
13) $2\tan^2 x$
14) $\sin^2 x$
15) $\tan x$
16) $\sin x$
17) $\sin x + \cos x$
18) $\sin x$
19) $\sec^2 x$
20) $\tan x$

Domain and Range of Trigonometric Functions

1) Domain: $(-\infty, +\infty)$
   Range: $[-5, -3]$
2) Domain: $(-\infty, +\infty)$
   Range: $[-4, -2]$
3) Domain: $(-\infty, \infty)$
   Range: $\left[\frac{1}{3}, 1\right]$
4) Domain: $(-\infty, +\infty)$
   Range: $[-3, 11]$
5) Domain: $[\pi n, \frac{\pi}{2} + \pi n) \cup (\frac{\pi}{2} + \pi n, \pi + \pi n)$
   Range $(-\infty, +\infty)$
6) Domain: $(-\infty, -1] \cup [1, \infty)$
   Range: $[0, \frac{\pi}{2}) \cup (\frac{\pi}{2}, \pi]$
7) Domain: $(-\infty, +\infty)$
   Range: $\left(-\frac{\pi}{2}, \frac{\pi}{2}\right)$
8) Domain: $(-\infty, -1] \cup [1, \infty)$
   Range: $[-\frac{\pi}{2}, 0) \cup (0, \frac{\pi}{2}]$
9) Domain $(-\infty, +\infty)$
   Range: $\left[-\frac{1}{3}, -\frac{1}{5}\right]$
10) Domain: $(-\infty, +\infty)$
    Range: $(0, \pi)$
11) Domain: $(-\infty, +\infty)$
    Range: $[3, 9]$
12) Domain: $(-\infty, +\infty)$
    Range: $[-14, -2]$

Chapter 15: More Topics Trigonometric Functions

Cofunctions

1) 55°
2) 10°
3) 22°
4) 17°
5) 48°
6) 35°
7) 65°
8) 57°
9) 16°
10) 43°
11) $\frac{3\pi}{8}$
12) 0
13) $\frac{\pi}{20}$
14) $\frac{7\pi}{20}$
15) $\frac{\pi}{6}$

Law of Sines

1) $x = 7.9$
2) $y = 27.6°$
3) $66.8°$
4) 41
5) $m\angle B = 142°, a = 15.1, b = 22.9$
6) $m\angle A = 86.1°, a = 18\ cm, c = 11\ cm$
7) $m\angle A = 45.4°, m\angle B = 59.6°, b = 17\ cm$
8) $m\angle B = 145°, b = 13.8, c = 5.4$

Law of Cosines

1) $x = 19.2$
2) $x = 6.8$
3) $x = 137.1°$
4) $x = 32.3°$
5) $m\angle A = 122.9°, m\angle B = 34°, m\angle C = 23.1°$
6) $m\angle A = 42.1°, m\angle B = 12.9°, c = 29.3$
7) $m\angle A = 25.2°, m\angle B = 96.4°, m\angle C = 58.4°$
8) $m\angle B = 26.3°, m\angle C = 46.7°, a = 30.2$
9) $m\angle A = 121.9°, m\angle B = 31°, m\angle C = 27°$

Chapter 15: More Topics Trigonometric Functions

Sum and Difference Identities

1) $\frac{\sqrt{6}-\sqrt{2}}{4}$

2) $\frac{1}{2}$

3) $\frac{\sqrt{6}+\sqrt{2}}{4}$

4) $\frac{\sqrt{6}+\sqrt{2}}{4}$

5) $2+\sqrt{3}$

6) $\frac{-\sqrt{6}-\sqrt{2}}{4}$

7) $\frac{\sqrt{2}-\sqrt{6}}{4}$

8) $\frac{2\sqrt{3}}{3}$

9) $\sqrt{3}-2$

10) $\frac{\sqrt{2}+\sqrt{6}}{4}$

11) $-2-\sqrt{3}$

12) $\frac{\sqrt{2}-\sqrt{6}}{4}$

13) $2-\sqrt{3}$

14) $\frac{-\sqrt{6}-\sqrt{2}}{4}$

15) $-\sqrt{6}-\sqrt{2}$

16) $-2+\sqrt{3}$

17) $\frac{-\sqrt{6}-\sqrt{2}}{4}$

18) -1

19) $2+\sqrt{3}$

20) $\frac{-\sqrt{3}}{2}$

21) $\frac{\sqrt{6}-\sqrt{2}}{4}$

22) $\sqrt{6}-\sqrt{2}$

23) $\frac{-\sqrt{2}}{2}$

24) $2-\sqrt{3}$

Double-Angle and Half-Angle Identities

1) $\frac{17}{25}$

2) $-\frac{24}{25}$

3) $-\frac{24}{25}$

4) $\frac{161}{242}$

5) $-\frac{3\sqrt{7}}{8}$

6) $\frac{\sqrt{2}}{10}$

7) $\frac{\sqrt{3}}{2}$

8) $\frac{\sqrt{2}-\sqrt{6}}{4}$

9) $-\sqrt{3-2\sqrt{2}}$

10) $\frac{\sqrt{6}-\sqrt{2}}{4}$

11) $\frac{\sqrt{2-\sqrt{2}}}{2}$

12) $\frac{-\sqrt{6}-\sqrt{2}}{4}$

13) $\frac{\sqrt{6}-\sqrt{2}}{4}$

14) $-2\sqrt{2+\sqrt{2}}+\sqrt{2}\sqrt{2+\sqrt{2}}$

Using the Law of Cosines to Find Angle Measure

1) 41.7°

2) 53.9°

3) 122.9°

4) 39.1°

Chapter 16: Graphs of Trigonometric Functions

Math Topics that you'll learn in this Chapter:

- ✓ Graph of the Sine Function
- ✓ Graph of the Cosine Function
- ✓ Amplitude, Period, and Phase Shift
- ✓ Writing the Equation of a Sine Graph
- ✓ Writing the Equation of a Cosine Graph
- ✓ Graph of the Tangent Function
- ✓ Graph of the Cosecant Function
- ✓ Graph of the Secant Function
- ✓ Graph of the Cotangent Function
- ✓ Graph of Inverse of the Sine Function
- ✓ Graph of Inverse of the Cosine Function
- ✓ Graph of Inverse of the Tangent Function
- ✓ Sketching Trigonometric Graphs

Chapter 16: Graphs of Trigonometric Functions

Graph of the Sine Function

✎ **Graph the following functions.**

1) $y = 2 \sin 2x$

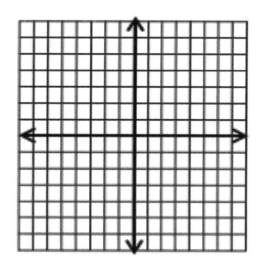

2) $y = -3 \sin x$

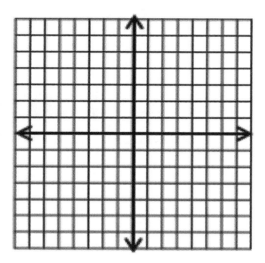

3) $y = -2 \sin^2 x$

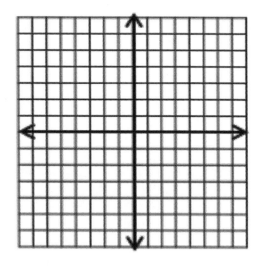

4) $y = 4 \sin 3x$

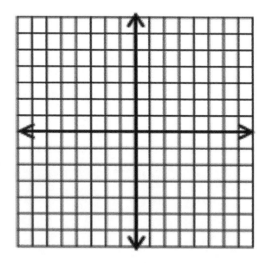

Chapter 16: Graphs of Trigonometric Functions

Graph of the Cosine Function

✎ *Graph the following functions.*

1) $y = 2 \cos x$

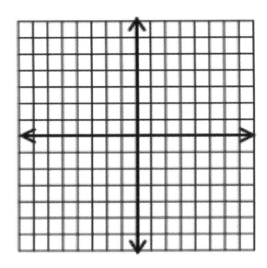

2) $y = 3 \cos 2x - 2$

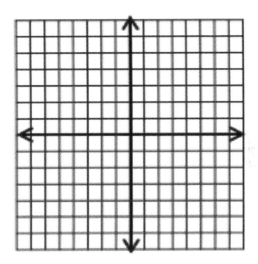

3) $y = \cos^2 2x$

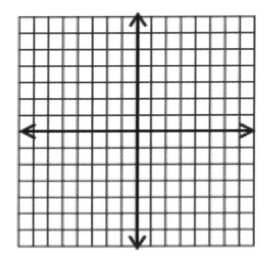

4) $y = -2 \cos 3x$

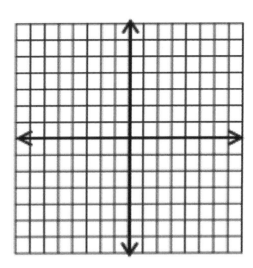

Chapter 16: Graphs of Trigonometric Functions

Amplitude, Period, and Phase Shift

✎ **Determine the amplitude, the period, and the phase shift of:**

1) $y = \sin\left(\dfrac{x}{3}\right)$

   Amplitude: _____
   Period: _____
   Phase shift: _____

2) $y = 4 - 2\sin\left(\dfrac{2x}{3}\right)$

   Amplitude: _____
   Period: _____
   Phase shift: _____

3) $y = 4\sin\left(2x - \dfrac{\pi}{2}\right) - 5$

   Amplitude: _____
   Period: _____
   Phase shift: _____

4) $y = 3\sin(6x - \pi) - 3$

   Amplitude: _____
   Period: _____
   Phase shift: _____

5) $y = \sin\left(x - \dfrac{\pi}{4}\right) - 2$

   Amplitude: _____
   Period: _____
   Phase shift: _____

6) $y = 3\cos\left(2x - \dfrac{\pi}{6}\right)$

   Amplitude: _____
   Period: _____
   Phase shift: _____

7) $y = -2\sin\left(\dfrac{2}{3}x - \dfrac{\pi}{3}\right)$

   Amplitude: _____
   Period: _____
   Phase shift: _____

8) $y = \dfrac{2}{3}\cos\left(2x + \dfrac{\pi}{3}\right) - 2$

   Amplitude: _____
   Period: _____
   Phase shift: _____

9) $y = 3\cos\left(2x + \dfrac{\pi}{2}\right) - 6$

   Amplitude: _____
   Period: _____
   Phase shift: _____

10) $y = -\dfrac{2}{5}\sin\left(3x - \dfrac{\pi}{4}\right) - 4$

    Amplitude: _____
    Period: _____
    Phase shift: _____

www.EffortlessMath.com

Chapter 16: Graphs of Trigonometric Functions

Writing the Equation of a Sine Graph

✎ *Determine the equation of the graph below.*

1) _____

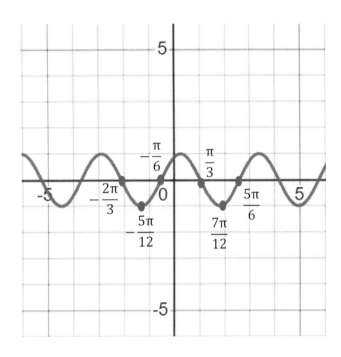

2) _____

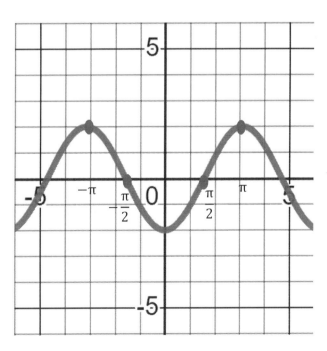

Chapter 16: Graphs of Trigonometric Functions

Writing the Equation of a Cosine Graph

✎ *Determine the equation of the graph below.*

1) _____

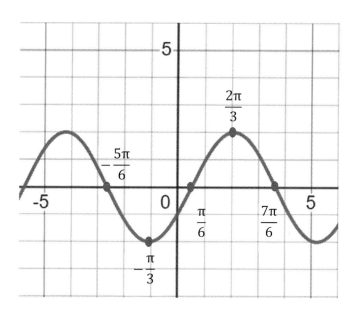

2) _____

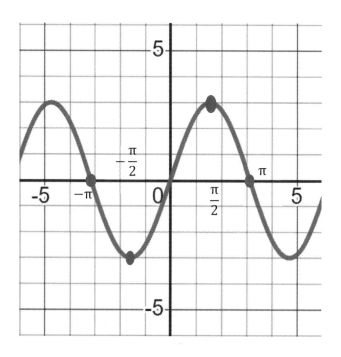

Chapter 16: Graphs of Trigonometric Functions

Graph of the Tangent Function

✍ *Draw the graph of equations.*

1) $y = tan\left(x - \frac{\pi}{2}\right)$

2) $y = tan\left(x + \frac{\pi}{4}\right)$

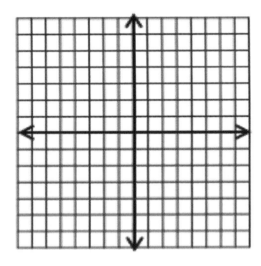
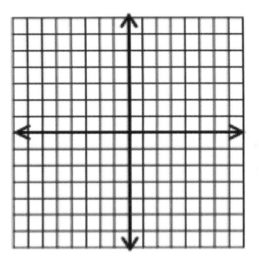

3) $y = tan\left(2x + \frac{\pi}{2}\right)$

4) $y = tan\left(\frac{x}{2} - \frac{3\pi}{4}\right) + 1$

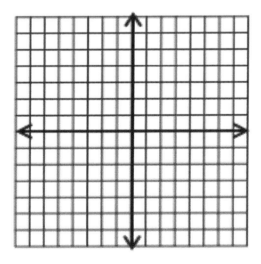
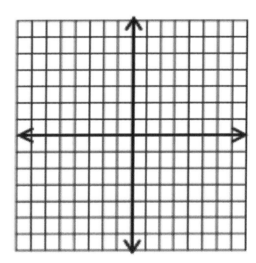

Chapter 16: Graphs of Trigonometric Functions

Graph of the Cosecant Function

✏️ *Draw the graph of equations.*

1) $y = -3\csc(4x)$

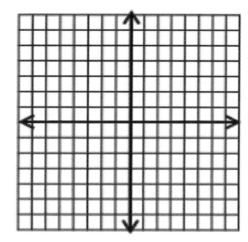

2) $y = 2\csc(3x)$

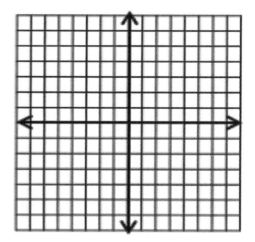

3) $y = \csc\left(x + \frac{\pi}{4}\right)$

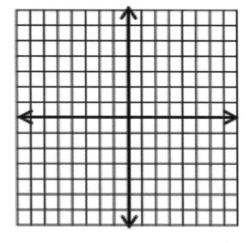

4) $y = 1 + 2\csc(x)$

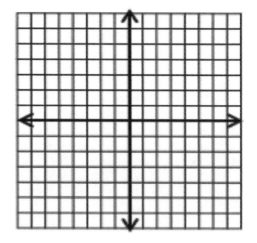

Chapter 16: Graphs of Trigonometric Functions

Graph of the Secant Function

✎ *Draw the graph of equations.*

1) $y = \sec\left(x - \frac{\pi}{2}\right)$

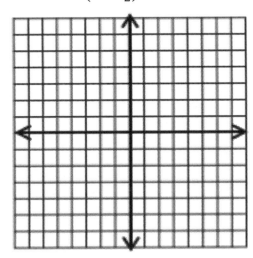

2) $y = \sec\left(x + \frac{\pi}{4}\right)$

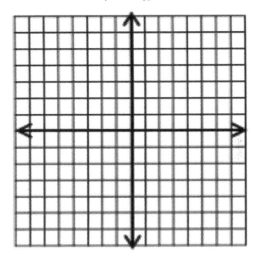

3) $y = \sec\left(2x + \frac{\pi}{2}\right)$

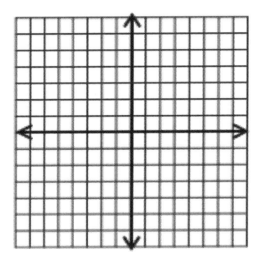

4) $y = -\sec\left(2x - \frac{\pi}{3}\right) + 2$

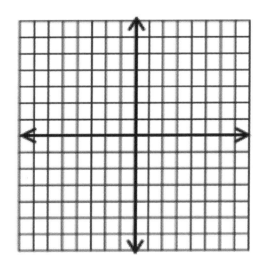

Chapter 16: Graphs of Trigonometric Functions

Graph of the Cotangent Function

✏️ *Draw the graph of equations.*

1) $y = \cot\left(x + \frac{\pi}{2}\right)$

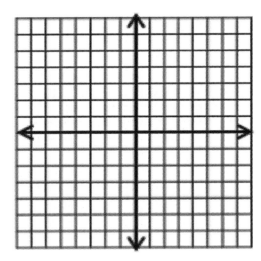

2) $y = \cot\left(2x - \frac{\pi}{4}\right)$

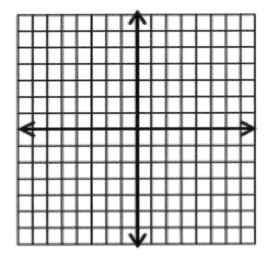

3) $y = 2\cot\left(x - \frac{\pi}{2}\right)$

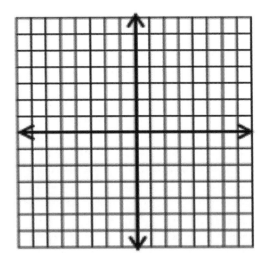

4) $y = -\cot\left(2x + \frac{2\pi}{3}\right) + 1$

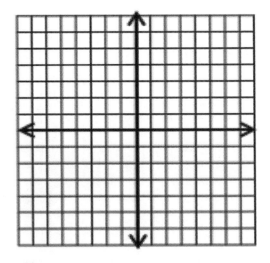

Chapter 16: Graphs of Trigonometric Functions

Graph of Inverse of the Sine Function

✎ *Draw the graph of equations.*

1) $y = \sin^{-1}(x + 1)$

2) $y = 3\sin^{-1}(x + 2)$

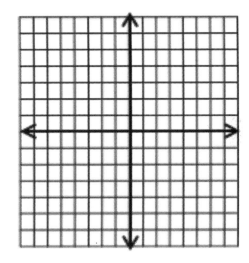

3) $y = \sin^{-1}\left(x - \dfrac{\pi}{3}\right)$

4) $y = 3\sin^{-1}\left(x + \dfrac{\pi}{2}\right)$

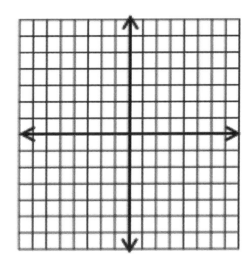
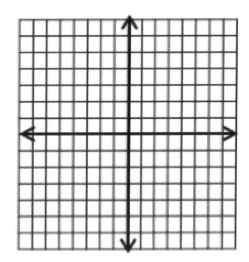

Chapter 16: Graphs of Trigonometric Functions

Graph of Inverse of the Cosine Function

✎ *Draw the graph of equations.*

1) $y = \cos^{-1}(x - 1)$

2) $y = 2\cos^{-1}(x + 1)$

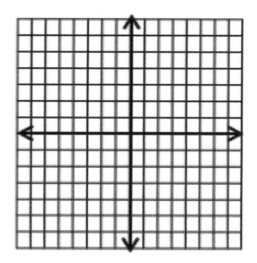

3) $y = -\cos^{-1}\left(x + \frac{\pi}{2}\right)$

4) $y = 3\cos^{-1}\left(x - \frac{\pi}{4}\right)$

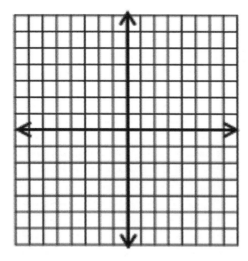
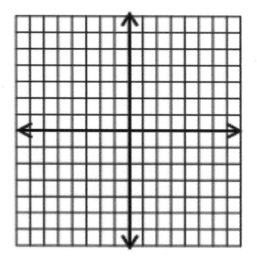

Chapter 16: Graphs of Trigonometric Functions

Graph of Inverse of the Tangent Function

✍ *Draw the graph of equations.*

1) $y = \tan^{-1}(x + 2)$

2) $y = -2\tan^{-1}(x - 1)$

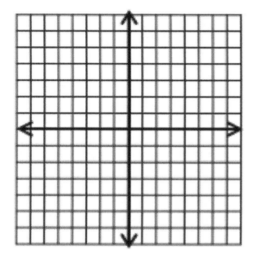
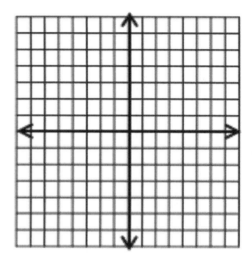

3) $y = 2\tan^{-1}\left(x - \frac{2\pi}{3}\right)$

4) $y = \tan^{-1}\left(x + \frac{\pi}{4}\right) + 2$

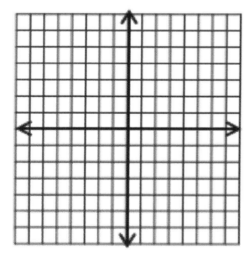
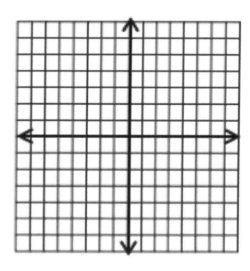

Chapter 16: Graphs of Trigonometric Functions

Sketching Trigonometric Graphs

✏️ *Draw two cycles of the graph.*

1) $y = \cos\left(x - \frac{\pi}{2}\right)$

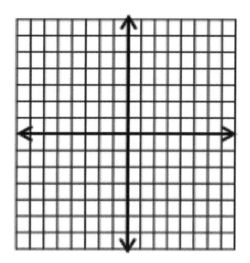

2) $y = \sin\left(x - \frac{\pi}{4}\right)$

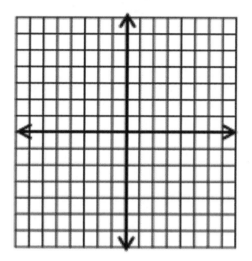

3) $y = 2\sin\left(x + \frac{\pi}{3}\right)$

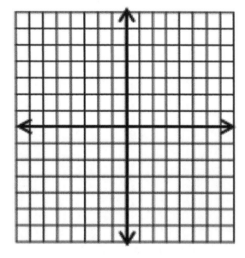

4) $y = -3\cos\left(x + \frac{\pi}{4}\right)$

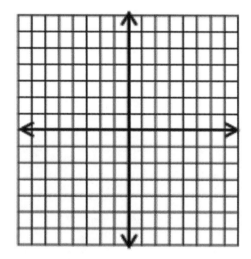

Chapter 16: Graphs of Trigonometric Functions

Answers – Chapter 16

Graph of the Sine Function

1)
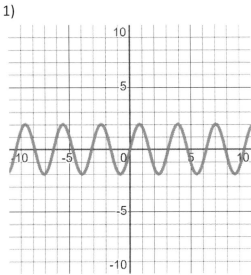

2)
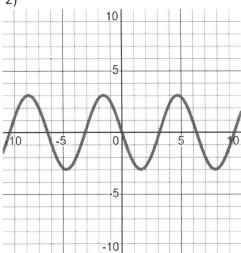

3)
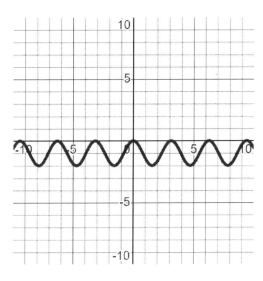

4)
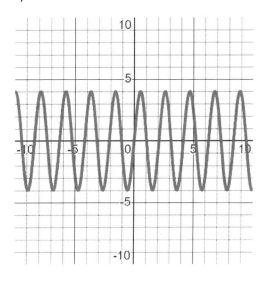

Chapter 16: Graphs of Trigonometric Functions

Graph of the Cosine Function

1) $y = 2\cos x$

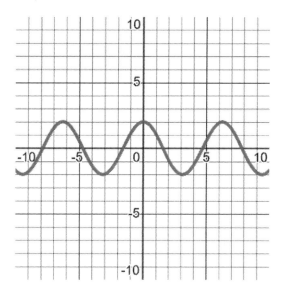

2) $y = 3\cos 2x - 2$

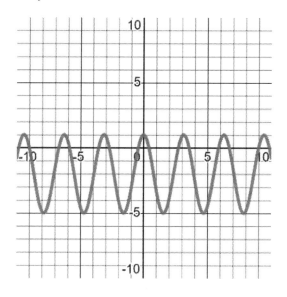

3) $y = \cos^2 2x$

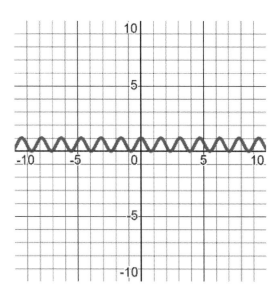

4) $y = -2\cos 3x$

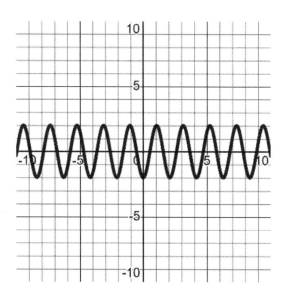

Chapter 16: Graphs of Trigonometric Functions

Amplitude, Period, and Phase Shift

1) Amplitude: 1
   Period: 6π
   Phase shift: 0

2) Amplitude: 2
   Period: 3π
   Phase shift: 0

3) Amplitude: 4
   Period: π
   Phase shift: $\frac{\pi}{4}$

4) Amplitude: 3
   Period: $\frac{\pi}{3}$
   Phase shift: $\frac{\pi}{6}$

5) Amplitude: 1
   Period: 2π
   Phase shift: $\frac{\pi}{4}$

6) Amplitude: 3
   Period: π
   Phase shift: $\frac{\pi}{12}$

7) Amplitude: 2
   Period: 3π
   Phase shift: $\frac{\pi}{2}$

8) Amplitude: $\frac{2}{3}$
   Period: π
   Phase shift: $-\frac{\pi}{6}$

9) Amplitude: 3
   Period: π
   Phase shift: $-\frac{\pi}{4}$

10) Amplitude: $\frac{2}{5}$
    Period: $\frac{2\pi}{3}$
    Phase shift: $\frac{\pi}{12}$

Writing the Equation of a Sine Graph

1) $y = sin\left(2x + \frac{\pi}{3}\right)$

2) $y = 2sin\left(x - \frac{\pi}{2}\right)$

Writing the Equation of a Cosine Graph

1) $y = 2cos\left(x - \frac{2\pi}{3}\right)$

2) $y = -3cos\left(x + \frac{\pi}{2}\right)$

Chapter 16: Graphs of Trigonometric Functions

Graph of the Tangent Function

1) $y = tan\left(x - \frac{\pi}{2}\right)$

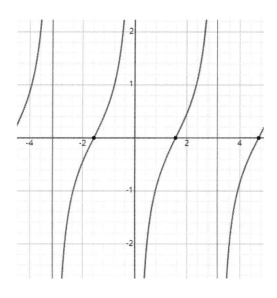

2) $y = tan\left(x + \frac{\pi}{4}\right)$

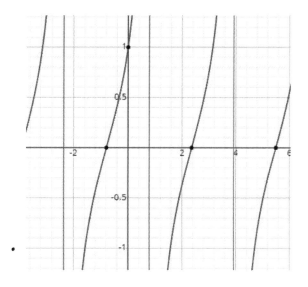

3) $y = tan\left(2x + \frac{\pi}{2}\right)$

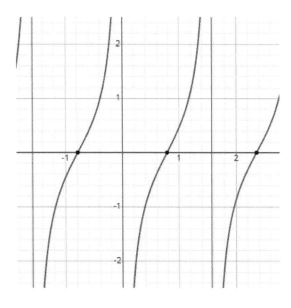

4) $y = tan\left(\frac{x}{2} - \frac{3\pi}{4}\right) + 1$

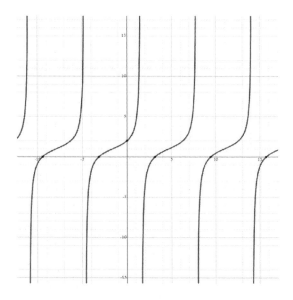

Effortless Math Education

Chapter 16: Graphs of Trigonometric Functions

Graph of the Cosecant Function

1) $y = -3\,csc\,(4x)$

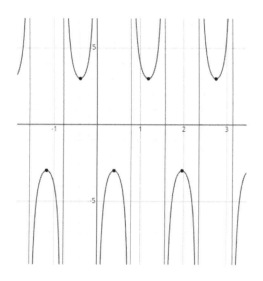

2) $y = 2\,csc\,(3x)$

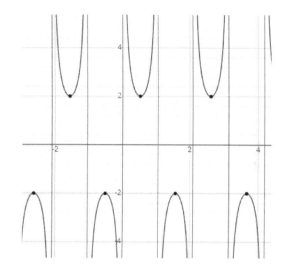

3) $y = csc\left(x + \dfrac{\pi}{4}\right)$

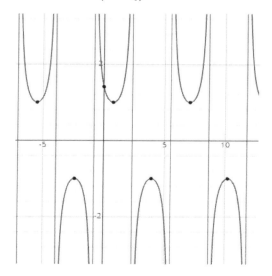

4) $y = 1 + 2\,csc(x)$

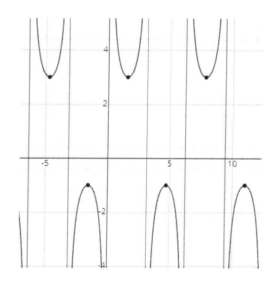

Chapter 16: Graphs of Trigonometric Functions

Graph of the Secant Function

1) $y = \sec(x - \frac{\pi}{2})$

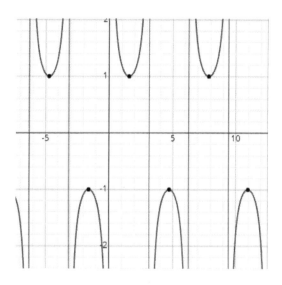

2) $y = \sec(x + \frac{\pi}{4})$

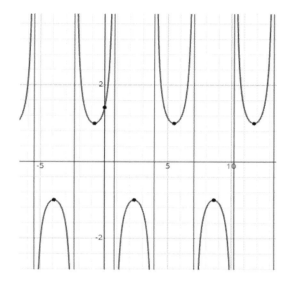

3) $y = \sec\left(2x + \frac{\pi}{2}\right)$

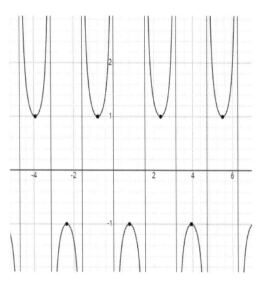

4) $y = -\sec\left(2x - \frac{\pi}{3}\right) + 2$

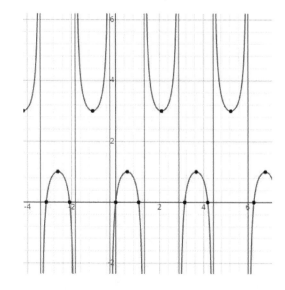

Chapter 16: Graphs of Trigonometric Functions

Graph of the Cotangent Function

1) $y = \cot\left(x + \dfrac{\pi}{2}\right)$

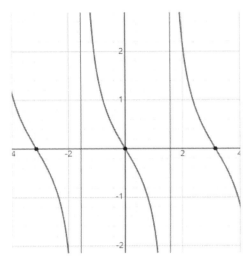

2) $y = \cot\left(2x - \dfrac{\pi}{4}\right)$

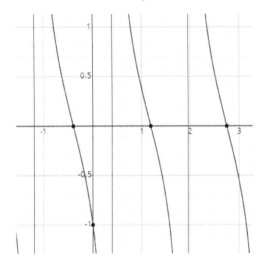

3) $y = 2\cot\left(x - \dfrac{\pi}{2}\right)$

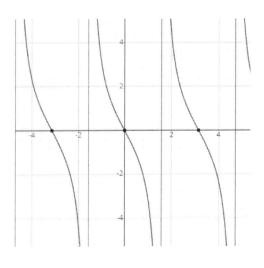

4) $y = -\cot\left(2x + \dfrac{2\pi}{3}\right) + 1$

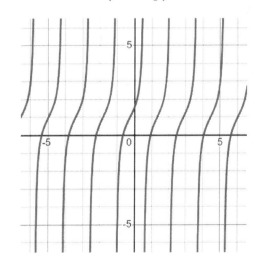

Chapter 16: Graphs of Trigonometric Functions

Graph of Inverse of the Sine Function

1) $y = \sin^{-1}(x+1)$

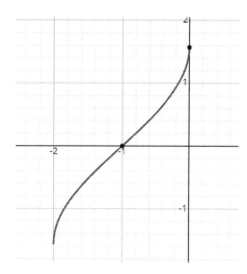

2) $y = 3\sin^{-1}(x+2)$

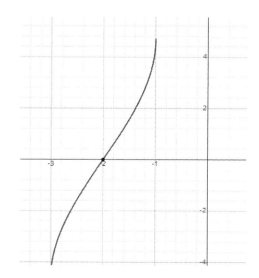

3) $y = \sin^{-1}(x - \frac{\pi}{3})$

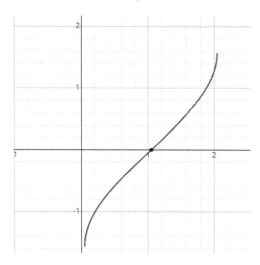

4) $y = 3\sin^{-1}(x + \frac{\pi}{2})$

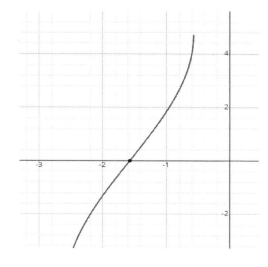

Chapter 16: Graphs of Trigonometric Functions

Graph of Inverse of the Cosine Function

1) $y = \cos^{-1}(x - 1)$

2) $y = 2\cos^{-1}(x + 1)$

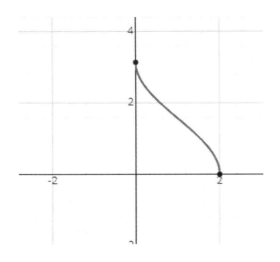
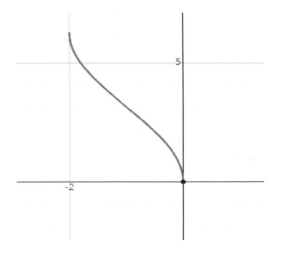

3) $y = -\cos^{-1}(x + \frac{\pi}{2})$

4) $y = 3\cos^{-1}(x - \frac{\pi}{4})$

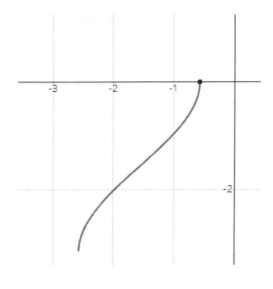
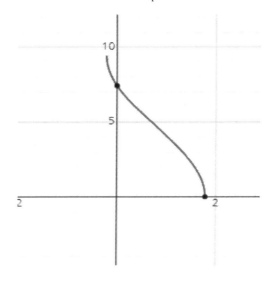

Chapter 16: Graphs of Trigonometric Functions

Graph of Inverse of the Tangent Function

1) $y = tan^{-1}(x+2)$

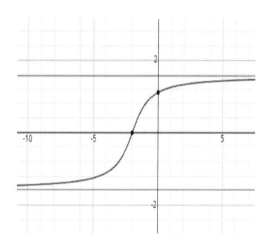

2) $y = -2\,tan^{-1}(x-1)$

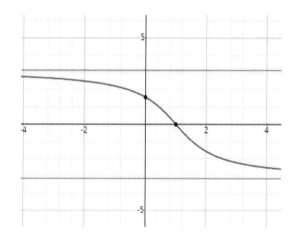

3) $y = 2tan^{-1}(x - \frac{2\pi}{3})$

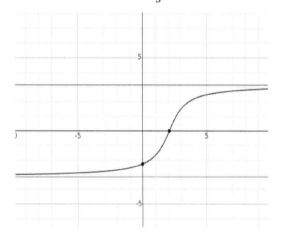

4) $y = tan^{-1}\left(x + \frac{\pi}{4}\right) + 2$

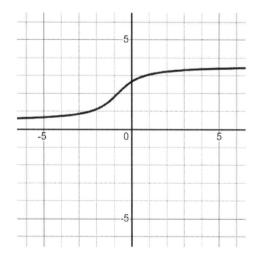

Chapter 16: Graphs of Trigonometric Functions

Sketching Trigonometric Graphs

1) $y = \cos(x - \frac{\pi}{2})$

2) $y = \sin(x - \frac{\pi}{4})$

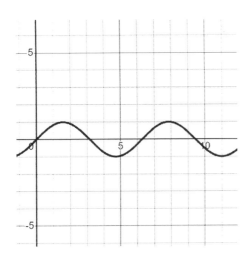
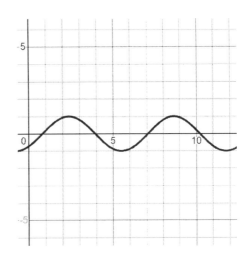

3) $y = 2\sin(x + \frac{\pi}{3})$

4) $y = -3\cos(x + \frac{\pi}{4})$

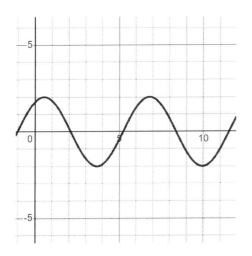
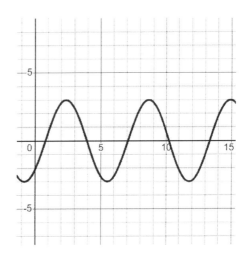

Chapter 17: Statistics

Math Topics that you'll learn in this Chapter:

- ✓ Frequency and Histograms
- ✓ Box-and-Whisker Plots
- ✓ Measures of Dispersion
- ✓ Organizing Data
- ✓ Data Distribution
- ✓ Central Limit Theorem and Standard Error

Chapter 17: Statistics

Frequency and Histograms

✎ *The graph below shows the distribution of scores of 40 students on a mathematics test.*

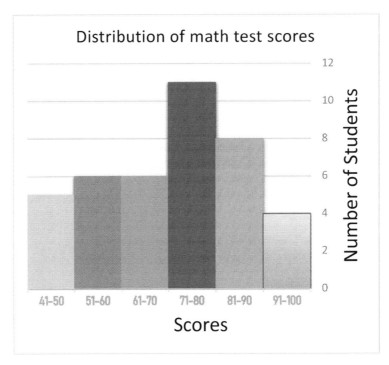

1) Complete the frequency table below using the data in the frequency histogram shown.

Scores	Frequency
41 – 50	
51 – 60	
61 – 70	
71 – 80	
81 – 90	
91 – 100	

Chapter 17: Statistics

Box-and-Whisker Plots

✍ *According to the following data, draw the related box-and-whisker plots.*

1) 9, 12, 15, 18, 20, 25, 29, 30, 34, 35, 38, 40

2) 5, 7, 11, 12, 14, 18, 22, 26, 28, 30, 31, 35, 36, 38

3) 52, 48, 62, 60, 42, 56, 54, 68, 44, 38, 66, 72, 70

4) 12, 9, 6, 2, 22, 23, 16, 6, 4, 10, 12, 24, 28, 32

5) 130, 42, 122, 114, 49, 58, 100, 102, 94, 95, 63, 57, 47, 78

6) 12, 9, 6, 2, 22, 23, 16, 6, 4, 10, 12, 24, 28, 32

Chapter 17: Statistics

Measures of Dispersion

✎ *Find the mean absolute deviation, standard deviation and variance of the data set.*

1) 36, 38, 42, 27, 46, 39, 43

   Standard Deviation: _____

   Mean Absolute Deviation: _____

   Variance: _____

2) 24, 28, 12, 15, 26, 29, 23

   Standard Deviation: _____

   Mean Absolute Deviation: _____

   Variance: _____

3) 56, 48, 28, 25, 36, 46, 60

   Standard Deviation: _____

   Mean Absolute Deviation: _____

   Variance: _____

4) 88, 96, 52, 74, 92, 38, 40

   Standard Deviation: _____

   Mean Absolute Deviation: _____

   Variance: _____

5) 122, 134, 159, 145, 123, 112, 118

   Standard Deviation: _____

   Mean Absolute Deviation: _____

   Variance: _____

6) 224, 240, 218, 239, 241, 221, 252

   Standard Deviation: _____

   Mean Absolute Deviation: _____

   Variance: _____

7) 62, 88, 96, 123, 69, 106, 118, 66

   Standard Deviation: _____

   Mean Absolute Deviation: _____

   Variance: _____

8) 190, 240, 280, 300, 420, 530, 630

   Standard Deviation: _____

   Mean Absolute Deviation: _____

   Variance: _____

Chapter 17: Statistics

Organizing Data

Solve.

1) Suppose that total of 45 horse riders participated in the race and their records were registered. The recorded points are normally distributed with a mean of 76 points and a standard deviation of 5.6 points. How many points will fall between 59.2 and 92.8?

   _____

2) In research, various types of blood groups (A, B, AB, and O) are studied. In which category of data organization should this data be placed?

   _____

3) In a survey, participants were asked questions about their height. We now have a data set containing the heights of 100 randomly chosen 30 years old boys (in cm). Into which category of data organization does this survey data fall?

   _____

4) If you want to measure the number of air pollutants over a month in parts per million (ppm), into which category of data organization would these from this measurement be classified?

   _____

Chapter 17: Statistics

Data Distribution

✎ **Solve.**

1) Which graph can be more suitable to display the data distribution of Outlier data?

2) In a data set, the data distribution is such that the mean of the data is equal to 25 and the mode of the data is equal to 10. Determine whether this data distribution follows the normal distribution or not.

3) Which chart is used to check for outliers and the normal distribution?

4) Which chart is most suitable better for multiple distributions?

5) What are the 3 types of frequency distribution graphs?

6) What is the most common distribution function?

7) A 5th grade class collected data on the number of letters in the first names of all the students in class. Here is the dot plot of data they collected:

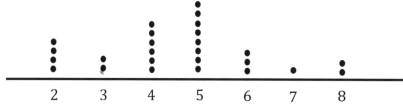

a) What is the shortest name length? _____

b) What is the most common name length? _____

Chapter 17: Statistics

Central Limit Theorem and Standard Error

✎ **Find the standard error of given observations.**

1) 33, 35, 37, 22, 41, 34, 36.

   standard error: _____

2) 17, 23, 25, 15, 31, 36, 29.

   standard error: _____

3) 8, 12, 16, 9, 5, 13, 25.

   standard error: _____

4) 44, 48, 28, 36, 24, 32, 41.

   standard error: _____

5) 14, 22, 15, 18, 27, 31, 35.

   standard error: _____

6) 25, 23, 29, 12, 32, 22, 42.

   standard error: _____

7) 44, 56, 65, 43, 59, 41, 67.

   standard error: _____

8) 66, 56, 62, 55, 73, 92, 42.

   standard error: _____

9) 88, 64, 58, 62, 68, 74, 80.

   standard error: _____

10) 99, 87, 56, 34, 26, 62, 73.

    standard error: _____

11) 112, 124, 118, 102, 108, 132, 101.

    standard error: _____

12) 194, 185, 162, 178, 199, 164, 178.

    standard error: _____

13) 222, 245, 264, 284, 224, 256, 212.

    standard error: _____

14) 334, 422, 212, 156, 321, 270, 189.

    standard error: _____

Chapter 17: Statistics

Answers – Chapter 17

Frequency and Histograms

Scores	Frequency
41 – 50	5
51 – 60	6
61 – 70	6
71 – 80	11
81 – 90	8
91 – 100	4

Box-and-Whisker Plots

1)

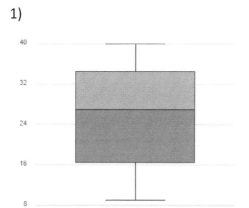

2)

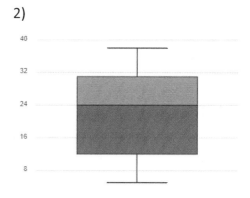

3)

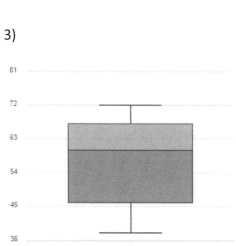

4)

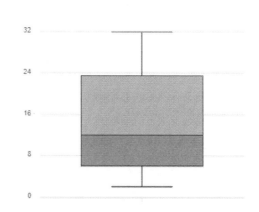

Chapter 17: Statistics

5)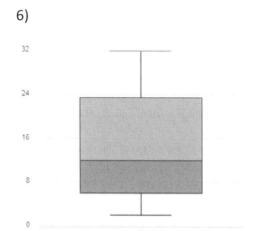

6)

Measures of Dispersion

1) Standard Deviation: 6.1

   Mean Absolute Deviation: 4.3

   Variance: 37.9

2) Standard Deviation: 6.5

   Mean Absolute Deviation: 5.1

   Variance: 42.2

3) Standard Deviation: 13.4

   Mean Absolute Deviation: 11.1

   Variance: 181.5

4) Standard Deviation: 24.9

   Mean Absolute Deviation: 21.6

   Variance: 622.2

5) Standard Deviation: 16.6

   Mean Absolute Deviation: 13.3

   Variance: 276.9

6) Standard Deviation: 12.6

   Mean Absolute Deviation: 10.7

   Variance: 159.6

7) Standard Deviation: 23.7

   Mean Absolute Deviation: 19.7

   Variance: 566

8) Standard Deviation: 162.2

   Mean Absolute Deviation: 134.2

   Variance: 26333.3

Chapter 17: Statistics

Organizing Data

1) 99.7%

2) The types of blood groups are qualitative data because you can't easily recognize them with real numbers.

3) The data obtained from the survey about the heights of 100 randomly chosen 30 years old boys (in cm) is included in the category of quantitative data because after being recorded it can be easily recognized with the real numbers.

4) The amounts of air pollutants during a month in parts per million (ppm) are placed in the category of quantitative data because, in this data set, you are dealing with real numbers.

Data Distribution

1) Considering that Minimum, First Quartile—$Q1$, Median, Third Quartile—$Q3$, and Maximum are specified in the box plot, this graph can give us better information about the existence of outlier data and determine their value.

2) In the normal distribution mean, median, and mode are equal to each other. So, this data distribution is not a normal distribution.

3) A histogram is a data visualization that shows the distribution of a variable. Outliers can be detected using a box plot or a scatter plot.

4) Boxplots are simple yet informative and work well when plotted side by side to visualize many distributions at once.

5) Frequency tables, histograms, or bar charts.

6) The Normal or Gaussian distribution.

7) a) 2 letters, b) 5 letters

Effortless Math Education

Chapter 17: Statistics

Central Limit Theorem and Standard Error

1) standard error: 2.22
2) standard error: 2.84
3) standard error: 2.47
4) standard error: 3.29
5) standard error: 3.06
6) standard error: 3.52
7) standard error: 4.1
8) standard error: 5.97
9) standard error: 4.04
10) standard error: 10.03
11) standard error: 4.34
12) standard error: 5.27
13) standard error: 9.82
14) standard error: 35.42

Chapter 18: Probability

Math Topics that you'll learn in this Chapter:

- ✓ Independent and Dependent Events
- ✓ Compound Events
- ✓ Conditional and Binomial Probabilities
- ✓ Theoretical Probability
- ✓ Experimental Probability

Chapter 18: Probability

Independent and Dependent Events

✏️ *Solve.*

1) A bottle contains 25 marbles: 15 are white, 5 are green and 5 are blue. What is the probability of picking a white and then a green marble without replacing the white marbel? _____

2) Two cards are chosen at random from a deck. What is the probability of getting a black ace and then a black queen without replacement? _____

3) In a file, there are 6 Math papers, 5 Geography papers, and 8 English papers. If you select three papers randomly, what is the probability of getting English and then a Geography paper from the file without replacing the first paper? _____

4) In a state, 30% of all people own a scooter, and 41% of all people have a scooter and bicycle. Find the probability of choosing a person that has a scooter and then choosing another person sequentially who has a bicycle and scooter. _____

5) Two cards are chosen at random from a deck. What is the probability of getting a King and then a Jack without replacing the first card? _____

6) In a factory, out of 12 products, 2 of them are defective. If the manufacturer chooses 2 products, what is the probability that both are defective? _____

7) In a survey, it was found that 4 out of 8 people read books in their free time. If 3 people are randomly selected with replacements, what is the probability that all 3 people read books in their free time? _____

Chapter 18: Probability
Compound Events

✎ *Solve.*

1) The probability of rain on Monday is 0.1. The probability of rain on Tuesday is 0.8. What is the probability of it raining on both Monday and Tuesday? _____

2) In a game, you choose a card from a box containing 4 red cards, 6 blue cards, and 5 yellow cards. You replace the first card in the box and then draw again. What is the probability of first choosing a red or blue card and then choosing a blue or yellow card? _____

3) A coin is tossed, and a die is rolled. What is the probability that the coin lands on tails and the die lands on 3? _____

4) A coin is tossed, and a die is rolled. What is the probability that the coin lands on heads and the die lands on an odd number? _____

5) In a game, you draw a card from a box containing 4 red cards, 6 blue cards, and 5 yellow cards. You do not replace the first card in the box before drawing again. What is the probability of choosing a blue card and then choosing a yellow card? _____

6) A bowl contains 10 red marbles, 3 blue marbles and 11 yellow marbles. Find the probability of first drawing a blue marble and then drawing a yellow marble. _____

Chapter 18: Probability

Conditional and Binomial Probabilities

✍ *Solve.*

1) A bag contains 3 black, 5 grey, and 8 white marbles. Two marbles are randomly selected. Find the probability that the second marble is black given that the first marble is grey. (Assume that the first marble is not replaced.)

   _____

2) What is the probability of getting 4 tails when you toss a coin 7 times?

   _____

3) In a group of 10 people, 4 people bought bananas, 3 people bought pineapples, and 2 people bought bananas and pineapples. If the buyer randomly bought bananas, use the conditional probability formula to find the probability that he also bought pineapples.

   _____

4) What are the chances of 2 heads, with 4 tosses?

   _____

5) A class has five students. What is the probability that exactly two of the students will travel during the last holiday?

   _____

6) Professors sometimes select a student at random to answer a question. If each student has an equal chance of being selected and there are 24 people in your class, what is the chance that she will pick you for the next question?

   _____

Chapter 18: Probability

Theoretical Probability

✎ *Solve.*

1) Donato's little brother Joseph is too small to see inside his sock drawer. Joseph has 2 pairs of white socks, 4 pairs of black socks, and 1 pair of blue socks inside his drawer. If the socks are not paired together, what is the probability that Joseph will reach inside his drawer and pick a black sock?

   _____

2) You are one of 30 people entering a contest. What is the probability that your name will be drawn first?

   _____

3) What is the probability of drawing a spade from a deck of 52 playing cards?

   _____

4) We have written the numbers 0, 2, 5, 7, 9, and 10 separately on 6 cards and put them in a bag. What is the probability that the number we will pick out is greater than 5?

   _____

5) The letters of the word "MATHEMATICS" are put in a bag. What is the probability of pulling out the letter "T" from the bag?

   _____

6) If a bag contains 7 red and 9 blue balls, then what is the probability of picking up a red ball?

   _____

Chapter 18: Probability

Experimental Probability

✎ **Solve.**

1) A manufacturer of smartwatches, after testing 100 smartwatches, finds that 95 smartwatches are not defective. What is the experimental probability that a smartwatch chosen at random has no defects? _____

2) A bookstore recently sold 12 books, 6 of which were novels. What is the experimental probability that the next book will be a novel? _____

3) A spinner has three unequal sections: red, yellow, and blue. The table shows the results of Nolan's spins. Find the experimental probability of landing on each color. _____

color	frequency
red	10
yellow	14
blue	6

4) John tossed a coin 15 times and got a head 10 times and a tail 5 times. Find the experimental probability of getting tails. _____

5) The following set of data shows the number of messages that Mike received recently from 5 of his friends. 6, 4, 3, 2, 5. Based on this, find the probability that Mike will receive less than 3 messages next time. _____

	Chapter 18: Probability
Effortless Math Education	Answers – Chapter 18

Independent and Dependent Events

1) $\frac{1}{8}$

2) $\frac{1}{663}$

3) $\frac{20}{171}$

4) 0.123

5) $\frac{4}{663}$

6) $\frac{1}{66}$

7) $\frac{1}{8}$

Compound Events

1) 0.08

2) $\frac{22}{45}$

3) $\frac{1}{12}$

4) $\frac{1}{4}$

5) $\frac{1}{7}$

6) $\frac{33}{552}$

Conditional and Binomial Probabilities

1) $\frac{1}{5}$

2) 0.27

3) 0.5

4) 0.375

5) 0.2975

6) $\frac{1}{24} = 0.0417$

Theoretical Probability

1) $\frac{4}{7}$

2) $\frac{1}{30}$

3) $\frac{1}{4}$

4) $\frac{1}{2}$

5) $\frac{2}{11}$

6) $\frac{7}{16}$

Experimental Probability

1) $\frac{19}{20}$

2) $\frac{1}{2}$

3) $\frac{1}{5}$

4) $\frac{1}{3}$

5) $\frac{3}{5}$

Time to Test

Time to refine your math skill with a practice test.

In this book, there are five complete Algebra 2 Tests. Take these tests to simulate the test day experience. After you've finished, score your test using the answer keys.

Before You Start

- You'll need a pencil a calculator to take the test.
- For each question, there are five possible answers. Choose which one is best.
- It's okay to guess. There is no penalty for wrong answers.
- Use the answer sheet provided to record your answers.
- **Calculator is permitted for Algebra 2 Test.**
- After you've finished the test, review the answer key to see where you went wrong.

Good Luck!

Algebra II Practice Test 1

2024

Total number of questions: 40

Total time: No time limit

Calculator is permitted for Algebra 2 Math Test.

Algebra II Practice Test Answer Sheet

Remove (or photocopy) this answer sheet and use it to complete the practice test.

Algebra II Practice Test 1 Answer Sheet

1	Ⓐ Ⓑ Ⓒ Ⓓ Ⓔ	21	Ⓐ Ⓑ Ⓒ Ⓓ Ⓔ
2	Ⓐ Ⓑ Ⓒ Ⓓ Ⓔ	22	Ⓐ Ⓑ Ⓒ Ⓓ Ⓔ
3	Ⓐ Ⓑ Ⓒ Ⓓ Ⓔ	23	Ⓐ Ⓑ Ⓒ Ⓓ Ⓔ
4	Ⓐ Ⓑ Ⓒ Ⓓ Ⓔ	24	Ⓐ Ⓑ Ⓒ Ⓓ Ⓔ
5	Ⓐ Ⓑ Ⓒ Ⓓ Ⓔ	25	Ⓐ Ⓑ Ⓒ Ⓓ Ⓔ
6	Ⓐ Ⓑ Ⓒ Ⓓ Ⓔ	26	Ⓐ Ⓑ Ⓒ Ⓓ Ⓔ
7	Ⓐ Ⓑ Ⓒ Ⓓ Ⓔ	27	Ⓐ Ⓑ Ⓒ Ⓓ Ⓔ
8	Ⓐ Ⓑ Ⓒ Ⓓ Ⓔ	28	Ⓐ Ⓑ Ⓒ Ⓓ Ⓔ
9	Ⓐ Ⓑ Ⓒ Ⓓ Ⓔ	29	Ⓐ Ⓑ Ⓒ Ⓓ Ⓔ
10	Ⓐ Ⓑ Ⓒ Ⓓ Ⓔ	30	Ⓐ Ⓑ Ⓒ Ⓓ Ⓔ
11	Ⓐ Ⓑ Ⓒ Ⓓ Ⓔ	31	Ⓐ Ⓑ Ⓒ Ⓓ Ⓔ
12	Ⓐ Ⓑ Ⓒ Ⓓ Ⓔ	32	Ⓐ Ⓑ Ⓒ Ⓓ Ⓔ
13	Ⓐ Ⓑ Ⓒ Ⓓ Ⓔ	33	Ⓐ Ⓑ Ⓒ Ⓓ Ⓔ
14	Ⓐ Ⓑ Ⓒ Ⓓ Ⓔ	34	Ⓐ Ⓑ Ⓒ Ⓓ Ⓔ
15	Ⓐ Ⓑ Ⓒ Ⓓ Ⓔ	35	Ⓐ Ⓑ Ⓒ Ⓓ Ⓔ
16	Ⓐ Ⓑ Ⓒ Ⓓ Ⓔ	36	Ⓐ Ⓑ Ⓒ Ⓓ Ⓔ
17	Ⓐ Ⓑ Ⓒ Ⓓ Ⓔ	37	Ⓐ Ⓑ Ⓒ Ⓓ Ⓔ
18	Ⓐ Ⓑ Ⓒ Ⓓ Ⓔ	38	Ⓐ Ⓑ Ⓒ Ⓓ Ⓔ
19	Ⓐ Ⓑ Ⓒ Ⓓ Ⓔ	39	Ⓐ Ⓑ Ⓒ Ⓓ Ⓔ
20	Ⓐ Ⓑ Ⓒ Ⓓ Ⓔ	40	Ⓐ Ⓑ Ⓒ Ⓓ Ⓔ

1) Which of the following is greatest?

A. $(2^3)^2$

B. $2^{(2^3)}$

C. $(3^2)^3$

D. $(2^3)^3$

E. $4^{(2^2)}$

2) Which of the following is one solution of this equation?
$$x^2 + 2x - 5 = 0$$

A. $\sqrt{2} + 1$

B. $\sqrt{2} - 1$

C. $\sqrt{6} + 1$

D. $-\sqrt{6} - 1$

E. $\sqrt{12}$

3) Divide: $\frac{16n^6 - 32n^2 + 8n}{8n}$

A. $2n^5 - 4n$

B. $2n^6 - 4n^2$

C. $2n^5 - 4n + 1$

D. $2n^6 - 4n^2 + 1$

E. $2n^6 - 4n^2 + n$

$$4x^2 + 6x - 3, \ 3x^2 - 5x + 8$$

4) Which of the following is the sum of the two polynomials shown above?

A. $x^2 + 5x + 4$

B. $4x^2 - 6x + 3$

C. $5x^2 + 3x + 4$

D. $7x^2 + x + 5$

E. $7x^2 + 5x + 1$

Algebra II Practice Test 1

x	1	2	3
$g(x)$	-1	-3	-5

5) The table above shows some values of linear function $g(x)$. Which of the following defines $g(x)$?

A. $g(x) = x + 2$

B. $g(x) = 2x + 1$

C. $g(x) = 2x - 1$

D. $g(x) = -2x + 1$

E. $g(x) = 2x + 2$

6) Which of the following expressions is equal to $\sqrt{\frac{x^2}{2} + \frac{x^2}{16}}$?

A. x

B. $\frac{3x}{4}$

C. $x\sqrt{x}$

D. $\frac{x\sqrt{x}}{4}$

E. $4x$

7) If $x \neq 0$ and $x = x^{-6}$, what is the value of x?

A. 1

B. 2

C. -2

D. 3

E. 4

8) Which of the following is equal to expression $\frac{5}{x^2} + \frac{7x-3}{x^3}$?

A. $\frac{6x+1}{x^3}$

B. $\frac{6x+4}{x^3}$

C. $\frac{10x+6}{x^3}$

D. $\frac{12x-3}{x^3}$

E. $\frac{13x+2}{x^3}$

9) Which of the following is equal to $m^{\frac{1}{2}} n^{-2} m^4 n^{\frac{2}{3}}$?

A. $m^2 n^{-\frac{4}{3}}$

B. $\dfrac{1}{m^{\frac{9}{4}} n^{\frac{4}{3}}}$

C. $\dfrac{m^{\frac{9}{4}}}{n^{\frac{4}{3}}}$

D. $\dfrac{m^{\frac{9}{2}}}{n^{\frac{4}{3}}}$

E. $\dfrac{1}{m^{\frac{9}{4}} n^{\frac{4}{3}}}$

10) For what value of x is the proportion true? $x:40 = 20:32$

A. 16

B. 20

C. 25

D. 28

E. 32

11) What is the 15th term of the arithmetic sequence $\frac{1}{2}x, \frac{1}{2}x + 3, \frac{1}{2}x + 6, \ldots$?

A. $\frac{1}{2}x + 15$

B. $\frac{1}{2}x + 18$

C. $\frac{1}{2}x + 21$

D. $\frac{1}{2}x + 42$

E. $\frac{1}{2}x + 45$

Algebra II Practice Test 1

12) Solve for x: $2 + \frac{3x}{x-5} = \frac{3}{5-x}$?

A. $\frac{4}{5}$

B. $\frac{6}{5}$

C. $\frac{7}{5}$

D. $\frac{8}{5}$

E. $\frac{9}{5}$

13) Which of the following expressions is equivalent to $2x(5 + 3y + 2x + 4z)$?

A. $7x + 5xy + 4x + 6xz$

B. $5x + 3xy + 4x^2 + 4xz$

C. $6xy + 4x^2 + 8xz + 10$

D. $10x + 6xy + 4x^2 + 8xz$

E. $14x + 6xy + 8xz$

14) If $f(x) = 3^x$ and $g(x) = \log_3 x$, which of the following expressions is equal to $f(3g(p))$?

A. $3P$

B. 3^p

C. p^3

D. p^9

E. $\frac{p}{3}$

15) The following table represents the value of x and function $f(x)$. Which of the following could be the equation of the function $f(x)$?

A. $f(x) = x^2 - 5$
B. $f(x) = x^2 - 1$
C. $f(x) = \sqrt{x+2}$
D. $f(x) = \sqrt{x} + 4$
E. $f(x) = \sqrt{x} + 6$

x	$f(x)$
1	5
4	6
9	7
16	8

16) What is the highest-degree term in the expansions of $\frac{(2x-2)^3 - 2x(x^3+3x)}{2}$?

A. $4x^3$

B. $-2x^4$

C. $-x^4$

D. $\frac{-x^4}{2}$

E. $\frac{4x^3}{2}$

17) Which graph shows a non-proportional linear relationship between x and y?

A.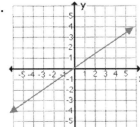

B.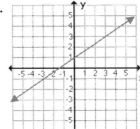

C.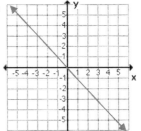

D.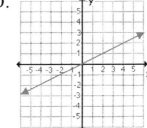

E.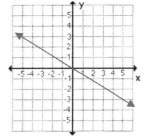

18) Which of the following is a factor of $12x^8 - 21x^4 + 3x^2$?

A. $3x^2$

B. $x - 1$

C. $3x + 1$

D. $4x^5 - 7x^2$

E. $4x^6 - 7x + 1$

19) If $4x + y = 25$ and $x - 2z = 24$, what is the value of x?

A. 0

B. 3

C. 5

D. 10

E. It cannot be determined from the information given.

20) Which of the following is equivalent to?
$$(4x^2 - 4xy - 6) - (-2x^2 - 4xy - 1)$$

A. $-6x^2 - 5$

B. $6x^2 - 5$

C. $2x^2 - 8xy - 5$

D. $2x^2 - 8xy - 7$

E. $6x^2 - 8xy - 5$

21) Where defined $\dfrac{\frac{x+3}{x^2-9}}{\frac{x-2}{x-3}}$?

A. $\dfrac{1}{(x-2)}$

B. $\dfrac{1}{(x-3)(x+3)}$

C. $\dfrac{(x-3)}{(x-2)}$

D. $\dfrac{1}{(x+3)(x-2)}$

E. $\dfrac{(x+3)(x-3)}{(x-2)}$

22) Which of the lines in the following figure is the graph of $x = -3$?

A. A

B. B

C. C

D. D

E. E

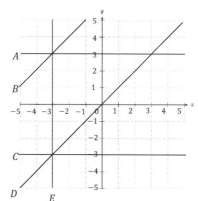

23) Which of the following graphs represents the solution of $|9 + 6x| \leq 3$?

A. 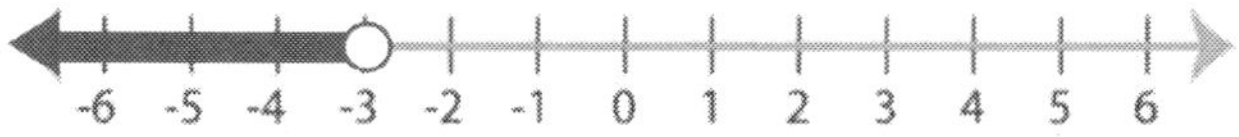

B. 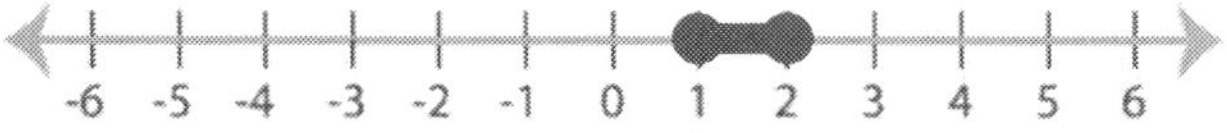

C. 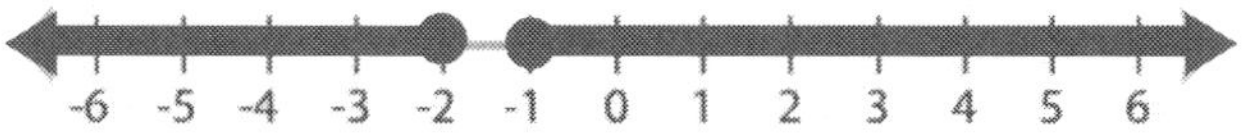

D. 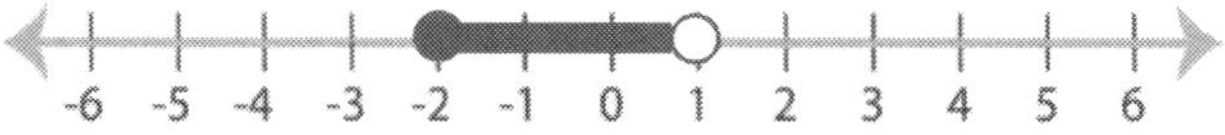

E. 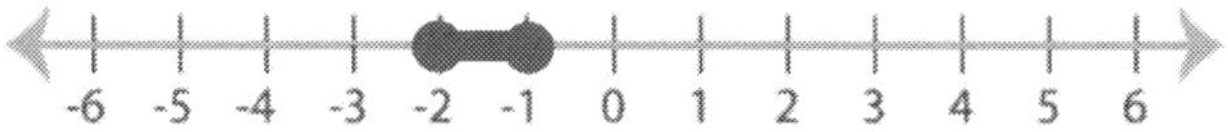

24) What are all real values of a in the following equation?

$$\frac{a}{4} + \frac{1}{2} = \frac{3}{a - 2}$$

A. $a = 4$

B. $a = 2, a = 4$

C. $a = 2, a = 6$

D. $a = -4, a = 4$

E. $a = 4, a = 8$

25) The graph of $y = f(x)$ is shown in the xy −plane below. Which the following equations could define $f(x)$?

A. $x^2 + 2x - 3$

B. $-x^2 - 2x + 3$

C. $(x - 2)(x + 3)$

D. $(x - 1)^2 + 3$

E. $(x + 1)^2 + 3$

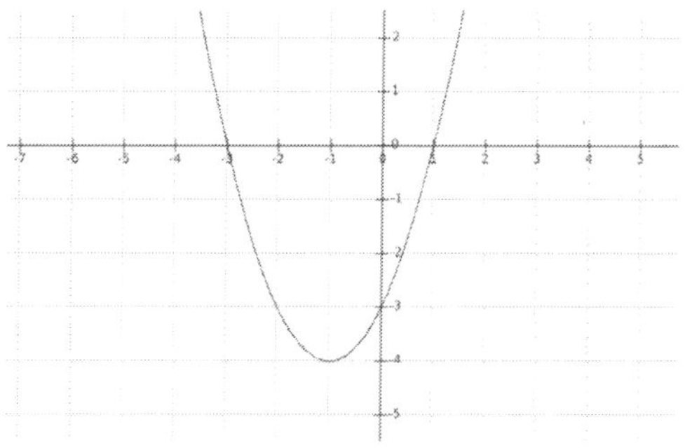

26) The shaded region in the figure below represents the intersection of the graphs of $x \geq 0$, $y \geq 0$, and which of the following inequalities?

A. $y \geq 2x - 1$

B. $y \leq x + 2$

C. $y \geq x + 2$

D. $y \geq x - 2$

E. $y \geq -2x + 1$

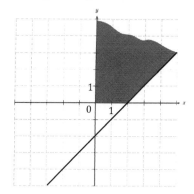

27) Which of the following is not an equivalent statement?

A. $x^{-2} = \frac{1}{x^2}$

B. $(x^2)^3 = x^6$

C. $x^6 - 5x^2 = x^2(x^3 - 5)$

D. $\left(3 - \frac{a}{6}\right)\left(3 + \frac{a}{6}\right) = 9 - \frac{a^2}{36}$

E. $4x^2 - 16x + 8 = (2x - 4)^2$

28) What is the simplified form of $\sqrt{3}(\sqrt{3} - 4)$?

A. $4 - \sqrt{3}$

B. $3 - 4\sqrt{3}$

C. $1 - 3\sqrt{3}$

D. $3 - \sqrt{3}$

E. $\sqrt{3} - 4$

29) If $h(x) = x + 8$ and $g(x) = 3x^2 + 24x$, what is the value of $\left(\frac{g}{h}\right)(x)$?

A. $3x + 8$

B. $x - 3$

C. $x + 8$

D. $3x$

E. $\frac{3x+24}{x+8}$

30) Find the perimeter of the figure.

A. $4x + 5y$

B. $3x + 5$

C. $9y - 2$

D. $9x + 3y$

E. $x + y + 5$

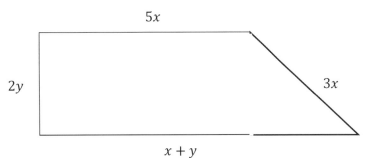

31) Write the following polynomial in standard form. $\frac{12x^2+8x^3+24}{4}$

A. $3x^3 + 2x^2 + 6$

B. $2x^3 + 3x^2 + 6$

C. $2x^2 + 4x^3 + 4$

D. $x^3 + 2x^2 + 3$

E. $2x^3 + 3x^2 + 8$

32) Rewrite $(-5)^{-3}$ with positive exponents.

A. 125

B. -125

C. $-\frac{1}{125}$

D. $\frac{1}{125}$

E. $-\frac{1}{25}$

33) Find the expanded form of $\log \frac{a^2 b^2}{c^4}$.

A. $\log ab - 4 \log c$

B. $2 \log a + 2 \log b - 4 \log c$

C. $2 \log ab - 4 \log c$

D. $\log \frac{a}{c} + \log \frac{b}{c}$

E. $2 \log a - 2 \log b + 4 \log c$

34) What is the domain of the function $g(x) = \frac{3x}{x^2-9}$.

A. All real numbers

B. All real numbers except 3

C. All real numbers except -3

D. All real numbers except 0

E. All real numbers except 3 and -3

35) Classify $-8x^2 + 5x^4 + 9 - 3x^3$ by degree.

A. constant

B. linear

C. quadratic

D. cubic

E. quartic

36) What is the vertex of the parabola $y = (x+9)^2 - 5$?

A. $(9, 5)$

B. $(-1, -9)$

C. $(-9, 1)$

D. $(-9, -5)$

E. $(5, -9)$

37) Find the area of a square whose sides are $1 + \sqrt{6}$.

A. $2 + \sqrt{5}$

B. $1 - \sqrt{6}$

C. $2\sqrt{6}$

D. $2 - \sqrt{6}$

E. $7 + 2\sqrt{6}$

38) Which of the following shows a rule for the following sequence?
5, 9, 13, 17, ...

A. $a_n = 4n$

B. $a_n = n - 4$

C. $a_n = 4n - 6$

D. $a_n = 4n + 1$

E. $a_n = n + 4$

39) What is the inverse of $g(x) = 5x - 7$?

A. $g^{-1}(x) = \frac{x+7}{5}$

B. $g^{-1}(x) = \frac{x+5}{7}$

C. $g^{-1}(x) = \frac{x}{5} + 7$

D. $g^{-1}(x) = x + 7$

E. $g^{-1}(x) = \frac{x-7}{5}$

40) Solve the following quadratic equation by using quadratic formula.
$x^2 + 7x + 6 = 0$

A. $-\sqrt{8}, -1$

B. $\sqrt{5}, -2$

C. $-6, -1$

D. $-\sqrt{5}, -2$

E. $6, -1$

End of Algebra II Practice Test 1

Algebra II Practice Test 2

2024

Total number of questions: 40

Total time: No time limit

Calculator is permitted for Algebra II Math Test.

Algebra II Practice Test Answer Sheet

Remove (or photocopy) this answer sheet and use it to complete the practice test.

Algebra II Practice Test 2 Answer Sheet

1	Ⓐ Ⓑ Ⓒ Ⓓ Ⓔ	21	Ⓐ Ⓑ Ⓒ Ⓓ Ⓔ
2	Ⓐ Ⓑ Ⓒ Ⓓ Ⓔ	22	Ⓐ Ⓑ Ⓒ Ⓓ Ⓔ
3	Ⓐ Ⓑ Ⓒ Ⓓ Ⓔ	23	Ⓐ Ⓑ Ⓒ Ⓓ Ⓔ
4	Ⓐ Ⓑ Ⓒ Ⓓ Ⓔ	24	Ⓐ Ⓑ Ⓒ Ⓓ Ⓔ
5	Ⓐ Ⓑ Ⓒ Ⓓ Ⓔ	25	Ⓐ Ⓑ Ⓒ Ⓓ Ⓔ
6	Ⓐ Ⓑ Ⓒ Ⓓ Ⓔ	26	Ⓐ Ⓑ Ⓒ Ⓓ Ⓔ
7	Ⓐ Ⓑ Ⓒ Ⓓ Ⓔ	27	Ⓐ Ⓑ Ⓒ Ⓓ Ⓔ
8	Ⓐ Ⓑ Ⓒ Ⓓ Ⓔ	28	Ⓐ Ⓑ Ⓒ Ⓓ Ⓔ
9	Ⓐ Ⓑ Ⓒ Ⓓ Ⓔ	29	Ⓐ Ⓑ Ⓒ Ⓓ Ⓔ
10	Ⓐ Ⓑ Ⓒ Ⓓ Ⓔ	30	Ⓐ Ⓑ Ⓒ Ⓓ Ⓔ
11	Ⓐ Ⓑ Ⓒ Ⓓ Ⓔ	31	Ⓐ Ⓑ Ⓒ Ⓓ Ⓔ
12	Ⓐ Ⓑ Ⓒ Ⓓ Ⓔ	32	Ⓐ Ⓑ Ⓒ Ⓓ Ⓔ
13	Ⓐ Ⓑ Ⓒ Ⓓ Ⓔ	33	Ⓐ Ⓑ Ⓒ Ⓓ Ⓔ
14	Ⓐ Ⓑ Ⓒ Ⓓ Ⓔ	34	Ⓐ Ⓑ Ⓒ Ⓓ Ⓔ
15	Ⓐ Ⓑ Ⓒ Ⓓ Ⓔ	35	Ⓐ Ⓑ Ⓒ Ⓓ Ⓔ
16	Ⓐ Ⓑ Ⓒ Ⓓ Ⓔ	36	Ⓐ Ⓑ Ⓒ Ⓓ Ⓔ
17	Ⓐ Ⓑ Ⓒ Ⓓ Ⓔ	37	Ⓐ Ⓑ Ⓒ Ⓓ Ⓔ
18	Ⓐ Ⓑ Ⓒ Ⓓ Ⓔ	38	Ⓐ Ⓑ Ⓒ Ⓓ Ⓔ
19	Ⓐ Ⓑ Ⓒ Ⓓ Ⓔ	39	Ⓐ Ⓑ Ⓒ Ⓓ Ⓔ
20	Ⓐ Ⓑ Ⓒ Ⓓ Ⓔ	40	Ⓐ Ⓑ Ⓒ Ⓓ Ⓔ

Algebra II Practice Workbook

1) Which of the following is a factor of $6x^2 - 4x - 10$?

A. $x - 1$

B. $3x - 2$

C. $3x - 5$

D. $4x - 2$

E. $6x - 2$

2) If $x = \frac{1}{3}$ and $y = \frac{9}{21}$, then which is equal to $\frac{1}{x} \div \frac{y}{3}$?

A. $\frac{1}{3}$

B. $\frac{1}{7}$

C. $\frac{1}{21}$

D. 9

E. 21

3) Which of the following answers represents the compound inequality $-4 \leq 4x - 8 < 16$?

A. $-1 < x \leq 6$

B. $1 \leq x < 6$

C. $2 \leq x \leq 6$

D. $-2 \leq x < 8$

E. $-4 \leq x < 8$

4) Which of the following is equal to x^{yz} for all values of $x, y,$ and z ?

A. $x^{(y+z)}$

B. $x^y z$

C. $x^y x^z$

D. $(x^y)^z$

E. xy^z

5) If $2x - 4 = 14$, what is the value of $3x - 3$?

A. 9

B. 12

C. 24

D. 28

E. 30

6) John works for an electric company. He receives a monthly salary of $4,500 plus 5% of all his monthly sales as bonus. If x is the number of all John's sales per month, which of the following represents John's monthly revenue in dollars?

A. $0.05x - 4,500$

B. $0.05x + 4,500$

C. $0.95x + 4,500$

D. $0.95x - 4,500$

E. $0.95x + 9,500$

7) If $f(x^2) = 3x + 4$, for all positive value of x, what is the value of $f(121)$?

A. 29

B. -29

C. -33

D. 37

E. 367

Algebra II Practice Workbook

8) If a and b are solutions of the following equation, which of the following is the ratio $\frac{a}{b}$?

$$(a > b)$$
$$2x^2 - 11x + 8 = -3x + 18$$

A. $\frac{1}{5}$

B. $-\frac{1}{5}$

C. 5

D. -5

E. -8

9) Integer x is evenly divisible by 4. Which expression below is also evenly divisible by 4?

A. $x + 1$

B. $2x + 1$

C. $2x + 4$

D. $3x + 2$

E. $4x + 1$

10) Which of the following is the expansion of $(3x + 2)^3$?

A. $3x^3 + 6x^2 + 6x + 2$

B. $3x^3 + 18x^2 + 18x + 8$

C. $3x^3 + 12x^2 + 18x + 8$

D. $27x^3 + 18x^2 + 12x + 8$

E. $27x^3 + 54x^2 + 36x + 8$

Algebra II Practice Test 2

11) If a parabola with equation $y = ax^2 + 5x + 10$, where a is constant, passes through point $(2, 12)$, what is the value of a^2?

A. 2

B. -2

C. 4

D. -4

E. 6

12) What is the solution of the following system of equations?
$$\begin{cases} \frac{-x}{2} + \frac{y}{4} = 1 \\ \frac{-5y}{6} + 2x = 4 \end{cases}$$

A. $x = 20, y = 50$

B. $x = 20, y = 48$

C. $x = 22, y = 48$

D. $x = 48, y = 22$

E. $x = 50, y = 20$

13) If $8 + 2x$ is 16 more than 20, what is the value of $6x$?

A. 40

B. 55

C. 62

D. 84

E. 88

14) Which graph corresponds to the following inequalities?

$y \leq x + 4$
$2x + y \leq -4$

A.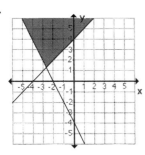

B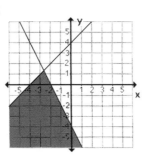

C.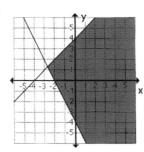

D.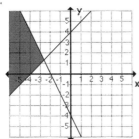

E.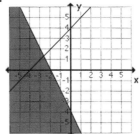

15) If $log_x 2 = \frac{1}{3}$, what is the value of x ?

A. $\sqrt{\frac{1}{3}}$

B. $\sqrt{2}$

C. 2

D. 4

E. 8

16) Find the equation of the horizontal asymptote of the function $f(x) = \frac{x+2}{x^2+1}$.

A. $y = 0$

B. $y = -1$

C. $x = 1$

D. $y = 2x$

E. $y = x + 2$

17) Given the right triangle ABC bellow, cos (β) is equal to?

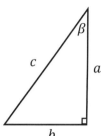

A. $\dfrac{a}{b}$

B. $\dfrac{a}{\sqrt{a^2+b^2}}$

C. $\dfrac{\sqrt{a^2+b^2}}{ab}$

D. $\dfrac{b}{\sqrt{a^2+b^2}}$

E. $\dfrac{b}{\sqrt{a^2-b^2}}$

18) Solve the following inequality. $\left|\dfrac{x}{2} - 2x + 10\right| < 5$

A. $-\dfrac{10}{3} < x < 10$

B. $\dfrac{10}{3} < x < 10$

C. $-10 < x < \dfrac{10}{3}$

D. $-10 < x < -\dfrac{10}{3}$

E. $-30 < x < 10$

19) Simplify $(3x - 5)^2$

A. $9x^2 + 30x + 25$

B. $9x^2 - 30x + 25$

C. $9x^2 + 25$

D. $9x^2 - 25$

E. $3x^2 + 25$

20) Which of the following are the solutions of the equation $3x^2 - 4x = 3 - x$?

A. $x = 3$ and $x = 1$

B. $x = 3$ and $x = -\frac{3}{4}$

C. $x = \frac{1+\sqrt{5}}{2}$ and $x = \frac{1-\sqrt{5}}{2}$

D. $x = \frac{3+\sqrt{5}}{2}$ and $x = \frac{3-\sqrt{5}}{2}$

E. $x = \frac{3+\sqrt{5}}{6}$ and $x = \frac{3-\sqrt{5}}{6}$

21) What is the value of x in this equation?
$$4\sqrt{2x+9} = 28$$

A. 7

B. 14

C. 20

D. 28

E. 40

22) The table represents different values of function $g(x)$. What is the value of
$3g(-2) - 2g(3)$?

A. -2

B. 3

C. -12

D. 13

E. 18

x	$g(x)$
-2	3
-1	2
0	1
1	0
2	-1
3	-2

Algebra II Practice Test 2

23) What is the equation of the following graph?

A. $y = |x| - 1$

B. $y = |x| + 1$

C. $y = -|x| + 1$

D. $y = |x + 1|$

E. $y = |x - 1|$

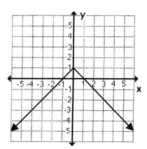

24) What is the sum of $\sqrt{x-7}$ and $\sqrt{x} - 7$ when $\sqrt{x} = 4$?

A. 0

B. -1

C. 3

D. -3

E. 6

25) In a right triangle $\sin A = \frac{1}{3}$, what is $\cos A$?

A. 1

B. $\frac{1}{2}$

C. $\frac{\sqrt{3}}{2}$

D. $\frac{\sqrt{8}}{3}$

E. $\sqrt{3}$

26) If $(x - 2)^2 + 1 > 3x - 1$, then x can equal which of the following?

A. 1

B. 3

C. 4

D. 6

E. 8

27) Solve for $x: \frac{3x}{5} = 27$?

A. 16.2

B. 31

C. 45

D. 55

E. 135

28) What is the solution of the equation $81 = 3^{2x}$?

A. $\frac{1}{2}$

B. $\frac{3}{2}$

C. $\frac{5}{2}$

D. 1

E. 2

29) $(2i - 3) - (2 - i)(i - 2) =$

A. $2i$

B. $-2i$

C. $2i - 1$

D. $-2i + 1$

E. $-2i - 1$

30) If $f(x) = \frac{4x^2 - 6x + 12}{9 - x}$, which of the following is NOT defined?

A. $f(0)$

B. $f(-4)$

C. $f(-6)$

D. $f(9)$

E. $f(-9)$

Algebra II Practice Test 2

31) Find the solution (x, y) to the following system of equations?
$$-3x - y = 6$$
$$6x + 4y = 10$$

A. $(14, 5)$

B. $(6, 8)$

C. $(11, 17)$

D. $(-\frac{17}{3}, 11)$

E. $(-6, 11)$

32) $\frac{3x-2}{x-3} - \frac{x-4}{3x-2} =$

A. $\frac{(3x-2)}{(x-3)}$

B. $\frac{(x-4)}{(x-3)}$

C. $\frac{8x^2-5x-8}{(x-3)(3x-2)}$

D. $\frac{8x^2-13x+16}{(x-3)(3x-2)}$

E. $\frac{10x^2-19x+16}{(x-3)(3x-2)}$

33) What is the sum of all values of n that satisfies $2n^2 + 16n + 24 = 0$?

A. 4

B. -4

C. 8

D. -8

E. -12

34) For $i = \sqrt{-1}$, what is the value of $\frac{3+2i}{5+i}$?

A. i

B. $\frac{32i}{5}$

C. $\frac{7+7i}{13}$

D. $\frac{17+7i}{26}$

E. $\frac{17-i}{5}$

35) Which of the point in the below figure represents the complex number $2 - 4i$?

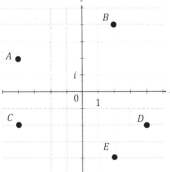

A. A

B. B

C. C

D. D

E. E

36) If $2x - 5y = 10$, what is x in terms of y?

A. $x = \frac{5}{2}y + 5$

B. $x = \frac{2}{5}y + 10$

C. $x = -\frac{5}{2}y - 5$

D. $x = -\frac{5}{2}y + 5$

E. $x = -\frac{2}{5}y + 5$

37) Which of the following is equivalent to $\frac{x+(5x)^2+(3x)^3}{x}$?

A. $16x^2 + 25x$

B. $16x^3 - 16x^2 + 1$

C. $16x^2 + 25x + 1$

D. $27x^3 + 16x^2 + 1$

E. $27x^2 + 25x + 1$

38) What is the range of the function shown below?

A. $-4 \leq x \leq 3$

B. $-4 \leq y \leq 3$

C. $-4 \leq x \leq 4$

D. $-4 \leq y \leq 4$

E. $-2 \leq y \leq 4$

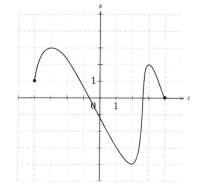

39) If $\tan x = \frac{8}{15}$, then $\sin x =$

A. $\frac{7}{15}$

B. $\frac{8}{17}$

C. $\frac{1}{2}$

D. $\frac{15}{17}$

E. It cannot be determined from the information given.

40) In which direction does the graph of the parabola $y = -6x^2$ open?

A. Right

B. Left

C. Up

D. Down

E. Given information is not enough.

End of Algebra 2 Practice Test 2

Algebra II Practice Tests Answers and Explanations

Now, it's time to review your results to see where you went wrong and what areas you need to improve.

Algebra II Practice Test 1				Algebra II Practice Test 2			
1	C	21	A	1	C	21	C
2	D	22	C	2	E	22	D
3	C	23	E	3	B	23	C
4	D	24	D	4	D	24	A
5	D	25	A	5	C	25	D
6	B	26	D	6	B	26	E
7	A	27	E	7	D	27	C
8	D	28	B	8	D	28	E
9	D	29	D	9	C	29	B
10	C	30	D	10	E	30	D
11	D	31	B	11	C	31	D
12	C	32	C	12	C	32	C
13	D	33	B	13	D	33	D
14	C	34	E	14	B	34	D
15	D	35	E	15	E	35	E
16	C	36	D	16	A	36	A
17	B	37	E	17	B	37	B
18	E	38	D	18	B	38	B
19	E	39	A	19	B	39	B
20	B	40	C	20	C	40	D

Algebra II Practice Test 1

Answers and Explanations

1) Choice C is correct.

A. $(2^3)^2$ $(2^3)^2 = 2^{3\times 2} = 2^6 = 64$

B. $2^{(2^3)}$ $2^{(2^3)} = 2^8 = 256$

C. $(3^2)^3$ $(3^2)^3 = 3^{2\times 3} = 3^6 = 729$

D. $(2^3)^3$ $(2^3)^3 = 2^{3\times 3} = 2^9 = 512$

E. $4^{(2^2)}$ $4^{(2^2)} = 4^4 = 256$

Choice C is the greatest value.

2) Choice D is correct.

$x_{1,2} = \frac{-b \pm \sqrt{b^2 - 4ac}}{2a}$ $ax^2 + bx + c = 0$

$x^2 + 2x - 5 = 0 \Rightarrow$ then: $a = 1$, $b = 2$ and $c = -5$

$x = \frac{-2 + \sqrt{2^2 - 4(1)(-5)}}{2(1)} = \sqrt{6} - 1$ $x = \frac{-2 - \sqrt{2^2 - 4(1)(-5)}}{2(1)} = -1 - \sqrt{6}$

3) Choice C is correct.

$\frac{16n^6 - 32n^2 + 8n}{8n} = \frac{16n^6}{8n} - \frac{32n^2}{8n} + \frac{8n}{8n} = 2n^5 - 4n + 1$

4) Choice D is correct.

The sum of the two polynomials is $(4x^2 + 6x - 3) + (3x^2 - 5x + 8)$

This can be rewritten by combining like terms: $(4x^2 + 6x - 3) + (3x^2 - 5x + 8) = (4x^2 + 3x^2) + (6x - 5x) + (-3 + 8) = 7x^2 + x + 5$

5) Choice D is correct.

Plugin the values of x in the choices provided. The points are $(1, -1), (2, -3)$, and $(3, -5)$

For $(1, -1)$ check the options provided:

A. $g(x) = x + 2 \to -1 = 1 + 2 \to -1 = 3$ This is NOT true.

B. $g(x) = 2x + 1 \to -1 = 2(1) + 1 \to -1 = 3$ This is NOT true.

C. $g(x) = 2x - 1 \to -1 = 2(1) - 1 = 1 \to -1 = 1$ This is NOT true.

D. $g(x) = -2x + 1 \to -1 = -2(1) + 1 \to -1 = -1$ This is true.

E. $g(x) = 2x + 2 \to -1 = 2(1) + 2 \to -1 = 4$ This is NOT true.

6) Choice B is correct.

Simplify the expression. $\sqrt{\frac{x^2}{2} + \frac{x^2}{16}} = \sqrt{\frac{8x^2}{16} + \frac{x^2}{16}} = \sqrt{\frac{9x^2}{16}} = \sqrt{\frac{9}{16}x^2} = \sqrt{\frac{9}{16}} \times \sqrt{x^2} = \frac{3}{4} \times x = \frac{3x}{4}$

7) Choice A is correct.

The easiest way to solve this one is to plug the answers into the equation.

When you do this, you will see the only time $x = x^{-6}$ is when $x = 1$ or $x = 0$.

Only $x = 1$ is provided in the choices.

8) Choice D is correct.

First find a common denominator for both of the fractions in the expression $\frac{5}{x^2} + \frac{7x-3}{x^3}$.

of x^3, we can combine like terms into a single numerator over the denominator:

$\frac{5x}{x^3} + \frac{7x-3}{x^3} = \frac{(5x) + (7x - 3)}{x^3} = \frac{12x - 3}{x^3}$

9) Choice D is correct.

$m^{\frac{1}{2}} n^{-2} m^4 n^{\frac{2}{3}} \to m^{\frac{1}{2}} \cdot m^4 = m^{\frac{1}{2}+4} = m^{\frac{9}{2}}, n^{-2} \cdot n^{\frac{2}{3}} = n^{-2+\frac{2}{3}} = n^{-\frac{4}{3}} = \frac{1}{n^{\frac{4}{3}}},$

$m^{\frac{9}{4}} \cdot \frac{1}{n^{\frac{4}{3}}} = \frac{m^{\frac{9}{2}}}{n^{\frac{4}{3}}}$

10) Choice C is correct.

Write the ratios in fraction form and solve for x: $\frac{x}{40} = \frac{20}{32}$

Cross multiply: $32x = 800$. Apply the multiplicative inverse property; divide both sides by 32: $x = \frac{800}{32} = 25$

11) Choice D is correct.

The difference of two terms in the sequence is 3. ($\frac{1}{2}x + 3 - \frac{1}{2}x = 3$)

To find any term in an arithmetic sequence use this formula: $x_n = a + (n-1)d$

a = the first term, d = the common difference between terms, n = number of items

Then, the 15th term is: $x_{15} = \frac{1}{2}x + ((15-1) \times 3) = \frac{1}{2}x + 42$

12) Choice C is correct.

First, find a common denominator for 2 and $\frac{3x}{x-5}$. It's $x-5$. Then:

$2 + \frac{3x}{x-5} = \frac{2(x-5)}{x-5} + \frac{3x}{x-5} = \frac{2x-10+3x}{x-5} = \frac{5x-10}{x-5}$. Now, multiply the numerator and denominator of $\frac{3}{5-x}$ by -1. Then: $\frac{3 \times (-1)}{(5-x) \times (-1)} = \frac{-3}{x-5}$. Rewrite the expression: $\frac{5x-10}{x-5} = \frac{-3}{x-5}$. Since the denominators of both fractions are equal, then, the numerators must be equal. $5x - 10 = -3 \rightarrow 5x = 7 \rightarrow x = \frac{7}{5}$.

13) Choice D is correct.

Use distributive property: $2x(5 + 3y + 2x + 4z) = 10x + 6xy + 4x^2 + 8xz$

14) Choice C is correct.

To solve for $f(3g(P))$, first, find $3g(p)$: $g(x) = \log_3 x \rightarrow g(p) = \log_3 p \rightarrow 3g(p) = 3\log_3 p = \log_3 p^3$. Now, find $f(3g(p))$: $f(x) = 3^x \rightarrow f(\log_3 p^3) = 3^{\log_3 p^3}$

Logarithms and exponentials with the same base cancel each other. This is true because logarithms and exponentials are inverse operations. Then: $f(\log_3 p^3) = 3^{\log_3 p^3} = p^3$

15) Choice D is correct.

A. $f(x) = x^2 - 5$ if $x = 1 \rightarrow f(1) = (1)^2 - 5 = 1 - 5 = -4 \neq 5$

B. $f(x) = x^2 - 1$ if $x = 1 \rightarrow f(1) = (1)^2 - 1 = 1 - 1 = 0 \neq 5$

C. $f(x) = \sqrt{x+2}$ if $x = 1 \rightarrow f(1) = \sqrt{1+2} = \sqrt{3} \neq 5$

D. $f(x) = \sqrt{x} + 4$ if $x = 1 \rightarrow f(1) = \sqrt{1} + 4 = 5$

E. $f(x) = \sqrt{x} + 6$ if $x = 1 \rightarrow f(1) = \sqrt{1} + 6 = 7 \neq 5$

Algebra II Practice Tests Answers and Explanations

16) Choice C is correct.

First simplify the numerator. Perfect cube formula:

$(2x-2)^3 = (2x)^3 - 3(2x)^2(2) + 3(2x)(2)^2 - 2^3$. Simplify: $8x^3 - 24x^2 + 24x - 8$

Expend: $-2x(x^3 + 3x) = -2x^4 - 6x^2$

And adding these together result in:

$8x^3 - 24x^2 + 24x - 8 - 2x^4 - 6x^2 = -2x^4 + 8x^3 - 30x^2 + 24x - 8$

Taking out a common factor of 2:

$-2x^4 + 8x^3 - 30x^2 + 24x - 8 = 2(-x^4 + 4x^3 - 15x^2 + 12x - 4)$

Then: $\frac{(2x-2)^3 - 2x(x^3+3x)}{2} = \frac{2(-x^4+4x^3-15x^2+12x-4)}{2} = -x^4 + 4x^3 - 15x^2 + 12x - 4$.

The highest-degree term is $-x^4$.

17) Choice B is correct.

A linear equation is a relationship between two variables, x and y, and can be written in the form of $y = mx + b$. A non-proportional linear relationship takes on the form $y = mx + b$, where $b \neq 0$ and its graph is a line that does not cross through the origin. Only in graph B does not pass through the origin.

18) Choice E is correct.

Factor the expression: $12x^8 - 21x^4 + 3x^2 = 3x^3(4x^6 - 7x + 1)$. Therefore, the correct listed factor is $4x^6 - 7x + 1$.

19) Choice E is correct.

We have two equations and three unknown variables, therefore x cannot be obtained.

20) Choice B is correct.

$(4x^2 - 4xy - 6) - (-2x^2 - 4xy - 1)$. Add like terms together: $4x^2 - (-2x^2) = 6x^2$

$-4xy - (-4xy) = 0, -6 - (-1) = -5$

Combine these terms into one expression to find the answer: $6x^2 - 5$

21) Choice A is correct.

$\frac{\frac{x+3}{x^2-9}}{\frac{x-2}{x-3}} = \frac{(x+3) \times (x-3)}{(x^2-9) \times (x-2)}, (x^2 - 9) = x^2 - 3^2 = (x-3)(x+3)$,

Then: $\frac{(x+3)(x-3)}{(x-3)(x+3)(x-2)} = \frac{1}{(x-2)}$

Algebra II Practice Workbook

22) Choice C is correct.

Line C is the graph of $x = -3$.

23) Choice E is correct.

Apply absolute equation rule $-3 \leq 9 + 6x \leq 3$. Add -9 to all sides. Then:

$-3 - 9 \leq 9 + 6x - 9 \leq 3 - 9 \rightarrow -12 \leq 6x \leq -6$. Now, divide all sides by 6:

$-2 \leq x \leq -1$. Choice E represents this inequality.

24) Choice D is correct.

To solve $\frac{a}{4} + \frac{1}{2} = \frac{3}{a-2}$, first multiply by the least common multiplier $4(a-2)$. Then:

$\frac{a}{4} \cdot 4(a-2) + \frac{1}{2} \cdot 4(a-2) = \frac{3}{a-2} \cdot 4(a-2)$. Now, simplify: $a(a-2) + 2(a-2) = 12 \rightarrow$

$a^2 - 2a + 2a - 4 = 12 \rightarrow a^2 = 16 \rightarrow a = \sqrt{16} \rightarrow a = -4, a = 4$

25) Choice A is correct.

The graph of $y = f(x)$ crosses the x-axis at $x = -3$ and $x = 1$, and crosses the y-axis at $y = -3$, and has its vertex at the point $(-1, -4)$. Therefore, the ordered pairs $(-3, 0)$, $(1, 0)$, $(0, -3)$, and $(-1, -4)$ must satisfy the equation for $f(x)$. Furthermore, because the graph opens up-ward, the equation defining $f(x)$ must have positive leading coefficient. All of these conditions are met by the equation:
$f(x) = x^2 + 2x - 3$

26) Choice D is correct.

First, find the equation of the line. Two points on the line are $(0, -2)$ and $(2, 0)$. The slope of the line is 1 and the equation of the line is: $y = x - 2$. Only Choices D is similar to the equation of the line.

27) Choice E is correct.

A. $x^{-2} = \frac{1}{x^2}$ This is true.

B. $(x^2)^3 = x^6$ This is true.

C. $x^6 - 5x^2 = x^2(x^3 - 5)$ This is true.

D. $\left(3 - \frac{a}{6}\right)\left(3 + \frac{a}{6}\right) = 9 - \frac{a^2}{36}$ This is true.

E. $4x^2 - 16x + 8 = (2x - 4)^2$ This is incorrect: $4x^2 - 16x + 16 = (2x - 4)^2$

Algebra II Practice Tests Answers and Explanations

28) Choice B is correct.
Take the number outside the parenthesis and distribute it to the numbers inside.

$$\sqrt{3}(\sqrt{3} - 4) = \sqrt{3} \cdot \sqrt{3} - \sqrt{3} \cdot 4$$

When multiplying a number inside and a number outside the radical symbol, simply place them side by side: $\sqrt{3} \cdot \sqrt{3} - \sqrt{3} \cdot 4 = \sqrt{9} - 4\sqrt{3} = 3 - 4\sqrt{3}$

29) Choice D is correct.
We know that $\left(\frac{g}{h}\right)(x) = \frac{g(x)}{h(x)}$. Since $g(x) = 3x^2 + 24x$ and $h(x) = x + 8$, we can find $\frac{g(x)}{h(x)}$ by simplifying $g(x)$: $\frac{g(x)}{h(x)} = \frac{3x^2 + 24x}{x+8} = \frac{3x(x+8)}{x+8} = 3x$

30) Choice D is correct.
The perimeter of the shape is the sum of all its sides:

Perimeter $= 5x + 3x + (x + y) + 2y$. Now, combine like terms:
$5x + 3x + (x + y) + 2y = 9x + 3y$

31) Choice B is correct.
First divide the numerator $(12x^2 + 8x^3 + 24)$ by 4: $\frac{12x^2 + 8x^3 + 24}{4} = 3x^2 + 2x^3 + 6$

Arranging the exponents in the descending order, we get the standard form of the polynomial: $2x^3 + 3x^2 + 6$

32) Choice C is correct.
Use the definition of a negative exponent. $x^{-n} = \frac{1}{x^n} \to (-5)^{-3} = \frac{1}{(-5)^3} = -\frac{1}{125}$

33) Choice B is correct.
Quotient rule: $\log \frac{x}{y} = \log x - \log y$, Product rule: $\log(xy) = \log x + \log y$,

Power rule: $\log x^n = n \log x$. Using the above rules, we can expand the logarithm.

$$\log \frac{a^2 b^2}{c^4} = (\log a^2 b^2) - (\log c^2) = \log a^2 + \log b^2 - \log c^4 = 2\log a + 2\log b - 4\log c$$

34) Choice E is correct.
When finding the domain of a fractional function, you must exclude all the x values that make the denominator equal to zero, because you can never divide by zero.

$$x^2 - 9 = 0 \to (x + 3)(x - 3) = 0 \to x = 3, -3$$

Domain = all real numbers except 3 and -3.

35) Choice E is correct.

The highest exponent will be the degree of the polynomial.

In expression $-8x^2 + 5x^4 + 9 - 3x^3$, the highest exponent is 4. Then, its degree is 4. So, choice E is correct.

36) Choice D is correct.

The vertex form of a parabola is $y = a(x - h)^2 + k$ where (h, k) is the vertex. So, $(-9, -5)$ is the vertex of parabola $y = (x + 9)^2 - 5$.

37) Choice E is correct.

One side of square $= a$

Area of square $= a \times a \rightarrow (1 + \sqrt{6})(1 + \sqrt{6}) = 1 + \sqrt{6} + \sqrt{6} + 6 = 7 + 2\sqrt{6}$

38) Choice D is correct.

You can use a general formula to find the formula for the sequence. The formula is: $a_n = a_1 + d(n - 1)$.

From the first two term and the difference between the first term and the second term is $9 - 5 = 4$. Just plug these numbers into formula and the simplify:

$a_n = 5 + 4(n - 1) \rightarrow a_n = 5 + 4n - 4 \rightarrow a_n = 4n + 1$

39) Choice A is correct.

First replace $g(x)$ with y. Then: $y = 5x - 7$

Next, replace all $x's$ with y and all $y's$ with x. $x = 5y - 7$

Now, solve for y. $5y = x + 7 \rightarrow y = \frac{x+7}{5}$

Finally replace y with $g^{-1}(x)$: $g^{-1}(x) = \frac{x+7}{5}$

40) Choice C is correct.

The standard form of a quadratic equation looks like this: $ax^2 + bx + c = 0$

Where $a, b,$ and c are the numerical coefficients of the terms of the quadratic, the value of the variable x is given by the following equation: $x = \frac{-b \pm \sqrt{b^2 - 4ac}}{2a}$.

$x^2 + 7x + 6 = 0$. In this equation, $a = 1, b = 7, c = 6$

Now, we can use the quadratic formula: $x = \frac{-b \pm \sqrt{b^2 - 4ac}}{2a}$

Just plug in the values of $a, b,$ and c, and do the calculations. $x_{1,2} = \frac{-7 \pm \sqrt{7^2 - 4(1)(6)}}{2(1)} = \frac{-7 \pm 5}{2} = -6, -1$

Algebra II Practice Tests Answers and Explanations

Algebra II Practice Test 2

Answers and Explanations

1) Choice C is correct.

$6x^2 - 4x - 10 = 2(x+1)(3x-5)$

2) Choice E is correct.

$x = \frac{1}{3}$ and $y = \frac{9}{21}$, substitute the values of x and y in the expression and simplify:

$\frac{1}{x} \div \frac{y}{3} \to \frac{1}{\frac{1}{3}} \div \frac{\frac{9}{21}}{3} \to \frac{1}{\frac{1}{3}} = 3$ and $\frac{\frac{9}{21}}{3} = \frac{9}{63} = \frac{1}{7}$. Then: $\frac{1}{\frac{1}{3}} \div \frac{\frac{9}{21}}{3} = 3 \div \frac{1}{7} = 3 \times 7 = 21$

3) Choice B is correct.

Solve for x. $-4 \leq 4x - 8 < 16$, Then, add 8 to all sides $-4 + 8 < 4x - 8 + 8 < 16 + 8 \Rightarrow$

$4 < 4x < 24$. Divide all sides by 4: $1 \leq x < 6$. Choice B represents this inequality.

4) Choice D is correct.

Choice D is the correct answer because $(x^y)^z$ is same as $x^{y \times z}$.

5) Choice C is correct.

$2x - 4 = 14 \to 2x = 18 \to x = 9$. Now, find the value of $3x - 3$.

$3x - 3 = 3(9) - 3 = 24$

6) Choice B is correct.

x is the number of all John's sales per month and 5% of it is: $5\% \times x = 0.05x$

John's monthly revenue: $0.05x + 4,500$

7) Choice D is correct.

$x^2 = 121 \to x = 11$ (Positive value)   Or $x = -11$ (Negative value)

Since x is positive, then: $f(121) = f(11^2) = 3(11) + 4 = 33 + 4 = 37$

8) Choice D is correct.

$2x^2 - 11x + 8 = -3x + 18 \to 2x^2 - 11x + 3x + 8 - 18 = 0 \to 2x^2 - 8x - 10 = 0$

$\to 2(x^2 - 4x - 5) = 0 \to$ Divide both sides by 2. Then: $x^2 - 4x - 5 = 0$, Find the factors of the quadratic equation. $\to (x-5)(x+1) = 0 \to x = 5$ or $x = -1$

$a > b$, then: $a = 5$ and $b = -1$ $\frac{a}{b} = \frac{5}{-1} = -5$

9) Choice C is correct.

Since integer x is evenly divisible by 4, substitute 4 for x in the answer choices to determine which expression is also divisible by 4: Let $x = 4$

Choice A: $\quad x + 1 = 4 + 1 = 5 \quad\quad\quad$ This is NOT divisible by 4.

Choice B: $\quad 2x + 1 = 2(4) + 1 = 9 \quad\quad$ This is NOT divisible by 4.

Choice C: $\quad 2x + 4 = 2(4) + 4 = 12 \quad\quad$ This is divisible by 4.

Choice D: $\quad 3x + 2 = 3(4) + 1 = 13 \quad\quad$ This is NOT divisible by 4.

Choice E: $\quad 4x + 1 = 4(4) + 1 = 17 \quad\quad$ This is NOT divisible by 4.

So, choice C is correct.

10) Choice E is correct.

Perfect cube formula: $(a + b)^3 = a^3 + 3a^2b + 3ab^2 + b^3$. Then:

$(3x + 2)^3 = (3x)^3 + 3.(3x)^2.2 + 3.(3x).2^2 + 2^3 = 27x^3 + 54x^2 + 36x + 8$

11) Choice C is correct.

Plug in the values of x and y of the point $(2, 12)$ in the equation of the parabola. Then: $12 = a(2)^2 + 5(2) + 10 \to 12 = 4a + 10 + 10 \to 12 = 4a + 20$

$\to 4a = 12 - 20 = -8 \to a = \dfrac{-8}{4} = -2 \to a^2 = (-2)^2 = 4$

12) Choice C is correct.

$\begin{cases} \dfrac{-x}{2} + \dfrac{y}{4} = 1 \\ \dfrac{-5y}{6} + 2x = 4 \end{cases} \to$ Multiply the top equation by 4. Then,

$\begin{cases} -2x + y = 4 \\ \dfrac{-5y}{6} + 2x = 4 \end{cases} \to$ Add two equations. $\dfrac{1}{6}y = 8 \to y = 48$, plug in the value of y into the first equation $x = 22$.

13) Choice D is correct.

The description $8 + 2x$ is 16 more than 20 can be written as the equation $8 + 2x = 16 + 20$, which is equivalent to $8 + 2x = 36$. Subtracting 8 from each side of $8 + 2x = 36$ gives $2x = 28$.

Since $6x$ is 3 times $2x$, multiplying both sides of $2x = 28$ by 3 gives $6x = 84$.

Algebra II Practice Tests Answers and Explanations

14) Choice B is correct.

For each option, choose a point in the solution set part and check it on both inequalities.

$y \leq x + 4, 2x + y \leq -4$

A. Let's choose this point $(0, 5)$ $5 \leq 0 + 4$, That's not true.

B. Point $(-4, -4)$ is in the solution section. Let's check the point in both inequalities.

$-4 \leq -4 + 4$, It works.

$2(-4) + (-4) \leq -4 \Rightarrow -12 \leq -4$, it works (this point works in both inequalities)

C. Let's choose this point $(0, 0)$ $0 \leq 0 + 4$, It works, $2(0) + (0) \leq -4$, That's not true!

D. Let's choose this point $(-5, 0)$,$0 \leq -5 + 4$, That's not true!

E. Let's choose this point $(-5, 0)$ $0 \leq -5 + 4$, That's not true!

Only choice B represents both inequalities.

15) Choice E is correct.

$log_x 2 = \frac{1}{3}$ (log rule: $log_a(b) = \frac{1}{log_b(a)}$), $\frac{1}{log_2 x} = \frac{1}{3}$,Using the cross multiplication: $1 \times 3 = 1 \times log_2 x \to 3 = log_2 x$.

(Use logarithmic definition: $log_a b = c \to b = a^c$) $x = 2^3 \to x = 8$

16) Choice A is correct.

In a rational function, if the denominator has a bigger degree than the numerator, the horizontal asymptote is the x −axes or the line $y = 0$. In the function $f(x) = \frac{x+2}{x^2+1}$, the degree of numerator is 1 (x to the power of 1) and the degree of the denominator is 2 (x to the power of 2). Then, the horizontal asymptote is the line $y = 0$.

17) Choice B is correct.

$Cos \beta = \frac{Adjacent\ side}{hypotenuse}$, to find the hypotenuse, we need to use Pythagorean theorem.

$a^2 + b^2 = c^2 \to c = \sqrt{a^2 + b^2}.$ $cos(\beta) = \frac{a}{c} = \frac{a}{\sqrt{a^2+b^2}}$

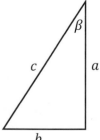

Algebra II Practice Workbook

18) Choice B is correct.

$\left|\frac{x}{2} - 2x + 10\right| < 5 \to \left|-\frac{3}{2}x + 10\right| < 5 \to -5 < -\frac{3}{2}x + 10 < 5$

Subtract 10 from all sides of the inequality. $\to -5 - 10 < -\frac{3}{2}x + 10 - 10 < 5 - 10 \to$

$-15 < -\frac{3}{2}x < -5$. Multiply all sides by 2. $\to 2 \times (-15) < 2 \times \left(-\frac{3x}{2}\right) < 2 \times (-5) \to$

$-30 < -3x < -10$. Divide all sides by -3. (Remember that when you divide all sides of an inequality by a negative number, the inequality sign will be swapped.)

$\to \frac{-30}{-3} > \frac{-3x}{-3} > \frac{-10}{-3} \to 10 > x > \frac{10}{3} \to \frac{10}{3} < x < 10$

19) Choice B is correct.

Use FOIL (First-Out-In-Last) method to simplify the expression:

$(3x - 5)^2 = (3x - 5)(3x - 5) = 9x^2 - 15x - 15x + 25 = 9x^2 - 30x + 25$

20) Choice C is correct.

Bring all values to one side of the equation. Add x to both sides:

$3x^2 - 4x + x = 3 - x + x \to 3x^2 - 4x + x = 3$. Subtract 3 from both sides:

$3x^2 - 4x + x - 3 = 3 - 3 \to 3x^2 - 4x + x - 3 = 0$. Now, solve using the quadratic formula:

For a quadratic of the form $ax^2 + bx + c = 0$, the solutions are $x_{1,2} = \frac{-b \pm \sqrt{b^2 - 4ac}}{2a}$

For this equation: $a = 3, b = -4, c = -3$. Then: $x_{1,2} = \frac{-(-3) \pm \sqrt{(-4)^2 - 4(3)(-3)}}{2(3)}$

$x_1 = \frac{-(-3) + \sqrt{(-4)^2 - 4(3)(-3)}}{2(3)} = \frac{3 + \sqrt{45}}{6} = \frac{3 + 3\sqrt{5}}{6}$. Cancel the common factor 3 $\to x = \frac{1 + \sqrt{5}}{2}$

$x_2 = \frac{-(-3) - \sqrt{(-4)^2 - 4(3)(-3)}}{2(3)} = \frac{3 - \sqrt{45}}{6} = \frac{3 - 3\sqrt{5}}{6}$. Cancel the common factor 3 $\to x = \frac{1 - \sqrt{5}}{2}$

Algebra II Practice Tests Answers and Explanations

21) Choice C is correct.

To solve for x, isolate the radical on one side of the equation. Divide both sides by 4. Then: $4\sqrt{2x+9} = 28 \to \frac{4\sqrt{2x+9}}{4} = \frac{28}{4} \to \sqrt{2x+9} = 7$. Square both sides: $\left(\sqrt{(2x+9)}\right)^2 = 7^2$. Then: $2x + 9 = 49 \to 2x = 40 \to x = 20$. Substitute x by 20 in the original equation and check the answer: $x = 20 \to 4\sqrt{2(20)+9} = 4\sqrt{49} = 4(7) = 28$

22) Choice D is correct.

Based on the table provided: $g(-2) = g(x = -2) = 3 \to g(3) = g(x = 3) = -2$

$3g(-2) - 2g(3) = 3(3) - 2(-2) = 9 + 4 = 13$

23) Choice C is correct.

The general form of absolute function is: $f(x) = a|x - h| + k$

Since the graph opens downward with a slope of 1, then a is negative one. The graph moved 1 unit up, so the value of k is 1. Then, choice C is correct. $y = -|x| + 1$

24) Choice A is correct.

$\sqrt{x} = 4 \to x = 16$, then; $\sqrt{x} - 7 = \sqrt{16} - 7 = 4 - 7 = -3$ and $\sqrt{x-7} = \sqrt{16-7} = \sqrt{9} = 3$

Then: $(\sqrt{x-7}) + (\sqrt{x}-7) = 3 + (-3) = 0$

25) Choice D is correct.

$\sin A = \frac{1}{3} \Rightarrow$ Since $\sin \theta = \frac{opposite}{hypotenuse}$, we have the following right triangle.

Then: $c = \sqrt{3^2 - 1^2} = \sqrt{9-1} = \sqrt{8}$. Then: $\cos A = \frac{opposite}{Adjacent} = \frac{\sqrt{8}}{3}$

26) Choice E is correct.

Plug in the value of each choice in the inequality.

A. 1 $(1-2)^2 + 1 > 3(1) - 1 \to 2 > 2$ This is Not true.

B. 3 $(3-2)^2 + 1 > 3(3) - 1 \to 2 > 8$ This is Not true.

C. 4 $(4-2)^2 + 1 > 3(4) - 1 \to 5 > 11$ This is Not true.

D. 6 $(6-2)^2 + 1 > 3(6) - 1 \to 17 > 17$ This is Not true.

E. 8 $(8-2)^2 + 1 > 3(8) - 1 \to 37 > 23$ This is true.

27) Choice C is correct.

To solve for the variable, isolate it on one side of the equation. For this equation, multiply both sides by 5. Then: $\frac{3x}{5} = 27 \rightarrow \frac{3x}{5} \times 5 = 27 \times 5 \rightarrow 3x = 135$

Now, divide both sides by 3: $x = \frac{135}{3} = 45$

28) Choice E is correct.

$81 = 3^{2x}$. Convert to base 3: $81 = 3^{2x} = 3^4 = 3^{2x}$. If $a^{f(x)} = b^{g(x)}$, then $f(x) = g(x)$

Therefore: $4 = 2x \rightarrow x = \frac{4}{2} \rightarrow x = 2$

29) Choice B is correct.

Use FOIL (First-Out-In-Last) method: $-(2-i)(i-2) = -2i + 4 + i^2 - 2i = -4i + i^2 + 4$. Combine like terms: $(2i - 3) - 4i + i^2 + 4 = -2i + i^2 + 1 = -2i + (-1) + 1 = -2i$

30) Choice D is correct.

In the function $f(x) = \frac{4x^2 - 6x + 12}{9 - x}$, the denominator cannot be zero. Then, $9 - x \neq 0 \rightarrow x \neq 9$. So, $f(9)$ is not defined.

31) Choice D is correct.

Multiplying each side of $-3x - y = 6$ by 2 gives $-6x - 2y = 12$. Adding each side of $-6x - 2y = 12$ to the corresponding side of $6x + 4y = 10$ gives $2y = 22$, or $y = 11$. Finally, substituting 11 for y in $6x + 4y = 10$ gives $6x + 4(11) = 10$, or $x = -\frac{17}{3}$.

32) Choice C is correct.

Find a common denominator and simplify: $\frac{3x-2}{x-3} - \frac{x-4}{3x-2} = \frac{(3x-2)^2 - (x-4)(x-3)}{(x-3)(3x-2)} =$

$\frac{(3x)^2 - 2(3x)(2) - 2^2 + (-x+4)(x-3)}{(x-3)(3x-2)} = \frac{9x^2 - 12x + 4 - x^2 + 3x + 4x - 12}{(x-3)(3x-2)} = \frac{8x^2 - 5x - 8}{(x-3)(3x-2)}$

33) Choice D is correct.

The problem asks for the sum of the roots of the quadratic equation $2n^2 + 16n + 24 = 0$. Dividing each side of the equation by 2 gives $n^2 + 8n + 12 = 0$. If the roots of $n^2 + 8n + 12 = 0$ are n_1 and n_2, then the equation can be factored as $n^2 + 8n + 12 = (n - n_1)(n - n_2) = 0$. Looking at the coefficient of n on each side of $n^2 + 8n + 12 = (n + 6)(n + 2)$ gives $n = -6$ or $n = -2$, then, $-6 + (-2) = -8$

Algebra II Practice Tests Answers and Explanations

34) Choice D is correct.

To perform the division $\frac{3+2i}{5+i}$, multiply the numerator and denominator of $\frac{3+2i}{5+1i}$ by the conjugate of the denominator, $5 - i$. This gives $\frac{(3+2i)(5-i)}{(5+1i)(5-i)} = \frac{15-3i+10i-2i^2}{5^2-i^2}$. Since $i^2 = -1$, this can be simplified to $\frac{15-3i+10i+2}{25+1} = \frac{17+7i}{26}$.

35) Choice E is correct.

The real part of the complex number is 2, and the imaginary part is $-4i$. We plot the ordered pair $(2, -4)$, in whichthat the real number (2) is plotted on the x−axis and the imaginary part $(-4i)$ is plotted on the y−axis. Point E represents the complex number $2 - 4i$.

36) Choice A is correct.

Solve for x: $2x - 5y = 10 \to x - \frac{5}{2}y = 5 \to x = \frac{5}{2}y + 5$

37) Choice B is correct.

Simplify the numerator: $\frac{x+(5x)^2+(3x)^3}{x} = \frac{x+5^2x^2+3^3x^3}{x} = \frac{x+25x^2+27x^3}{x}$

Pull an x out of each term in the numerator. $\frac{x(1+25x+27x^2)}{x}$

The x in the numerator and the x in the denominator cancel:

$1 + 25x + 27x^2 = 27x^2 + 25x + 1$

38) Choice B is correct.

The possible y values are between -4 and 3. Range: $-4 \leq y \leq 3$

39) Choice B is correct.

$tanx = \frac{opposite}{adjacent}$, and $\tan x = \frac{8}{15}$, therefore, the opposite side of the angle x is 8 and the adjacent side is 15. Let's draw the triangle.

Using the Pythagorean theorem, we have:

$a^2 + b^2 = c^2 \to 8^2 + 15^2 = c^2 \to 64 + 225 = c^2 \to c = 17$

$sinx = \frac{opposite}{hypotenuse} = \frac{8}{17}$

40) Choice D is correct.

The vertex form of a parabola is $y = a(x - h)^2 + k$, where (h, k) is the vertex. The variable a has the same value and function as the variable in the standard form. If $a > 0$, the parabola opens up, and if $a < 0$, the parabola opens down. $-6 < 0 \to$ the parabola opens down.

Effortless Math's Algebra II Online Center

... So Much More Online!

Effortless Math Online Algebra II Center offers a complete study program, including the following:

- ✓ Step-by-step instructions on how to prepare for the Algebra II test

- ✓ Numerous Algebra II worksheets to help you measure your math skills

- ✓ Complete list of Algebra II formulas

- ✓ Video lessons for Algebra II topics

- ✓ Full-length Algebra II practice tests

- ✓ And much more...

No Registration Required.

Visit **EffortlessMath.com/Algebra2** to find your online Algebra II resources.

Build Your Math Skills: Our Top Book Picks!

Download eBooks (in PDF format) Instantly!

Download

Our Most Popular Books!

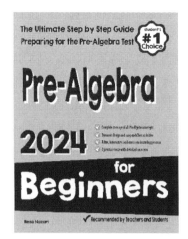 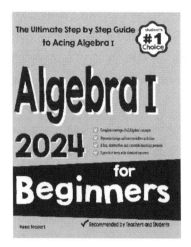 

   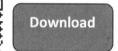

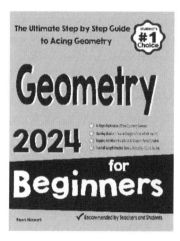 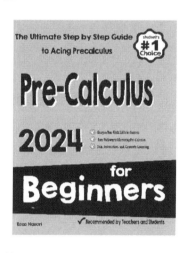 

  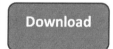 

Our Most Popular Books!

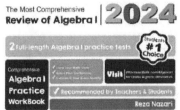

Receive the PDF version of this book or get another FREE book!

Thank you for using our Book!

Do you LOVE this book?

Then, you can get the PDF version of this book or another book absolutely FREE!

Please email us at:

info@EffortlessMath.com

for details.

Author's Final Note

I hope you enjoyed reading this book. You've made it through the book! Great job!

First of all, thank you for purchasing this study guide. I know you could have picked any number of books to help you prepare for your Algebra II course, but you picked this book and for that I am extremely grateful.

It took me years to write this study guide for the Algebra II because I wanted to prepare a comprehensive Algebra II study guide to help students make the most effective use of their valuable time while preparing for the final test.

After teaching and tutoring math courses for over a decade, I've gathered my personal notes and lessons to develop this study guide. It is my greatest hope that the lessons in this book could help you prepare for your test successfully.

If you have any questions, please contact me at reza@effortlessmath.com and I will be glad to assist. Your feedback will help me to greatly improve the quality of my books in the future and make this book even better. Furthermore, I expect that I have made a few minor errors somewhere in this study guide. If you think this to be the case, please let me know so I can fix the issue as soon as possible.

If you enjoyed this book and found some benefit in reading this, I'd like to hear from you and hope that you could take a quick minute to post a review on the book's Amazon page. To leave your valuable feedback, please visit: https://rb.gy/zkc5w

Or scan this QR code.

I personally go over every single review, to make sure my books really are reaching out and helping students and test takers. Please help me help Algebra II students, by leaving a review!

I wish you all the best in your future success!

Reza Nazari

Math teacher and author

Made in the USA
Columbia, SC
07 September 2024